Heal Trauma

How to Feel It, Unlock Patterns, and Release It

Alyson Quinn

HAMILTON BOOKS
AN IMPRINT OF
ROWMAN & LITTLEFIELD
Lanham • Boulder • New York • London

Published by Hamilton Books
An imprint of The Rowman & Littlefield Publishing Group, Inc.
4501 Forbes Boulevard, Suite 200, Lanham, Maryland 20706
www.rowman.com

86-90 Paul Street, London EC2A 4NE, United Kingdom

All art by Brooke Kelly, used with permission, unless otherwise stated.

This book is a revised and expanded version of *Reclaim Your Soul: Your Path to Healing* published in 2014 by University Press of America.

British Library Cataloguing in Publication Information Available

Library of Congress Cataloging-in-Publication Data

Names: Quinn, Alyson, 1959- author.
Title: Heal trauma : how to feel it, unlock patterns, and release it / Alyson Quinn.
Other titles: Reclaim your soul
Description: Lanham : Hamilton Books, [2023] | "This book is a revised and expanded version of Reclaim your soul : you path to healing published in 2014 by University Press of America"—Verso. | Includes bibliographical references and index. | Summary: "Heal Trauma: How to Feel it, Unlock Patterns and Release It, is a life companion for healing past trauma. The book guides the reader to understand and release challenging feelings, build resilience, identify helpful and unhelpful patterns and release embodied emotion that can impact our growth for decades"—Provided by publisher.
Identifiers: LCCN 2022053104 (print) | LCCN 2022053105 (ebook) | ISBN 9780761873464 (paperback ; alk. paper) | ISBN 9780761873471 (epub)
Subjects: LCSH: Emotions. | Self-actualization (Psychology) | Psychic trauma.
Classification: LCC BF531 .Q56 2023 (print) | LCC BF531 (ebook) | DDC 152.4--dc23/eng/20221212
LC record available at https://lccn.loc.gov/2022053104
LC ebook record available at https://lccn.loc.gov/2022053105

∞™ The paper used in this publication meets the minimum requirements of American National Standard for Information Sciences—Permanence of Paper for Printed Library Materials, ANSI/NISO Z39.48-1992.

Heal Trauma

*To all the clients with whom I have worked with over the years; thank you.
Thank you for educating me about your experience, giving words to feelings,
patterns, and the impact of trauma that diminishes us all and intensifies
our suffering. It is yours and my inner work that created the seeds for
this book to flourish and hopefully help us all on our healing journey.*

Contents

Figures

Acknowledgments

First, I would like to acknowledge Hamilton Books and Brooke Bures for all her help and guidance - I am deeply appreciative of your support. To Sam Brawand for her dedication re-editing and her incisive red pen. I would also like to thank Brooke Kelly for her skill, immense creativity, and dedication in taking on the role of illustrator, am so grateful for your artistic contribution. Thanks also to Aminda D'Sena and Shelley Hall for all of your help—much appreciated. And most importantly, to family and friends who have encouraged and inspired me to fulfill my furthest dreams and deepest desires, I am forever grateful.

A Note from the Author

Many clients who have read the first edition, *Reclaim Your Soul: Your Path to Healing* (2014), have commented that it is a book to be used throughout their lives, to assist in bringing unconscious processes to conscious awareness so that they can be processed, resolved, and integrated into their bodies. I hope the book will be used as *medicine in the moment*. For example, when you feel a feeling, or observe a pattern, you can go to the book right away to get a deeper understanding in that moment. If, for instance, you feel sad or hurt, I hope by reading the vignettes on both of those feelings you can acknowledge them, understand their depth, discover what they relate to, and then use a visual to release their impact. I hope the book can be a companion by your bedside helping to reduce the aloneness we often feel with traumatic experiences, and that it provides a tool you can reach for over and over again to release layer upon layer of embodied emotion related to past trauma.

Chapter 1

A Conversation with Our Feelings

Feelings: everyone has them; it is what makes us human. Feelings help us relate to each other and develop relationships; to make critical decisions about our lives; to choose our partners in life; to form bonds with children we bring into the world; and to form connections with animals and the natural world around us. In essence, they are everything, as critical as the blood pulsating through our veins.

If having feelings is as fundamental to the human condition as breathing, why do many of us (and there are multitudes) do whatever we can to numb, distract, run away from, ignore, suppress, and sequester the very essence of what makes us authentic? One word comes up time and time again: fear.

But there are many reasons, a variety so complicated, so multilayered, so often lost in the tissues of our body, that they may remain in the unconscious forever. Sometimes the tragedies and traumas that occur in our lives come with so many overwhelming emotions that we just block them all; and so we lose ourselves and our capacity to heal. Consequently, when it comes to living life, we tend to keep busy, so we don't have to feel too much, and therefore the result is that we lose ourselves somewhere out there in the ether. We become amorphous entities floating freely through life, unsure of our direction or purpose, making decisions not based on anything that feels solid, finding ourselves at the end of our lives overwhelmingly confused, likely sad and filled with regret that things didn't turn out as planned.

Feelings, then, are guideposts illuminating the way, much like a lighthouse in a blackened ocean, treasured clues as to how we should act, what we need to say to be true to ourselves, what decisions and actions we might make to improve our lives and the lives of those around us. Listening and responding to them are the crucial steps that light the path of our lives, bringing us closer to our soul and its desires. If we honor our feelings, they can lead us to our highest self. Feeling every feeling along the way is the road to our enlightenment and liberation. By doing so we have the capacity to form bonds that are so deep that we cement ourselves in what is real in the bedrock of life and learn the ever-inspiring and daunting art of loving another, starting with loving ourselves and honoring all that we feel.

So, if feelings are our anchor against the storm of life, our guideposts that instruct us on a definitive path when we are uncertain, how can we make sure we get them, honor them, feel them, deal with them so our habits of distraction are bridled, especially when the waves of distress start to appear on the horizon? What advice would our feelings give us? What would they say if we took off their muzzle at last and just listened?

I imagine this:

We are showing you anger, despair, joy, sadness, elation, confusion, inadequacy, resentment, determination and so the list goes on. We show these for a reason. If you had no reactions to anything, how on earth would you figure out anything in life? You would be a lost soul, moving here and there with little purpose or direction. You need us. You often pretend you don't, and that confuses us a great deal. Why bury us under a mountain of food that you don't need, or hold your breath to squash us into your hips or stomach?

Another habit is to get so busy, so distracted that you don't even know us anymore, or (worse still!) pretend we weren't there in the first place. We hear people ask you how you are; we know deep down how you feel, but you put on a mask and say in your cheeriest possible voice, "I'm fine." You know it's not true, we know it's not true, so how long are you going to fake it through life? It's your life, not ours; you are the one staring in the mirror, not us.

So let's make a deal: If you acknowledge us every day and tell others about how you are feeling, or share us in some other way, we promise not to build up like a mountain inside of you. When we have been suppressed for so long, we can't help building up. We know that when we grow so big, you are overwhelmed, clueless how to let our myriad faces glimpse the sun; instead, we burst out all over the place so you feel completely out of control. We know you want to feel in control; that's natural. But if you keep suppressing us, you know as well as we do that you never will. Remember, if you catch us early, we are like small waves washing over you. We know it's hard to feel some of us when we push our way up, but we are here for a reason. Remember, too, we only stick around for a short time if you allow us to rise and you acknowledge us.

Now that you are listening, can we tell you our wish list so that together we can make a pact to improve your health from now on?

- Slow down! We can't rise if you are rushing around like one of those headless chickens gone mad on speed.
- Pay attention to your body. Wherever you feel tight or heavy, that is where one of us is. If you stretch the area, the feeling can rise and quit being locked, frustrated, inside your tissues.

- Breathe, for goodness sake take time to breathe! How about some stillness and meditation? Then we have time to rise to the surface. The breath is like a vehicle that carries us to your conscious awareness, so please take long deep breaths that go deep into your body and draw us to the surface.
- Be alert when you see a pattern repeating; it can keep you stuck for years, even decades. Sometimes we show up in patterns you know, like obsessive compulsive behavior, martyrdom, perfectionism, etc. These are clues that tons of us have been suppressed; otherwise the pattern would be easier to break.
- Be honest! You really know how much it costs to deceive others and yourself. We know you want to please all those people out there, but what is the point of pleasing them and losing yourself? Isn't that futile?
- Take time each day to write out your feelings for five or ten minutes to start; it will help you recognize us and release us along the way. Also make a list to record traps like busyness, any other distraction, or numbing behaviors so you will be on high alert when they show up. Brainstorm ways to drain the feelings and disarm the traps. We want to work with you!
- Remember, we can help you a lot if you let us guide you. Often we come into your stomach (your second brain); that's why it's called a "gut reaction." It's a feeling helping you to make a good decision. Honestly, we are on your side; if you will listen to us, we are there for you.
- Whatever happens, don't let us build up, or it will mean trouble for your body down the road. There are many illnesses that crop up from tension in the body, because so many feelings have been suppressed. If you have pushed us down and your body feels tense, have a massage or acupuncture to release us. Both of these break us out of the tissue walls where we are trapped. We can be locked in there for years, sometimes decades.
- The last wish on our wish list is really the most important: Just let us be what we are. You feel angry, confused, resentful etc. for a good reason; be curious as to what that reason may be. Be our friend, and you can trust us to guide you through life, helping you to heal along the way. In time, we will help you grow and move towards some of your favorite feelings: joy and peace.

Giving a voice to our feelings, imagining their needs and acknowledging them can be a way to get back to being ourselves at last. We must consolidate the self, know the self, before we can take the liberating step of transcendence and rise to our ever-expansive, limitless, ego-less state, where we remain intensely in touch with all of our feelings all of the time.

Chapter 2

Cultural Trends That Can Suppress and Numb Our Feelings

Lifestyle is a key piece to address regarding the change process. This chapter highlights some cultural trends that can create barriers to the healing process.

THE BUSYNESS TREND

Henry Miller asked the question in 1945 that is overwhelmingly relevant today "This frenzied activity which has us all, rich and poor, weak and powerful, in its grip—where is it leading us?" He continues "There are two things in life which it seems to me all men want and very few ever get (because both of them belong to the domain of the spiritual) and they are health and freedom.

The druggist, the doctor, the surgeon are all powerless to give health; money, power, security, authority do not give freedom. Education can never provide wisdom, nor churches religion, nor wealth happiness, nor security peace. What is the meaning of our activity then? To what end? (Miller, 1945: p29). Busyness can be a cultural disease, and if one listens deeply to our use of language, there can be cultural pride in wearing this badge of frenzy. "Where did the summer go?" is a common question "Where did the year go? I can't believe it is already"—is a common refrain.

Busyness is often driven by an underlying fear of slowing down, with an assumption that difficult feelings will arise, and so it is better to keep on going. Fear of connecting fully with self seems to drive the flurry of activity; but it leaves people feeling less and less in touch with who they are—and, in time, feeling lost and empty. Sometimes busyness is a financial necessity and is part of financial survival, however many are locked into busyness as a coping technique to deal with past traumatic experiences. This is profoundly disturbing because with busyness as the solution to many problems someone can live like this for decades. Moving around life like an autumn leaf that is

5

picked up by this wind and that, forever changing direction, perhaps partners, perhaps careers or geographical location, in desperation to find that anchor from the winds of life. Avoiding a life filled with feelings and fixating on the external world can result in an inner dialogue that is haunted by the mantra 'If only.' "If only I had bought that house, or put my money in shares, or married that person instead of this one, or had more children, or taken a different career - then I would be happy."

If an entire society has given over to this way of being then it's hard to buck the trend, to stop, to listen inside, to take the time to connect to oneself, to acknowledge the feelings of emptiness, the void, the meaninglessness of it all. It also becomes challenging to move at a different rhythm as there can be intense loneliness and alienation when one steps out of the whirlpool of activity and slows down.

INFLUENCE OF TECHNOLOGY
ON OUR FEELING STATE

In theory, advances in technology should be giving us more free time to connect meaningfully with others. However, it seems the opposite is occurring, and as a result, our capacity to relate to one another and to our core selves is diminishing dramatically. Television, along with social media, has people wiling away their hours engrossed in external worlds with a neglect of their internal world, and the consequent numb feelings.

Another aspect of technology is an increased exposure to violence on a screen which can trigger unconscious implicit memories and lead to nervous system dysregulation. The degree of violence that the average person is exposed to on screen has increased with violent video games contributing to the impact. The American academy of Child and Adolescent Psychiatry in their research states the average American child will have watched two hundred thousand violent acts, and sixteen thousand murders by the time they are eighteen years old. In an article by Melinda Hawkins on how the media is desensitizing children, she quotes the American Academy of Child and Adolescent Psychiatry as stating, "the overwhelming amount of violence seen by the typical child can desensitize him to violence by reducing his natural feelings of shock at real acts of violence, and by deteriorating his ability to empathize with victims. Violent video games also allow children to participate in what the Academy calls 'virtual violence,' in which they have an interactive role in creating the violent images they consume" (Hawkins, 2011: p. 2). When an individual is numb and disconnected, they can be more susceptible to hurting and harming others. The problem again becomes disconnection from self, and all the consequent suppressed emotions that often trigger impulsive behavior.

Cell phones are also having an impact on one's ability to focus and connect to self. Many are bombarded by the constant demand of incoming messages and so it can be challenging to concentrate. Most inner work requires an intense focus, and an ability to sequester the outer world to explore within. It was only two hundred odd years ago that most of us spent hours wiling away our time on family farms with few distractions. The opposite is the case these days with a myriad of distractions available at one's fingertips. Sadly, this can also impact our ability to have an intimate connection with someone in our lives given our limited capacity to be focused on another. This is when technology that could improve our communication is undermining our ability to 'be human' with each other. Connecting meaningfully with others is an art form and is also key to the healing process. As Bonnie Badenoch states, "It is different, however, when we are with a receptive, responsive other. . . . My emerging fear and pain can be embraced by the wide window of your receptive ventral presence, and in this space, healing potentially unfolds" (Badenoch, 2018, p. 71).

In a 1993 book, Technopoly: The Surrender of Culture to Technology, Neil Postman imagines the impact that we are observing today. He defines a technopoly as a society in which technology is deified, meaning "the culture seeks its authorization in technology, finds its satisfactions in technology and takes its orders from technology." (Postman, 1993: p 71–72).

SPEED FILLED LIVING

In the northern hemisphere this is overwhelmingly evident. It is likely one of the reasons people go to countries with more relaxed rhythms for vacations, where they are forced to slow down, despite the internal conflict inside. Speed is seen as all good, fast food, fast cars, and even speed dating. For those with a trauma background the pressure of speedy living can trigger and lead to nervous system dysregulation, given the demands of quick action and quick decision making. Speed has also taken over the way people speak. It is as if some are trying to crash all their thoughts into short time frames, because they know instinctively few people have time to really listen.

Devotion to speed fosters impatience, impatience in listening to others, hoping they get to the point quickly, impatience with messy contradictory feelings and impatience in life in general. Malidoma Some in his book *Ritual: Power, Healing and Community* reflects on speed in the developed world. "Speed is a way to prevent ourselves from having to deal with something we do not want to face. So, we run from these symptoms and their sources that are not nice to look at . . . I believe that the difference between the indigenous world and the industrial world has mostly to do with speed" (Some, 1993: p. 17). Milan Kundera, a Czech writer, in his book *Slowness* states "There is a secret bond between slowness and memory, between speed and forgetting. . . . In existential mathematics, that experience takes the form of two basic equations: the degree of slowness is directly proportional to the intensity of memory; the degree of speed is directly proportional to the intensity of forgetting" (On the virtues of slowness, 2012: p. 2).

Fixation with speed also influences the healing process profoundly. Many attend therapy sessions expecting a quick fix, somehow someone will do something to fix them, or they will have the insight of all insights, and all will be healed. Healing is often messy, implicit memories and embodied emotion are challenging to access. Accessing 'sensation as a way of knowing' requires intense concentration and a willingness to explore subtleties that are often below consciousness. Some leave therapy thinking it is not for them as progress is not happening quickly enough and they are unwilling to slow down.

OVERWORKING

The norm of weekly work hours in the developed world is varied going up and down according to the economy. From the time of industrialization in Britain, deemed to be the 'workshop of the world' working hours were dictated by those in power. Conditions were so brutal that in 1802 a law was passed which barred certain children (those who did not live with their parents) from working more than twelve hours a day.

Regarding working through trauma, the demands of the workweek can make it extraordinarily difficult to maintain a self- connection. When one has finished a day of work it is rare that the day's tasks are finished. Parents are just gearing up for family commitments. The weekend is often barely enough time to administer life, have some social time, or recover from the exhaustion of the week. An added layer is living in cities and commuting which could be up to two hours a day. Consequently, it can be highly challenging to acknowledge sequestered feelings and unmet needs that may have accumulated for years. Necessity drives most to not contemplate any other reality, and essentially suck it up, as one needs to pay a mortgage or rent, buy food and other necessities to sustain life. This accepted norm is a significant contribution to the glaring statistics on mental health. There are staggering numbers of people on psychiatric medication, their moods a constant battleground, and their sense of core self-buried under the pile of daily demands from the world around them.

THE TREND OF EXCESS ACTIVITY

When there is trapped embodied emotion related to past trauma individuals can be prone to behavior that is excessive, rather than balanced. The activity itself may be benign, or benign in small doses, but when done to excess it can contribute markedly to disconnection from self and a numb state. The person may enjoy running, but when they do it for long hours every day the body starts to wear out and emotionally there is a cost. Any activity of excess is at times a desire for adrenaline and the consequent escape from self. Some activities have a greater emotional cost than others; gambling being a good example, but any activity done to excess for lengthy periods can eventually leads to some sort of burn out or emotional crisis.

In my work as a group therapist, I often brainstorm with the group ways of disconnecting from feelings. The clients mention working too much or eating and sleeping too much or too little. They talk about drinking too much, taking too much medication, and watching too many movies. Some have mentioned reading, it seems benign, but clients have talked about escaping their reality through reading and ignoring what they need to do. Others talked about excessive talking and not listening to others. Blaming others repeatedly and fighting. Shopping comes up often and clients mention retail therapy gives them a short term high. Social commentator Jonathon Freedman reiterates this point "above the poverty level, the relationship between income and happiness is remarkably small. Yet when alternative measures of success are not available, the deep human need to be valued and respected by others is acted out through consumption. Buying things becomes a proof of self-esteem (I'm worth it chants one advertising slogan) and a means to self-acceptance" (Durning, 1991; p. 48).

Another area of excess or addictive behavior that clients talk about is 'falling in love' or sexual addiction. Human relationships have become increasingly co modified for the market through online dating sites. One is now selling oneself, talking up one's best characteristics in the hope of a date with someone special. There are also serial daters; people who use dating as their drug of choice. It is the chase; the newness of the encounter, the sexual experiences with a new person, and then when messy emotions get in the way of the frivolity of it all the person is dumped. Clients recognize that the cycle is the magnet, pulling themselves further and further away from who they really are and what they feel.

THE SEDUCTION OF STIMULANTS

To survive and keep pace with a speed filled, fast-talking world it can be helpful to have some stimulants. Coffee and alcohol are norms in today's world, and it can be hard to stick to reasonable limits. Whenever one feels exhaustion coming on there is always caffeine. It has become the drug of choice fueling the workers to work that extra hour, that extra day, and keeping exhaustion at bay for at least a little while longer. Alcohol and drugs also contribute significantly to numbed feelings. For some it is one of the few times individuals experience relaxation and so the temptation is strong, particularly in social situations when one has lost confidence in connecting with others.

MATERIALISM

"Early in the post-world war two age of affluence, an American retailing analyst named Victor Lebow proclaimed 'Our enormously productive economy. . . . demands that we make consumption our way of life, that we convert the buying and use of goods into rituals, that we seek spiritual satisfaction, our ego satisfaction, in consumption. . . . We need things consumed, burned up, worn out, replaced, and discarded at an ever-increasing rate" (Durning, 1991; p 45). This myth has been hot wired into the psyche of many cultures that large amounts of money will buy long term happiness. It is not to say that one can live comfortably in poverty, but it is the striving for the faster car, the bigger house, the sizable boat, the expensive jewelry, all those extra items that encourage one to give away those extra hours to work, to satisfy the insatiable cravings of more. The more one is driven for acquisition for its own sake, the more one is likely to move away from a sustained inner journey. For those with trauma there can be substantial pressure to keep up and disconnect from self. Advertisers ever on the lookout to get their messages out there are creative in their bombardment. Traditionally it was television, now it is on the bank teller machine, computers, cell phones, all over public transit, even sadly in schools. Children are targeted unapologetically; they are the future to the consumer markets; and it is serious business to get across the message that one will only be truly happy if they can buy the next item of impulsive need.

CEREBRAL COMMUNICATION

Many nowadays are so busy, so caught up in the speed of life, or responding to the latest gadgets clicks and beeps that their communication has become a waterfall of ideas. They are essentially 'talking at' people rather than 'talking with someone.' Their minds are often full so when they see a person willing to listen, they start to vent the latest whirlpool of thought swirling around. There is little to no feeling in their speech, rather it is often fast paced, multi tangential, and the rant can go on for ages. There is often a desperation to connect, but given the ideas are disconnected from feeling, it is hard to communicate at a deep level and the recipient can feel drained.

Martin Jacques in an article entitled 'The death of intimacy' talks about "the very idea of what it means to be human is being eroded. The reason we no longer feel as happy as we once did is that the intimacy on which our sense of well-being rests—a product of our closest, most intimate relationships, above all in the family—is in decline." (Jacques, 2004). Along with this trend is a trend to more and more talkers and fewer listeners. A myth has developed that if we are talking, we are getting out what we need to, and we will feel better. Many a client comes to therapy with this idea. Their goal is to tell the therapist as much as possible and then somehow, they will feel better. When a client is talking at me in this way it is critical to ask the client to stop, take breaks, breathe, and resource the body, as a stream of consciousness can re-traumatize and trigger, and consequently move the person outside their window of tolerance.

Chapter 3

How to Feel It

"To feel all your feelings, to acknowledge them, to reflect on them, and to release them is your path to wholeness. It is how you grow and reclaim all your humanity, residing patiently in your soul."

Some feelings are more challenging to feel than others. We know they are there, lurking like furtive ghosts, wanting full recognition before they will disappear into the ether. At times we fear that if we acknowledge them, they will get bigger, take over our lives, and leave us whimpering in a discombobulated mess waiting for help. When feelings have been suppressed for some time, they do threaten like a raging waterfall. However, when we get through the buildup, as we eventually will, we can start to practice daily recognition of feelings. When we choose to clear them regularly by our consistent attention, feelings become our allies in life, guiding us effortlessly through the maze of our existence.

FEAR

"Fear invites us to be small and contracted and to give in to it completely. By doing the very thing that scares us the most, we give fear the boot and drain its toxic ooze."

Fear can come up every day. Every day we have invitations to give it power to drain us, to give ourselves over to it. It can cast a long shadow over our day, and even if we are not conscious of its victories, the unconscious has it recorded in our dreams and in the tension in our bodies.

Do we have the courage to step out and be intimate with someone, not just to open our body physically but to open up the core of our being to the moment? Looking that deeply into the mirror is frightening stuff: what of the

Figure 3.1. Fear.

parts we don't like? Fear also moves into relationships with friends, relatives, or colleagues at work. How much do we reveal and still ensure acceptance? The horror of rejection reverberates. Who can bear the loneliness of being ostracized from the group? The mere thought of that builds more fear.

Fear, it has to be said, has numerous allies. It relies heavily on them to ensure it is the dominant player in a mortal's life. Fear can often be seen holding hands with "routine"– their relationship has been long-term. If I don't take risks, then my life will feel more predictable. Routine–I will have a routine that I have chosen. Routine has powerfully seductive magnets. It seduces us into an illusion of predictability. Our love of routine at some point takes over from our power to change it, and it begins to carve a deeper furrow into the marrow of our being. Initially, it appears somewhat harmless–there is that sitting-on-a-velvet-cushion feeling. We start out the weekend with the tried and tested recipe. Soon, without full awareness, we notice how invitations to break the routine are turned down for the comfort of the familiar. After a while, the wobbly jelly begins to set into a hard, crusty consistency. The grooves we have chosen in life now appear bigger than the spirit's ability to shift the pattern.

Once that trap has been experienced fully, we start to feel we have lost command of the wheel of our ship. The ship heads for waters full of obsessive whirlpools. Each day in theory is a fresh new beginning, but not for a mind that has been colonized by worry. We wake up and the record goes on: How will I cope with today's demands? We start to ponder all the potential doom scenarios and wonder which strategy we will employ to deal with each one. Fear knows this record well and relishes the playing. This is fear's chance to take a firmer hold. Fear throws seeds into the imagination and sits back to watch them flourish.

For instance, you are going on a trip and the initial worry is how you will manage to get everything ready in time. Then fear throws the seed: what if you have an accident on the trip? Imagination runs riot with this idea–soon you are lying on a road with no help in sight. Or the hospital you are taken to has run out of the medication you need. Imagination takes another swipe at you and remembers the latest terrorist threats–what if your plane gets hijacked and, worse still, passengers are shot? It is a fresh new day, but already you have ratcheted up the tension in your body, and your anxiety thermometer is reaching near the top. Your chest feels tight now, and there is a knot at the bottom of your spine you hadn't noticed before. Getting out of bed is going to be a challenge today–it now feels like you have a huge backpack on your back that you are going to have drag around all day.

When we feel this buried in life, the obvious cure seems to be to share our load, but this often has mixed results. There are some precious people in our lives who know the weight of the moment and can sense that we are buckling under it. They give us the feeling they are holding our hand, hoping we can marshal our resources for the challenge. Others though, often innocently, shower us with platitudes: "Oh, you'll be fine," or "Don't worry; there haven't been any plane fiascoes in Canada. Just go and have fun!" So now you not only have your backpack of obsessive worry (dictated routines and fear that is starting to feel insurmountable), but you have waves of alienation and you are feeling misunderstood by the human family. How does one get out of this trap, which you intuitively know could last months, years or even decades?

Well, it makes sense to be on hyperalert, wide awake to routine's seductions in the first place. Life is full of risk. Loving is risky. Caring about others, your life and your desires are all risky because we face roads full of potholes of disappointment. Taking a risk, even a minute risk, when we are virtually paralyzed by fear, sends a loud message to our soul: the contraction program is no longer being chosen; we are opting for expansion. Initially, such small steps are hard to celebrate. We step into mud that sucks at our feet, and pulls us down so our progress appears minimal. However, we begin to notice after a while that the mud has less suction, and then, unbelievably, a path appears ahead with only a cracked surface. Our footwear is able to grip this terrain. Occasionally we notice a spring in our step, and then a drier road ahead. We have endured, and the resilience which has been demonstrated offers some protection against the next time fear and routine try to seduce us with their advertising for a predictable life.

LONGING

"Longing in the soul says there is more mystery to come. Listen deeply—it is your soul diligently working to bring about a depth of connection that you hadn't imagined possible."

Figure 3.2. Longing.

If you are silent enough with yourself, you can feel the longing deep, deep inside. When you have your finger on its pulse, there it is, that unmistakable wave of longing. Longing for the other, longing for completion, longing for that "I have come home" feeling. It is hard to feel the ache, as there is pain with it, and once you start to feel it, the ache can take over your body, colonize your pores, and infuse your blood–it has the power to go everywhere.

When we feel the longing, it is natural to imagine or see "the other" who with their presence might fill the gaping hole. It may not be a union with shrieks of excitement, or storms of chaos, but instead soothing medicine that injects into the soul's wound a healing balm to fill the emptiness. "Aah, at last," we say, "my soul is drowning in peace." Sometimes the need to find "the other" is so strong that the blessed union is imagined; holes are filled in zealously in order to convince ourselves that the missing one has been found, the soulmate of soulmates. The path then is one of unbridled fantasy and disappointment. The mortal behind the mask is revealed in time, and the longing intensifies again as we realize that the search is still before us.

We as humans are born with this longing, and when we feel it, our first impulse is to put a seal over it. Quickly we move into activity or into superficial desires, hoping to fill the empty space. Longing can take on the power of an engine in full throttle, sending waves of aching sensations. To honor it we need to acknowledge it–it is human not to feel complete. We know intuitively that if we did not have this feeling there would be no desire, and therefore no growth. "Desires are seeds waiting for their season to sprout. From a single seed of desire, whole forests grow" (Chopra, February 5th, 1998). So embrace the longing! Put your arms around it, hold it and honor it! It is your body's way of saying that there is more richness to come. Hold on, be patient and notice what is unfolding right now, and give it your full attention.

One way for you to endure the longing is to feel your aloneness and try to accept it, to feel the sense of separation from others, even those very close to you. Perhaps it recaptures the feeling of being connected to your mother, but all alone in the womb. It is also the sensation experienced in sickness. No one can be in your skin, feeling your disconnection from the human family when your body insists on marching down a road of attrition, or clinging to disease. Our way of caring for each other is to focus wholeheartedly on taking the physical pain away, lessening it with medicinal help. What about the emotional need? How might we help drain that vortex of grief?

When I feel longing, the ache can be intense; I try to soothe it with stillness and silence. I monitor impatience and try to stay with what is, knowing the torment will increase if my imaginings run riot. Also I remind myself that throughout my life I will need skills to handle longing. For those lucky enough to find "the other," if the experience is pure then the other needs freedom: freedom to be themselves, freedom from having to soothe another's longing, freedom to live their moments fully. So, in essence, longing is a shadow friend, dancing quixotically throughout our lives, reminding us that we came here alone, and we leave alone, no matter the depth of connection during our lifetime.

STRESS

"Stress feels as if all the cells in your body contain time bombs, and they have contrived to explode together any minute for maximum impact."

Figure 3.3. Stress.

It feels like a cooker inside you that has just come to a boil. Each time it spills over, it sends another surge of intensity. How many more can you bear? The challenging aspect of stress is that others don't seem to recognize when you are at your limit. Can't they see you have had it? That the tests have superseded your abilities? That grace is departing as irritability enters with forcefulness? On a societal level it would be helpful if there were an external sign that warned others, "(S)he/they are maxed out—give a wide berth." It's confusing for others, too; just a short while ago you appeared as if you were skipping through life, gaily rising to any challenge. A brief time later, and you look as if hot coals are burning your feet. You're jumpy, restless, and discombobulated. What happened?

Well, that is the insidious character of stress. It creeps up on you like a stealth attacker, leaving a pile of detritus behind that has to be sorted out and worked though. Sometimes the demands for internal work seem endless. Where is the end? Before the question forms in your mind, you know that there is no destination point, death being the ultimate stressor for most of us. So why do we struggle so much? Do we have more stress than our ancestors before us? How could our stress possibly compare to pioneering and setting up homesteads in inhospitable terrain, or to surviving war and the Great Depression, or to suffering any number of maladies that we now have "quick fixes" for? What makes our own stress feel so great, when, some would argue, our challenges seem so much smaller? What has changed?

What has changed is the unrelenting nature of the demands on our psyche. Historically one spent one's waking hours looking at the land; it bored into the mind and soothed the eyes. It was a daily dose of soulful medicine. It is only in the last several decades that invitations for our attention have begun to come from an endless supply of sources. Since Alexander Bell's invention, it has chiefly been the phone. It was once the postal service. Before that, one scanned the horizon for smoke signals, or perhaps it would be a ferocious animal's howl that triggered one's fight-or-flight reaction. Nowadays, grasshopper attention is all we have because of the relentless interruptions from mobile phones, faxes, emails, post, texts, television, advertising and even outrageous marketers who have the temerity to knock on our door with a sale in mind.

It doesn't stop there, either–as technology advances, one practically needs a night school course to figure out the microchip inventions in just about everything. There is now a whole digital maze for us to figure out before a task is done, whether getting our clock radio to wake us up or toasting a piece of bread. Where did simplicity go? No wonder so many of us by the time we get to our beach vacation are human slabs, incapable of coherent decision making. Finally, on vacation we can move into the driver's seat and stare at each wave spewing foam for days on end. At last our deepest self, after being sequestered for eons, has an opportunity to start influencing the course of our life again.

It does make sense that we are stumbling in the egg and spoon race of our life. We have our legs tied by all our demands, and unless we focus, the egg is bound to slide off the spoon. Then we have all manner of reparations to make.

Attention, concentration, focus, a calm mind; ancient religions recognized these vital attributes and developed religious tenets to help us keep them in mind. Without focus we are like a child's spinning top. Oh, sure, we pick up speed, but where are we going? Hopefully not down another pointless track in life. When we are scattered, we are more likely to indulge in activities that compound our fragmented attention. Aldous Huxley recognized this in his book *Brave New World*. His fear was that we would become "a trivial culture preoccupied with some equivalent of the feelies, the orgy porgy and the centrifugal bumble puppy" (Postman, 1985:intro).

What is the way through so our stress becomes more manageable and our overstimulation contained, so they are not stripping us of peace throughout the day? We need a "technological timeout" every day; so that the candlelit, foam-frothing soak in the tub is not rudely interrupted by an electronic buzzer. We need to regroup, to get ourselves to ourselves, to give silence the credit it is due, to feel our minds free-falling in the still moments, to recharge. In a more peaceful state, we are alert to the smorgasbord of demands, and are more likely to say, "No, not now; I need some downtime." From an alternative perspective, we need "time for our souls to catch up with our bodies." Imagine saying that to your boss when the latest work demand hits the inbox! Perhaps we cannot go that far, but nothing stops us from taking a meditative, technology-free lunch, night or weekend, from creating an intrapsychic vacation today, right now, and leaning back into the velvet cushion of a pause as a whole new beginning.

LUST

"Lust demands full obeisance and full fantasy, but the cost can be high when we wake up to its tricks."

It's as if someone has taken an eggbeater to your brain and scrambled it. It is no longer possible to think in a straight line. Hormones are running amok, saying with unbridled glee, "We're in charge. You can't think your way out of this one." Adrenaline surges through your body in pondering the other. Fantasies electrify the adrenaline, and it becomes an increasing challenge not to lift off into full-scale levitation. It's hard even to have an ordinary conversation when there is this much stimulation occupying your brain cells.

You are now immersed in a frothing sea of excitement, and the other looks like perfection: their eyes, their hair, and my goodness the way that blue stonewashed shirt hangs on their shoulders! Their jeans, too, hug them "just right"–it almost becomes too much to contemplate, the rush of it all. It's impossible to imagine that this intense excitement will not last forever.

Figure 3.4. Lust.

Granted, you have only just met, and you barely know him or her: but your body and your psyche say emphatically, "This must be the one!" With all this drama going on, it's clear that fate has blessed you stupendously.

So the energy fields (and everything else) merge, and the union feels blessed from on high. Sexual union becomes the penultimate high and the glow of it all affects everything. The most mundane activity with the other is fascinating when hormones are all aflow.

Then, unexpectedly, irritations and disappointments start to burst onto the sublime surface. It was all so perfect; how is it possible that the couple now find themselves on thin ice with gaping cracks emerging? When the hormones are in the driver's seat, all manner of difference or challenge is glided over, as a figure skater glides across a smooth, frozen rink. You didn't even notice or remember hearing that (s)he/they had just broken off a long-term relationship, so intimacy of any depth would be impossible. You also had not taken full cognizance that the other was at an entirely different stage of life in terms of focus and priorities. It came, too, as a horrifying shock that relationship commitment was not where they were headed; rather they liked the sound of "serial dater." Why not? It comes with all the rush, full adrenaline charge, and as soon as the negotiations begin, a high tail is in order.

Online dating makes the serial dating choice so easy. At a couple of clicks of the mouse there is another man or woman to be hooked with one's best bait. Of course, online one puts one's best foot forward, making sure it is a glossy shoe, recently polished and in the latest captivating style. The other won't notice the scratches from previous romantic scraps, or the detritus stuck to the bottom of the footwear, residue from past exploitations where one entered the ring, cavorted, mumbled all manner of sweet sounds, and then quickly escaped through the ropes. As soon as the tone shifted from "being in the moment" to questioning "where might this be going," the shoes knew instinctively to make a quick exit.

Lust doesn't take heartfelt emotion into consideration. Lust doesn't honor past hurts and unresolved rejection. Lust pays little to no attention to trust issues, and doesn't want to be burdened by ideas of love. No, lust is fully in the moment; its overriding goal is sex with no strings attached, and it will play any number of tricks to get its way. Lust knows how to tamper with hormones, and encourage obsessive fantasy to dominate the psyche. Lust is totally disinterested in practical considerations like "the other is married" or "the other is continents away." These are minor details for lust, certainly nothing that should get in the way of another tempestuous time.

Lust, if it had its way, would discourage lovers from wanting to get to know each other fully, because this is where the problems can start. Lust tries to cajole lovers to leave quickly after their blissful romp, and then spend all their waking moments imagining and engineering the next liaison. One of lust's greatest allies is email and text messages. Both emails and texts provide an illusion of communication and seduce the lovers into thinking they are on track to "getting to know each other." In essence, they provide titillation with minimal substance, and so the fantasy of "the other" can be sustained for that much longer.

The internet, from lust's point of view, has made shopping for sex so easy. Lust is navigating right from the moment that the lonely heart scrolls down the smorgasbord of tantalizing choices. By the time one has zeroed in on one or two fish to bait, one's sensory organs are in full salivation, breathlessly impatient to get a response.

Lust recently overheard a conversation between daters that was alarming: One of the daters was asserting the need for a friendship first, so that they could get to know the person more fully. They also wanted to take note of any relationship patterns that might be a barrier to connecting fully. Lust was incensed and prayed obsessively that this radical idea would not catch on. From lust's point of view, it would drag us back to the dark ages of Victorian times. No sex before marriage? "Total hell!" lust bellowed. Daters would have to genuinely like or love each other before they indulged, and lust knew that if this happened, it would be bridled once again, trapped behind those ropes of self-discipline, caged, imprisoned. Lust pondered this for a while, and then a wry smile took over. Perhaps the odd couple would go this route, but with its tools of online dating, emails and texts it was already gloating over the idea of a full-scale bombardment of unsuspecting mortal brains.

ARROGANCE

"I am right. I always will be. Others just don't know as much as I do."

Figure 3.5. Arrogance.

Arrogance sits on the face with an upturned sneer. The wearer tilts their head upwards slightly, looks down their nose, and then expresses their superiority with a disapproving grimace on their mouth. The look says, "You are beneath me." The other is pushed into a box with an enormous label on the front. The label may be—loser, jerk, or some other perceived pathological flaw. The label is the first task in the necessary dehumanization of others; it is essential if arrogance is to be maintained and sustained over time.

The labeled and judged often rebel against the arrogance of quick judgment. How dare they? Who do they think they are? They ponder feverishly all the ways they could get back at the arrogant one. The energy is wasted, however–the arrogant often are removed from the feeling world and so one has to bore through a steely armor to have an impact. Banging on the metal shield won't help either; it is an exercise in futility. The only solace for the judged is that there are many others alongside them in other boxes. The experience, however, is demeaning. The entire range of one's personality is boiled down into a reductionist, demeaning word or phrase. Any obvious strengths are ignored or put aside, and the label is given strobe lighting. It is an injustice that needs gallons of soothing liquid to force it down the throat of the victimized.

So what would motivate someone to sit on a cushion of arrogance, constantly seeking opportunities to affirm their superiority? First of all, it is a facade. One need only scratch the surface of the arrogant to see their paint peel. Their upturned sneer has been boiled in a pot of cynicism. Life has given them numerous reminders of their inadequacy, so they have sought out a suit of protection. Sometimes the armor can be the "intellect." If they move into their mind, away from all those frail, fragile feelings of inadequacy, then they have conjured up an escape of sorts. They believe that sitting solely in the mind gives them an advantage: others are slower, as connection with feelings slows down the mental processes. The arrogant one does not want to reflect deeply, but to be out there in a daily game of one-upmanship. This is the major stimulant in their world; it is their necessary shot of caffeine.

Arrogance and perceived superiority have "justified" war, cruelty, and death; they have underpinned systems like colonization. The colonizers' psyche was a well-oiled intellectual machine, spewing out cerebral ideas of superiority like a manufacturing plant. Ethics and integrity were sequestered. Now was a time to bring their royally sanctioned flags and plant them proudly in the new land, stating it was now theirs. One could only commit such a heinous act if arrogance were drip-fed into ones' veins on a regular basis.

On arrival in the new land, the labeling strategy was exercised fully. Complex cultures were deemed primitive, the people mere savages. This would justify all manner of brutality and dehumanization. The slave trade is one example of people being treated like animals, apparently incapable of feeling, tied up and chained in horrendous conditions and transported to the apparently "civilized" lands and their people. Once there, the Africans were perceived as working mules, capable of daunting physical tasks with minimal food.

Humankind has a long history of using perceived superiority and arrogance to justify death and destruction. The Greeks and Romans believed in their superiority. Indigenous cultures have used it, too, to attack a neighboring tribe. Shine light on the past and injustices are exposed. The superior stand on shaky ground with their veins of inadequacy exposed for all to see.

For the truly elevated, equality is the central tenet. They believe race, class, culture, religion, gender, and sexual orientation should not divide us, that each human being has a unique offering for the world, has their own collection of stories that can add meaning to the human recipe of "where are we going and how will we get there?" The arrogant one instead feels a need to step up to the plate and let those around them know their flaws. We all have our shadow sides, which are more obvious than we realize. Our shadows are found in our vulnerability, and in vulnerability, the beauty of the human spirit is revealed for all to see. Then our inner magnificence has an opportunity to hold hands with tenderness and fragility. Only then can we rise like a firework with embers that glow brightly in darkness, bursting with hope and possibility.

HURT

"We cower with it, lick the painful spots over and over, and curl into a ball, our nerve endings tender with the ache of it all."

Hurt sits in the heart with a dull ache. When we think about the hurt, it intensifies and the ache goes deeper. The desire to mask it, ignore it and disconnect ourselves from it is strong, as there is soul pain with it. One of the hardest challenges about hurt, if it was inflicted by another, is acknowledging that the person did this to us intentionally. By drinking this bitter potion we are waking up to the idea that the world is not a safe place, that bad things happen to good people, that kindness and genuine caring are not protection from the mean-spirited intention of another. Good karma, therefore, is not enough. In fact, kindness and positive karma can attract even more those with a desire to hurt; the brightness of others may be their trigger to hurt and lash out. Those who intentionally hurt, however, soon find themselves under glaring lights highlighting their own inadequacy. The light illuminates their deficits, and sends out warning signals to others.

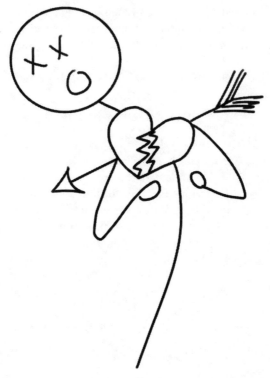

Figure 3.6. Hurt.

The one who inflicts hurt often has their barbs at the ready—they know about hurt and can't handle it, but need company nonetheless. Unlike others, they cannot secure friendship the easy, natural way of flowing in a river of affirmation and companionship. Their way of developing community is increasing the pool of victims. They strategically inflict a painful attack on an unsuspecting person when they appear off balance, vulnerable. Their intent is for the cruel words or action to linger, to corrode a sense of peace. This way, the attacked person wears the hurt like a hairshirt close to their skin, rubbing away at the tender spots. Why should one stew in the pot of hurt all alone? Surely it is reasonable to want others to join you; loneliness makes the state even more unbearable.

The victim has a choice to make:

They can ignore the hurt and live in hope they don't relive another hurtful experience anytime soon. Superficial forgiveness can be their thin gauze of protection: "Where there is hatred let me sow love," potent words from a prayer attributed to the thirteenth-century saint, Francis of Assisi. This is a powerful and effective shield against bitterness and cynicism, but what if it happens again and again and again? Can we keep sowing love and forgiveness when our heart is increasingly weighed down with corrosive balls of slowly dripping acid that leach the goodness out of the moment?

Another choice is to take the hurt on fully, to feel its full impact and to strip away the distorted lens that has one innocently expecting the best from all. With the rose-colored lens shattered in shards around them, they begin to let go of their childlike assumption that their world is a safe and secure one. They begin to acknowledge that the cruelty they hear of in other places could happen in their world too. They, too, could experience that degree of pain from a tormentor whose overriding intention is to make them suffer. They start to admit fully that the earth has many pariahs of pain whose pleasure is to have other sufferers around them.

To step fully into adulthood, one needs to witness both the light and the dark. One needs to acknowledge both loving kindness and acts of cruelty. They exist side by side, dancing together in an uneasy rhythm on the world stage for all to witness. From Kahil Gibran's perspective, the "black thread and the white are woven together. And when the black thread breaks, the weaver shall look into the whole cloth, and he shall examine the loom also" (Gibran, 1968:41–42).

So next time the inflicter of hurt sends off another arrow of venom, one is protected by a deep knowledge that it happens, that hurt is possible at any moment. The mere act of acceptance of it helps the hurt slide off like oil begging for a grip.

JEALOUSY

"'If only I were' can ring forever if we don't wake up to the importance of healing our areas of inadequacy."

Jealousy nibbles at peace and starts to tear holes in the fabric of our equilibrium. It has corrosive powers; and if fed by a thermometer drip of insecurity and low self-esteem, it can colonize our thought processes and build its tormenting powers. Jealousy likes to get in the middle of human relationships. Ironically, it is the love of the other that can drive the devouring feeling. Unbridled jealousy, however, can push away a cherished one. It can smother as it seeks to control, and the other suffocates in the claustrophobic, stifling atmosphere. On the up side, jealousy can be a driver for one to make necessary change in one's life; it can be a sharp pointer to holes of internal deficit that need attention.

Figure 3.7. Jealousy.

Jealousy has the power to drive a wedge between people. What were once valued characteristics of the other now become threats to one's identity. If only they didn't shine so brightly, weren't so good or obviously talented in an area in which we are struggling to build prowess, then we might feel better about ourselves. The resentment starts to build, and that sends a signal to jealousy that its momentum is on the rise.

Jealousy's partner in crime is competitiveness. Instead of an atmosphere of mutual appreciation, competitiveness takes hold. One-upping becomes the chosen game and tension increases dramatically. The topic of conversation may be benign, but the underlying theme is, "My opinion is right, my research is more reliable, and my values are the right values." How sad, with the myriad gifts we have to uplift each other and expand our understanding of the world, that competitiveness sneaks in and encourages us into a game of diminishing returns. Everyone loses–even the self-declared "winner." He or she will find loneliness, and potential alienation from the human family, a high price to pay for hierarchical status.

When considering jealousy and its impact, we also need to focus on the experience of the one who attracts jealous rivalry. Sometimes they are intent on being "better than" others, and so with that win/lose game in mind have attracted protagonists that will go to battle with them. Often, though, they are innocent in the game and have no desire to illuminate others' inadequacy. The fact is they have been blessed with gifts which have secured a strong self-esteem, and they effortlessly glow. They value closeness and mutually sharing relationships. When jealousy rears its head, the cooperatively inclined person is often dismayed when faced with competitive intentions. They have no desire to get into the ring and battle it out.

Even if they want to take away the others' perceived inferiority, there is nothing they can do. The realization that one's mere presence illuminates holes of inadequacy in another is an undermining and painful experience for them, particularly if they are craving closeness. The fear of rejection also haunts them. They know intuitively that if the competitor is not able to build themselves up in time, the relationship is on the line.

One strategy used by the competitor to push away the other may be to issue constant waves of criticism. They may also set up an argument that will be intentionally magnified, so as to threaten the foundation of the relationship. Techniques used by the competitor are likely to fall under passive/aggressive behavior. For instance, phone calls are not returned, and so silence is used as a weapon. They may talk about a person to others, trying to get them to reject or criticize the person, too. All in all, it is a battle of attrition: Attrition of human connection, attrition of self-worth and attrition of self-respect. In this game, the essence of the person in the world shrinks; they have become what they feared: small, and increasingly invisible.

At some point, they may want to resist jealousy's manipulations; foremost then it is important to shift ones' thinking on revealed inadequacy. Though the experience of having another illuminate our deficits is painful, we can turn it to our advantage. Clearly it bothers us because we wish we had prowess in these aspects. This then is a clear, direct message that pierces through the fog of our limited self-awareness: If we pay attention and work at these areas, perhaps in time we can shine in our own unique way. This is how we can experience breakthroughs: not by working on all of ourselves at once, but by picking an area of inadequacy and expanding it. Without those around us that seem to carry spotlights shining directly on those parts we don't like, we would not know where to start in our rebuilding process.

For those that experience projections of jealousy and competitiveness, a quote used by Nelson Mandela at his inauguration could be a soothing balm. He knew one of his tasks as a moral leader of a country, savaged by divisiveness based on race, was to encourage all citizens to rise and transcend smallness.

"Your playing small doesn't serve the world. There is nothing enlightened about shrinking so that other people won't feel insecure around you. We have been born to manifest the glory of God that is within us. It's not just in some of us; it's in everyone, and, as we let our light shine, we unconsciously give other people permission to do the same. As we are liberated from our own fear, so our presence automatically liberates others" (Williamson, 1992:190–191).

TRUST

"To grow, thrive and evolve as human beings, we have to take the big leap into the unknown, hoping with all our might that the leap is the right one—trust demands faith-based living."

Figure 3.8. Trust.

Trust is a bit like spreading our arms wide, our heart exposed and breathing fully, feeling completely open to the world. On the days we trust fully, we are at ease; there is openness in our hearts, and others are to be embraced without hesitation. In fact, life is to be embraced without hesitation, and all is just as it should be, certainly for that moment in time when our trust is high. When our trust is high, we are more expansive, see more opportunity, take more risks, love more and reach out. In that state, we attract others to us; they sense an open door and so they walk in, filling our lives with plenty. We grow, evolve, become unrecognizable to ourselves in a fully trusting state. In fact, with the trust thermometer high, there are no limits to our dreams and possibilities.

If trust is such a revered state how can we ensure it is with us always? How can we build it and protect ourselves against its contraction or annihilation?

First of all, we need to look at our expectations around trust. Some of us believe deeply that if I trust this or that person they SHOULD honor that trust forever, and that nothing should ever happen to affect that trust. How we view trust is often like a child who has been hurt: If anyone forsakes our trust, they are the devil incarnate. It's a black and white situation, with no grey; they are rejected and in the doghouse ad infinitum. Any love we had for them now turns to hatred, and we are willing to employ all sorts of legal help to drain them of their resources. Then they will really know we that we are not accepting what happened, not just rolling over passively. So trust has become an all-or-nothing idea in our mind, either total trust or total mistrust.

Total trust forever is an odd idea. Of course we want to believe it, but as humans we are in a state of constant change. Sure, we were trustworthy at that moment in time when life had sent us few challenges. However, when the tsunamis roll in and we buckle, then the ability to trust ourselves is diminished, let alone the ability to be trustworthy for others. It is so easy to forget that trust is not set in stone. It is more like putty: solid when things are cool, but when the heat is on formless and unrecognizable.

This idea creates havoc in long-term relationships. Although we said "in sickness and in health, until death us do part," that was when the relationship was in the fresh meadows of life, full of spring flowers and the possibility of growth. Inevitably the winds of change swirl around the relationship; a mate who once seemed strong seems to struggle with themselves, even trying to run away from the whirlpool of confusing emotion by distancing from themselves. That is when all manner of distress occurs: "They said they loved me and would cherish me, but now they are drinking excessively, staying out all night, perhaps with someone else." Also, they are lying, most often to themselves as well as their partner, and now trust is on the slide to hell.

When this happens or when some other event happens in our lives to break trust, we, much like an innocent and vulnerable child, say directly to our hearts, "I will never trust fully again. This person has betrayed me and so I will never take that kind of a risk again." We then think that the wise part of ourselves has kicked in and saved us from unfathomable hurt. However, what we sometimes don't realize is that we have now chosen a path of increasing cynicism, fear, and mistrust. We feel small, and we think small. Our risk-taking ability is dramatically reduced; our choice shrinks our world as well as our heart. We feel diminished but take succor in the fact that we are safe, but are we?

In that state, paranoia can set in. Then any challenge from the outside world is perceived as a threat against us. We barricade ourselves deeper in, soon losing touch with what is a real threat and what is perceived. This puts our body into a heightened state of hypervigilance, acid coursing through us due to the internalized anxiety of who is about to get us or trip us up. In time, this can plant the seeds of war, which are often about emotional or physical self-destruction taking over.

So how do we hold onto our ability to trust lifelong, given that it is such a critical ingredient for our growth and self-esteem? First, we must recognize that the most important person to trust is ourselves. If we step up to the plate and nurture ourselves consistently, taking care of our wounds when we feel fragile and compelled to cower in a corner, then we send a resounding message to ourselves that even when our trust is dishonored, we are in secure hands. To get on in life, we have to trust others.

Of course we are likely to be more discerning next time around, but that doesn't mean we need to retreat and erect a concrete wall. We can experience the sadness and hurt when life goes awry, but we can heal and become stronger than ever before, and therefore less likely to attract those that are likely to run when life sends them a tidal wave. The message we send ourselves then is, "Although it hurt and (s)he/they made a big mistake, I can heal and move on. I can also make a decision whether I want that person in my life in the future, and if so, in what way." We then know at a deep level that we have the capacity to deal with life's challenges, and nothing is more liberating and trust-inducing than that.

SHAME

"Shame wants our whole identity—it wants us to give over to its vice grip forever."

Shame is often meted out by an internal judge and jury, always at the ready for an excoriating attack. When one feels shame, it often consumes the psyche, douses the whole body in a shower of embarrassment and dis-ease. The impulse is to try to crawl away from it, run from it, but it is like a shadow following us down the dark alleyways of our mind. It can surprise us with attacks around the corner, trapping us in overwhelming negativity so that our ability to remember one positive characteristic of self is impossible. So why does shame take such a hold? Why does it go from zero to one hundred in moments and feel like we will never escape its grip?

Shame is perfectionism's long-time buddy; they ganged up a long time ago and work in tandem. Shame is the feeling; perfectionism is the pattern

Figure 3.9. Shame.

borne on a bedrock of shame. Shame often accumulates during childhood and waits patiently for an embarrassing moment or dreadful deed. Then its attack is ferocious. It says, "How could you? You are a really bad person, no one will want to be friends with you now, you are undeserving of anything, hide, run, but don't think you can run from me because I know your every move." Shame takes over the voice of our self-critic. By the time shame has finished with us, we don't want to go out ever again. The only solution that is remotely appealing is crawling up in a ball in some forgotten corner, and staying there forevermore, hoping the world will forget about us.

So, if shame has its way with us, what works to protect us, or fight back at those moments of extreme attack? Our first defense is recognizing that shame's voice is not to be trusted fully. Yes, we made a grave mistake; perhaps we hurt or harmed others in the process. The best we can say about a serious error is that we are learning from it, taking full responsibility. We reacted impulsively. We have re-lived the horror of our deed over and over again, and we deeply regret our actions, but it is part of being human.

Shame has us worrying incessantly about how others will view our actions. It was a heinous act, but does that make me a heinous individual? Desmond Tutu bore witness to the Truth and Reconciliation commission in South Africa after apartheid, an era of profound darkness in the history of the country. He came to the conclusion, "These were heinous acts and not heinous individuals." He cautioned, "When we see others as the enemy, we risk becoming what we hate. When we oppress others, we end up oppressing ourselves. All of our humanity is dependent on recognizing the humanity in others" (Tutu; 2004:139).

We can also explore how shame accumulated in the first place and fired up the voice of perfectionism. We can release the hurt that piled up from parents or bullies at school or those who consciously or unconsciously hurt us. We may want to try writing a letter that we don't send to those who scarred us, telling them about the pain of the seeds they planted and how it has impacted us over time. Once we have drained the toxicity of shame from the past, we then are free to see some positive aspects of shame. Shame and guilt are part of our conscience; if we felt neither, we might give in more to impulsivity in our decisions. Shame encourages more self-reflection. It says, "Take a while to figure out the consequences of your action before acting." Shame lets us know that we impact each other every day of our lives.

Let's tread carefully, keeping shame in mind as a guide to lead us to the better path, the nobler act. In the words of Desmond Tutu, a role model of forgiveness and compassion, "because we will hurt especially the ones we love by some wrong, we will always need a process of forgiveness and reconciliation to deal with those unfortunate yet all too human breaches in relationships. They are an inescapable characteristic of the human condition" (Tutu; 2004:57). He expands, "True reconciliation is based on forgiveness, and forgiveness is based on true confession, and confession is based on penitence, on contrition, on sorrow for what you have done" (Tutu; 2004:53).

JOY

"Joy knows no limits; it keeps reaching for a vision of our lives that elevates higher and higher."

Figure 3.10. Joy.

Joy from the heart is unique among human experiences. The heart has let go of excitement, of the need for the ego to be continually inflated, of the need for something new to be happening all the time. Joy in the heart is a quiet glee that radiates deep within, and it is an ebullient peace. It splashes over the heart, washing it with an immeasurable contentment; nothing else needs to happen, for all is just as it should be. Joy from the heart is full satiation with "what is."

We often crave spikes of joy. We are human, after all, and who hasn't desired with all their being a conquest of some sort? Coming first in the race of the Olympic athletes, winning money, landing the much sought-after job, getting the publishing contract, going on a date with our perfect partner—when these spikes happen, we are altered instantly, and that is the point. We often want something to take us away from the humdrum of life, from a feeling of mediocrity, of predictability. The spike does that and it does it well, but it's temporary. The gold medallion on the shelf only shines for so long; the novelty of buying anything at whim fades quickly, as unimaginable as that may sound. The ideal job or partner, when discovered fully, may have some sharp stones in the imagined backpack of complete delight. Life's treasures are rarely one color, all rosy pink with no slivers of darkness. So if our lives become a continual quest for spikes of joy, we find repeated troughs of disappointment along the way. Impermanence is the way ahead, even though we have buried our faces completely in the desert sand to avoid fully acknowledging its presence.

"Not getting what you desire and getting what you desire can both be disappointing," Kornfield states in his Buddhist phrase book (Kornfield, 1994:56). Desires for more joy often contribute to a tunnel vision, whereby all manner of beauty on the undiscovered path is missed along the way. Joy from the heart, however, is lingering memory. It comes up, unnoticed, of its own accord. It doesn't need events to heighten its state; it just is, a quiet overflowing cup that is sated effortlessly because the soul is known. When the heart is known and honored on the path of life, then acceptance is much easier. We let go of "what should be," "what I should be," "what should be happening now," and move gently, securely into "what is."

Khalil Gibran spoke about the interweaving of joy and sorrow: "Some of you say 'joy is greater than sorrow,' 'nay, sorrow is the greater.' But I say unto you, they are inseparable. Together they come, and when one sits alone with you at your board, remember that the other is asleep upon your bed" (Gibran, 1968:30).

So in essence all feelings, like joy and sorrow, are neither good nor bad, to be the desired ones and the not-desired ones. Every feeling, be it despair, loneliness, joy or elation, is part of the rainbow of feelings. They are all there because of the presence and acceptance of other feelings. If we only craved joy, then sorrow and misery would likely be the state we experienced the most. Like a wave crashing over the shore of our soul, all feelings want to be known; they want acknowledgment for who they are. "Let us be," they say. "Honor us because we are all the colors, none better than the other, none to stay permanently, all fleeting, each feeling a treasure in the path of getting to know the deepest part of you; all essential in this life of the slowly discovered magnificence of you." Feelings, just for a moment, feel a heart filled joy.

PATIENCE

"Patience is determined to bring out the best in us. It is the inexorably slow, unfolding rhythm that makes our final form breathtaking in all of its beauty."

Figure 3.11. Patience.

Patience is like sitting in treacle. You can feel the stickiness all around you. Your spirit needs air; it is suffocating, yet you sit still. You sit alert, yes waiting, waiting, waiting, and waiting past when you thought you could possibly wait; and yet you still wait, watch and observe; all the while hoping, hoping for that desire to be assuaged at last, hoping that the wait will be worth your while, and that the patience was not for naught.

Patience sits gracefully in a sea of frustration. To get to the bedrock of patience, one has to swim through all the muck, waves of frustration so high that you felt you would drown in the eddies of it all. Irritation is also swirling around. You can see the goal in your mind. It is almost within your reach, but you need some more time to get there. Then there are other internal barriers that make the reach harder. The greater the internal barriers, the deeper the frustration and irritation, and that is when impatience can take over and make an impulsive move. Impatience screams out, "You deserve it now! You shouldn't have to wait." Anger builds which is hard to quell. Once that anger is unleashed with entitlement, patience becomes an elusive eel snaking through a sea of toxic frustration.

With the long struggle to patience, often internal barriers get exposed. One might be the percolator drip of "Do I deserve this?" taking up space in the unconscious, triggering self-sabotage. You were just about there, making a humongous effort to stay the course, sitting under a mushroom of not knowing but still holding on, and then out of the blue you slide backwards from your own action. You do something that you know will make the hill steeper now, the peak achingly high. So with every ounce of your strength you dive back into the whirlpool of challenging emotions, determined to seize back patience. You know instinctively that once you get to a waiting spot you will be all right. The wait will somehow be more bearable then. You will stay in the moment but keep your eye on the prize, your gaze unwavering, and your spirit resolute.

Once you experience patience rising in you, the holding on will feel more effortless, because the bedrock of patience has a foundation of acceptance, acceptance that all is unfolding in exactly the right time and manner. You start to tentatively believe that perhaps there is a higher wisdom at work that you cannot access in your earthly form. Perhaps that makes the learning of patience not only worthwhile, but an essential ingredient to the peace you are able to create in your lifetime. On the bedrock of patience you have more of a bird's-eye view of your predicament; sometimes you reckon the process is as important as the goal. If the prize had been easy to get, would it be as valued? Would you be able to reach as high again without this opportunity to inhale patience deep into your being and birth it into every cell of your body? So patience at last has become an ally, not the dreaded tormentor. Patience and meaning weave beautifully together. They do a dance up the highest mountain, reveling in the hard-fought views, the higher plane. They take the next step to a more boundless perspective, a path of awe-inspiring achievement and the peak of grace.

CONFUSION

"Confusion is to be expected even though we rail against it. Every time we expand and grow, confusion takes over as a way of inviting us to explore ever deeper and mine our full splendor."

Figure 3.12. Confusion.

So you are all in a muddle, out of focus, scattered, a bit like jigsaw pieces lying on the carpet in disarray. Where do you even begin to get a handle on yourself, to chart a course that can help you move out of this morass? Thinking about it can cause even more confusion; the phrase "overanalysis leads to paralysis" comes to mind. As for the mind, well, that is the problem right there: it has become your archenemy in getting to know yourself. It sends so many dizzying, contradictory tangents that you can't even fathom a feeling. Feelings seem to be in some subterranean layer of your psyche, where thoughts are intentionally blocking the way. All the thoughts, too, seem to have one destination in mind: "Stucksville."

You have been stuck before; you remember another time being intimidated to even take one step out of the veritable cement you found yourself in. It's frightening because you know there is no quick fix to this stuff; no one is going to be coming along with a cement dissolver anytime soon. No, this is going to mean a mammoth effort on your part. The first massive challenge is figuring out the first step. It is also acknowledging that confusion seems to trigger past confusion. We start to remember all those periods in our lives when we were at sea, lost and clueless as to where we were going. Most often it is not one layer of confusion we are working through, but a lifetime of layers, a veritable vortex of not knowing. The deeper we go, the more frightening the feelings and the unknown.

So how do we end up on the lonely, debilitating road of confusion in the first place? One of the assured ways of getting there is to lose ourselves in the day to day of life. Whether it is busyness, or drowning in others' problems, or becoming obsessed with this or that activity, the ways are endless but the result is the same: Essentially we have lost connection with our essence, and then suddenly we hit a wall. Like a bird that flies into a window, we sit stunned for days, months and even years. We are immovable. Nothing (or very little) feels meaningful anymore. Our life has lost momentum, and we are forced to face the brutal reality of the emptiness of our existence. The questions that emerge at that time are endless: Where did I take a wrong turn? What was I doing that was so unhealthy that it contributed to this state? What should I have done instead? Which decisions do I regret? How on earth am I going to return to a life that resembles some normality and meaning?

Confusion can be an overall sign that all is not well, or that our life has changed dramatically and that we need to start anew. Confusion is a natural result of any grief. It educates that there is incongruence inside; our souls are still soaked in "what was" and we have not accepted yet "what is." For all of its challenges, ironically confusion also provides us with a rich opportunity to recreate our lives. We can potentially find a richer route to an uplifting endpoint, wherever the "end" is. However, first we need to figure out how on earth to get out of the cement.

Each person has to figure out the first action that makes sense to them. I remember the immense confusion I felt after immigrating to three countries and three continents in a space of ten years. By the time I arrived in Canada, my mind was coiled like spaghetti, and meaninglessness plagued me like an ever-present ghost, never leaving my side. I remember saying to myself at the time, "I need to create meaning; no one is going to give it to me. It will be my effort alone, and it will take some time. A new activity in a new country in a new home with a new job will all feel weird." I felt like I had invaded a far-off planet, where the people and customs seemed overwhelmingly foreign in spite of speaking the same language. Although there was boundless natural beauty, I couldn't feel it. For instance, I had never seen forests before and they were everywhere; the yearned-for African bush was clearly continents away.

In time each new activity, whether it was a sport or a pastime, started to slowly build up familiarity. Familiarity over time can start to build a brick of meaning in the foundation of one's psyche. Then, the more bricks of meaning one constructs, the more confusion finally starts to dissipate. It is like a mist that no longer shrouds the mind and the heart, but disappears into the ether, leaving a trail of clarity and richness in its wake. Through the process, one also has dived deeper and reclaimed more of oneself. Each reclamation celebrates protection against confusion's dizzying techniques that have us spinning in meaningless circles to oblivion.

HELPLESSNESS

"We are born helpless, and the feeling of helplessness never leaves our side even though we try to ignore it. Helplessness educates us continually about our limits, particularly with those we care about; it says we are vulnerable and unable to change others' circumstances, no matter the depth of our love."

Figure 3.13. Helplessness.

Try as you might, helplessness is a feeling you make a big effort to avoid. When you feel it even for a microsecond, you seem to be flooded with all those times you felt overwhelmed by your powerlessness, and childlike iner- tia takes hold. If you care about other people, there is no getting away from helplessness; inevitably others will trigger it, for example if they go down a self-destructive path and all you can do is watch. We should know the feeling well; when we think of our childhoods, many of us were immersed in help- lessness daily. Our cries weren't attended to all the time; it was all we had to get things going our way. Often, we were faced with parents who just didn't get it, didn't get why we were so unhappy; didn't get how hard it is to linger in a river of helplessness day after day, moment after moment.

When helplessness overwhelms us, it feels as if it will stay forever. It's also really uncomfortable to acknowledge it because the question arises "What do you do? Sit in its rocking chair and get paralyzed forever?" Helplessness talks in loud tones, saying, "There is nothing you can do; there is no point in trying. Just sit here and get used to it, because I am here to stay." Well, who is going to accept that state of affairs? "No," you retort, "I can give advice. They will listen to me when I tell them that what they are doing is killing themselves, a slow suicide, inch by inch."

"Painful" isn't the word that aptly describes this play. No, this is pure hor- ror! You love this person with all your heart, and now, before your eyes they are disintegrating, disappearing, because of either some grotesque illness or a self-destructive pattern. As a result, you have to watch with helplessness coursing through every vein in your body, in spite of your resistance.

What are our options when helplessness takes hold to this degree? Do we have any options other than to suffer in silence and get as depressed as the sufferer? The first step is likely the hardest: accepting "what is" and that there is nothing you can "do" about it. It is a huge step to acknowledge that you don't have the magic pill or the words of a sage that will turn it all around. The sufferer is sometimes under the illusion that you do, and it is a wakeup call for them to find that you don't, especially if they are actively undermin- ing their health. For the one who is terminally ill, your admitting your help- lessness helps prepare them for their exit from this life and eases them gently to face the final curtain. These may not feel like options at the time. Certainly they are the lesser of evils; there are no sandcastles on the beach in this sce- nario. However, they are a courageous position on your part, and a helpful nudge to the sufferer about their current doom laden reality.

Quite often when we are faced with helplessness, many of us deny it and give advice. It seems to bring out the doctor in all of us: Do this, do that, have you thought of this; as if it is likely that a quick panacea exists and will trans- port everyone to another reality overnight. The sufferer has likely heard this all before. From their perspective, no one seems to be really listening to them, or understanding how hard this is. There are countless internal obstacles ahead of them, and they sense these are bigger than their capacity to jump. Yes, they know helplessness well; their lives have become a living testament to it, and they may feel they are helpless to even communicate, which intensifies the feeling astronomically.

Helplessness has a habit of becoming a wedge between sufferer and caregiver. It can undermine one's ability to communicate the gap, the chasm splitting wider and wider until a plane can fly through it. If the dance of denying helplessness continues, despair sets in; and then helplessness has taken over, colonized both brains, dragging them to darkness.

Helplessness loses power instantly when it is expressed. It knows we think it is wrong to feel it; it takes advantage of that. To sit next to one you love and to feel the helplessness, to acknowledge it verbally, says volumes. It says you have the courage to face the full consequences of the situation, that you can hold their hand and lovingly stroke it, putting a lifetime of tenderness in the moment. Then, somehow, both are soothed. The outcome may still be one of great pain, but neither person is aching in loneliness, and that is the best medicine against helplessness that there ever was.

LONELINESS

"Loneliness says you are all alone, that it is only you who feels this way. It's not true; many in the human family have felt the pain of loneliness. If we reach out for another hand we can help heal each other—it is what being human is all about."

The ache of loneliness sometimes feels like it is going to devour your heart, eat you from the inside, and nibble away so that in time you are only pain, only ache, a submerging island in a vast ocean of others. The gap between the other and you seems ever widening. No one will ever understand the full suffering of your experience, so what is the point of even trying to communicate? It feels beyond communication, as if your very soul is steeped in a lonely stew that is slowly but inexorably swallowing you up.

Loneliness feeds on loneliness; it is its own mother's milk. The longer the lonely state, the more firmly loneliness is in charge. It is advising you continually that this is only happening to you; in this vast world of over eight billion people, only you are feeling the way that you do. You long for connection, but it is too big a risk. Given how vulnerable you feel, any rejection now could really send you into a vortex to hell. Then you would never come back from this outback lonely planet, back into society.

Come to think of it, you don't want anything to do with society; everyone else looks freaky to you. They are all running around with purpose, even

Figure 3.14. Loneliness.

smiles on their faces. You can't stand the whole charade of it all. Everyone
sounds like they are on happy pills, like Prozac is being injected into the
water from somewhere; only you are not getting what everyone else is on.
You can't relate; as soon as they open their mouths, their voices are all so
high-pitched you could scream. With this all-consuming ache in your heart,
you need a world that is real, not some bubblegum, squeaky, saccharine-filled
world full of nauseatingly peppy people. When you listen to yourself, you are
no longer really speaking to others. It is more like grunting, barely forming
words so you can hide deeper in the recesses of the curtain of life. No going
onto the main stage with the masses and making real sounds! That's way too
scary from this place of overwhelming solitude and pain.

One day, however, it feels a bit different. It is the same sky and the same
neighbors doing their thing, but everything looks a bit more approachable,

even the neighbors. Oddly, they seem a bit more receptive. You don't know why and you are suspicious of it, but there is definitely something different. Instead of spending the morning sleeping more, the day wandering aimlessly around the apartment until it's dark, and the night furtively scouring the streets in your darkest hat and coat so that you are more of a moving shadow than a person, this time you decide to get dressed early. What will you wear? You don't want to put on the dark coat, so you choose clothes you haven't worn in months since the loneliness took a vice grip on your heart. You spend a long time washing your face, as if layers of detritus have built up all around you, shrouding you in a veil of secrecy and lonesomeness.

The step outside in the daylight feels positively scary. Your neighbor looks at you and then quickly away, but you caught some kindness in her eyes so you take a risk and form a "hello" you hear reverberating forever in your psyche. The neighbor looks startled but says hello back and that, quite frankly, has made your day. You feel a smile form on your face, a creaky smile, like it needs oiling and it may be cracking your entire face, but you felt it nonetheless.

As you walk down the road, you hear the birds chirping; a purple finch is positively belting it out, its chorus filling the early morning with its piercing melody from heaven. Nothing has ever sounded so inspiring of goodness; you wish you could kiss the bird for this gift so freely given. It feels like nectar poured into the lonely chambers of your heart, like molten honey oozing into a dry crevice and moistening it all forever. You are almost ecstatic now for no real reason except for the friendly neighbor and the angelic finch; you haven't felt this alive in months, and you can't remember when you felt life around you feeding you in this way. You notice your feet are not shuffling along the pavement anymore, each step seems to have some energy in it, naturally higher, skirting the surface below. You wonder if you got some of that Prozac, after all, getting a bit overwhelmed with the promise of it all.

When you eventually return home, you look at your apartment with fresh new eyes. The whole place seems grubby. Dust balls flee as you walk past them, forming alliances as they gather together. You can't stand it. How on earth did you hang out here for day and night on end, not talking to anyone, spending endless hours in a stupor in front of the computer or television, soaking in your cynicism about the world and its inhabitants? In the cocoon of loneliness, this was your retreat, the only place you felt safe, and your hide-away from everything. Now it's all changed. You imagine going on a cleaning frenzy, rebooting the place with a sparkly shine, opening the windows at last, letting the wind blow things about, its freshness transporting you away from your self-imposed exile into the living, breathing planet filled with at least some people you might like, and certainly with joy-filled purple finches.

UNCERTAINTY

"'Uncertainty' is our middle name, much as we would deny it. How can it be otherwise? Who are we, where are we going and what we will be when we get there is all a mystery?"

Figure 3.15. Uncertainty.

Uncertainty is everywhere. Live a life of striving, and it is your shadow, chasing after you, drowning you in a sea of not knowing what the future brings. You can know yourself fully yet swim in incessant uncertainty, not knowing which direction you are going, only that it felt right to move this way, no matter the outcome. It's different from confusion: confusion is a specific feeling that has a certainty to it, where uncertainty is nebulous, ethereal, ill-formed, amoebalike. It has no real shape. It's as if the ground beneath you is jelly and each step is indefinite, to an unknown place and a destination that is unheard of, that may or may not exist.

So if one were to judge uncertainty, much like a jury in a court, would one say it is a good thing or a bad thing, to be embraced or wholeheartedly rejected? From my own understanding, I believe there is a relationship between uncertainty and living life to the full. The more we are able to embrace it, to hold it in our arms loosely, not clinging to anything, the more alive we feel in life. Uncertainty is here to stay; it is nonnegotiable. After all, we will all die at some point and we don't even know how or when. We don't know where we are going, if anywhere, when we die. We don't even know if we will like where we go when we die, if we do in fact go somewhere. So in fact all the critical questions in our lives remain unanswered, sitting like towering question marks over our heads every day. Uncertainty permeates our lives much like a misty sky of not knowing, never leaving this or that moment of our lives. It is a basic fact of everyone's life. Unless one has had a near-death experience or is a seer, uncertainty is certain, and that can have a profound impact, consciously or unconsciously, on our daily lives.

Some choose to bury uncertainty, put it underground in a steel vat, lock it firmly, throw away the key and imagine it is gone. When that happens, our lives get smaller as we take fewer risks; we want to know what is going to happen before we even get there. If that is the case, then packaged holidays become more attractive than adventure travel to some wild, untrammeled spot on Planet Earth. So too is living in a gated community: there are guards, keys, locks, and big dogs, all the accoutrements one needs for a certain path, a well-traversed road in life, a definite destination. One plans as if there were no unforeseen circumstances in life: this is what I will do next month, next year and by the next decade. Life is mapped out like a chart, all these definite events and milestones, nothing uncertain about that. One moves "into the seasonless world where you shall laugh, but not all of your laughter, and weep, but not all of your tears" (Gibran, 1968:12).

Living this way, one can delude oneself that all is certain. Except (and one has to say "except") when there is an earthquake, or a tsunami heaven forbid, or what about an illness that has no cure—no one, not even one's insurance, ventured down that road. An accident, some fluke occurrence: the only meteorite in the sky lands on your car and smashes your arm to smithereens. What then of those well-made plans?

It was only two hundred years ago when there were no cars, and housing was a lot more fragile, and the wild animals were still roaming; then all of us had a much better handle on uncertainty and how it pervaded every moment of every life. Our cocooning in cement or strong structures that can handle most gale force winds and in the ever-reliable automobile that is made for the backroads of life has in essence created illusions of certainty: the certain job (until the economy buckles), or the certain relationship (unless, of course, they find love down the road in some far-off place). Even someone that has planned for retirement like a mathematician can be thrown off the cozy rug onto the hard floor of nails in an instant by some devious shenanigans from one of the company's investors.

It is not my intent to be doom and gloom here; the hope is that love will last and that the money saved will be a handsome pot of gold for all that one desires in the future. However, to consider these visions static and ossified in eternity is to subscribe to an overwhelming illusion of life and its unpredictable nature. Ask any person living off the land about uncertainty; they will likely answer that it is in the hands of the gods whether they live or die the next day or hour, and that they have accepted that reality.

So if one were the jury, what would one advise, given that uncertainty is not in question, but our ability to acknowledge it fully and live consciously with it is the issue? The real issue is whether we will acknowledge the mystical uncertainty lurking everywhere, or deny it and pretend that it is for other people's lives and that somehow, we are immune to its influence. Kahil Gibran is clear in his advice: "Do we desire to live in a seasonless world?" So, if we have known that state, kept our world small, felt stifled by the stale air of the predictable moment, by the life of one considered wooden step after the next in a certain direction to the known lands, then how do we change? How do we move in another direction? How do we get away from this habit of being magnetized to predictability at all costs?

To ask the question is the first step, and it is a big one. All of a sudden the ground is not so solid and the path has taken a turn in a new direction. You start to take risks, small ones at first and then bigger and bigger. More questions start to flood the brain: "What did I always want to do with my life but never had the courage? What are my dreams?" Now it really starts opening up, and although uncertainty seems to be all around, following you now like a best friend, so too does opportunity. Strange coincidences pop up all over the place. "How weird is that?" you say to yourself, but secretly you love it. You feel more alive, like a kid again running into the forest without a care in the world. Even your hair has loosened, and your smile, long buried under a grimace of expectation and predictable moments, looks gleeful.

Even though you don't know for sure where you are going, your instincts seem to have taken over. Your heart is also on your side and says softly to you, "Give it a try!" in spite of the palpitations you have in your chest. Yes, you are feeling more for sure, and isn't that what distinguishes you from a robot? Robots are all pre-programmed; certainty their middle name. You, however, have chosen a different path, full of twists, turns, unforeseen companions and events along the way. "My goodness," you say to yourself one moment of one day, "wow, this is intense but exhilarating! I wouldn't have it any other way."

DETERMINATION

"Determination is an arrow thrown into the future with the will and desire to follow its path to glory."

Figure 3.16. Determination.

Determination is cut from steel. It is resistant, it is powerful, and it is overwhelmingly committed to stay the course. Determination flares up in the veins and says to the mind, "We are in it for the long haul; no matter the journey, we are staying the course." Determination married resilience a long time ago; they are in a sublime partnership, one bolstering the other intermittently. Between them they achieve great things and are able to sustain their inhabitants in the worst and best of times.

If determination is so great, then how does one get it, build it in the mind and the body so that when one needs it, it flows like a tap with an ever-plentiful supply? Determination isn't just given to us, as if some people got it in the virtue sweepstakes and others lost out. Determination is nurtured by discipline, one of its biggest friends, along with resilience. Determination is accumulated drop by drop from one moment to another. For example, a drop is added to our reserve when we know we need to exercise and, in spite of feeling lethargic, wanting to watch TV for hours on end, we get off the comfy couch and onto our bicycle, renewing our body and also renewing the spirit with another dousing of determination. When we act time and time again for our higher interest, the reserves of determination start to build, like a whirlpool of nourishing substance sitting in the body waiting for the moment it is needed. Determination is like a well of inspiration, strength, discipline, and resilience all mixed together, a quixotic brew, pickling in ideas and healthy choices that bolster us when life sends us a humdinger.

Determination is our ally and best friend when we get an illness that requires time to heal. Ask those who have experienced cancer and come out the other side, how helpful determination was when they were overwhelmed by the magnitude of the fight before them. Determination is necessary for the dedicated sports heroes and heroines. Their practice sessions are never-ending, and the elusive number of seconds shaved off their time would make all the difference between a first-place win and the back of the field. Determination gets them back at the racetrack time and time again, bursting over the hurdles as if they were doing it for the first time, their vigor and enthusiasm palpable for each practice session.

Determination is also coursing through the veins of the refugee who is fleeing a homeland that offers instability, and possibly death, for the foreseeable future. Packing a few bags and bringing the whole family in tow is an enormous act of courage and determination. It is determination that helps them all put one foot in front of another on the road out, not knowing where they are heading and what they will experience when they get there. Determination by the truckload is evident in the natural world; how else could one interpret the wildebeest calf who flees on newly born fragile legs with the wind, sensing the hungry lion only meters behind?

Given the necessity of determination to the everyday existence of most creatures and humans that inhabit this planet, let us all rise up and commit to building it daily. Build its reserves so there is nothing that gets in the way of our dreams that sit patiently in our souls. Veer away from those habits that keep us stuck in mediocrity and survival. Let's go for the gusto, get out there and start living to our fullest potential, using determination every step of the way.

SADNESS

"Sadness begs for attention. It is a great teacher if we let it guide us throughout our lives. It is tired of being pushed away, unacknowledged; it wants full expression, and it wants it today."

Figure 3.17. Sadness.

It is hard to admit sadness, but it is there. The heart knows; the heart reveals it with a heavy feeling. It is as if your heart has weights hanging off it, heavy weights, weights that aren't going away anytime soon. The heaviness reveals something; if it could talk it would say it needs exploration, like a miner digging deeper and deeper for what has not surfaced. You sometimes fear that if you dig, all manner of sadness will surface, that the sadness will consume you and take over your life, drown you in its turbulent eddies and whirlpools. Instead, you deny the heaviness, pretend it isn't there even though it seems to follow you everywhere. It is with you when you are surrounded by friends. It puts a barrier between you and them that is hard to cross without acknowledging how you really feel. It leaves you with a false sense that you are not genuine with others and they are not genuine with you.

Sometimes, you have to take a risk and say, "I don't always like my life, where I am going, or who I am, or who I will be when I get to the end." Sometimes, you have to give voice to the heaviness in your heart that acknowledges your unrealized dreams; to the weight carried in your heart for the relationships that never happened despite your effort; to the loneliness you sometimes feel; to the resounding emptiness that achingly haunts you even though you try to lower your expectations for a successful life. Sometimes you have to say, with the honesty of a truth-warrior, "All is not right with me. I don't know why I am sad. I just know, when I listen to my heart and feel the weight, that I am not right; that I am off kilter; that I am not at peace with myself."

Sadness comes up also when you lose yourself to someone or something and it doesn't work out. You dedicated all your time to winning a competition, and then it is over; or to caring for a relative, and then they are gone. You feel gutted by sadness, and when you feel the sadness, the regret comes, followed by disappointment, hurt, shame, rejection, abandonment and so the list goes on. Sadness seems to sit on top of a container of buried emotion; once the sadness is acknowledged and expressed, all manner of feelings rise. Sadness is the first wave, and then the others emerge, eager for air, eager for expression. Sadness took charge of the floodgate a long time ago; it put itself in charge and refused to allow other feelings to pass until it was first expressed. Then its generosity took over and it opened up the gates, releasing all to rise.

Sadness is sometimes concerned with what could have been, might have happened and was supposed to occur. At times, sadness has a lot of wisdom, if only we would let it guide us. With sadness, we know that things matter: the relationship that didn't work out, a job we left or a dream we let go of. Sadness says that something was important; our heart held it close and now can let it go with ease, knowing that the memory is cauterized forever.

Sadness also allows us to transition from one thing to another. Perhaps we change countries, change villages, change towns; wherever we go, sadness comes too, for a while. Sadness likes to acknowledge fully what went before. It has a reputation for being thorough; sadness wants a full acknowledgment of our history. Sadness knows this is how we arrive at peace. Sadness says, "Stop awhile; let's honor what was memorable, even if it was never fully realized." Sadness hones in on the experiences held in the heart, the ones that made the blood quicken in our veins or set our heart aflutter when we took the risk to "go for it!" In that way sadness has immeasurable wisdom: it knows full well that when we come to the end of our lives and look back, all of those memories of beauty will be intact, like jewels locked in a treasure chest, sacred moments protected to nourish our soul repeatedly as we savor each one.

So next time you want to speed up when your heart feels heavy, remember that sadness is on your side. It wants you to remember the precious moments, the times steeped in meaning and fulfillment. It is guarding them against the rush and torrent of life lest they get lost in oblivion, and all manner of emptiness fill the void. Sadness is your ally and companion throughout life, your preserver of meaning, a best friend of sorts, no matter what happens, steadfast with you to the end, helping you to hold onto what is real.

GUILT

"Guilt runs around with a big stick, wanting to whip us into shape. The question is, do we like its vision of our lives or does it just want to dominate?"

Guilt is a two-edged sword; guilt and our conscience weave together in a tightly twisted bond. Our conscience is built on our values, values passed on through the generations. Some are helpful, some not, but they are our values. When we go against them, act as if they were not there, then guilt lets us know. It rears its head, fills our mind with self-dread and self-incrimination. It bellows unequivocally that a line has been crossed, and that here is one of the costs: a long, protracted dance with guilt.

For instance, suppose that we were raised by someone who was, above all, a role model of loyalty, but then found ourselves talking meanly about another, our tongue wildly wagging with derisive detail. Guilt lets us know immediately that we have wronged another, been unfaithful to who we are, let our team down. Even if no one else is aware, guilt is, and that is judge and jury enough. In that way, guilt can be helpful; it can bring out our best behavior, and when we have strayed can give us a sharp awakening to guide us in a more positive direction. Some guilt is necessary for humankind to flow together: we learn there are consequences for hurting each other. We realize we leave a trail of open wounds in our wake when we barrel through life recklessly, having tossed any guilt out the window and far beyond.

Figure 3.18. Guilt.

However, guilt also has a dark side, a side that keeps us stuck in an endless perseveration cycle. It can contribute to self-loathing, lead us to self-punishment, take us down a road where our soul feels it is shriveling and drying up like crackling leaves. This kind of guilt is born from a rocky road in childhood. Some felt guilty for being alive, their parents reminding them, "I never wanted a child, a boy, a girl. You have taken away my enjoyment of life." A statement like that to an innocent child can scar the soul deeply; guilt then is felt for mere existence. With this overwhelming amount of guilt, the child's focus becomes to be as invisible as possible, so as to avoid the devouring beast that will swallow them up if it is aroused. Guilt, when it is on the attack and it knows the foundation is cracked, can have a field day. One can feel guilty then for any kind of enjoyment whatsoever. Guilt works from the presumption, "You don't deserve enjoyment and haven't earned it."

Guilt can also stop a partner from leaving an abusive situation. If they believed they deserved a better life, then it might be easier, but guilt and self-incrimination keep the person in glue for years; the longer they stay, the worse it gets. Guilt can say to the guilt-ridden person, "It was 'to love and cherish till death do us part.'" So guilt persuades them to stay, and they live a living death, in which their spirit has dried on the vine because of the torturous circumstances they drink in daily.

In situations like this, guilt is our enemy, dragging us to ever-greater degrees of self-punishment. When we are in this kind of a lock with guilt, how on earth can we break free? Guilt is no different from other challenging feelings in that way; it needs to be wrestled down, fought back, tackled, undermined, shocked and drained. If it is intent on bringing out the worst in us, then we need to release it in any way we can. To give in to it continually is a path of destruction. Slowly we implode inside, trying to do what guilt tells us is right, but in essence depriving our soul of the sustenance it needs to live the life we desire.

We need to be aware that when guilt is on a destructive path there is no letting up: We eat our favorite meal, and we feel guilty. We don't exercise one day a week, and guilt takes over our conscience. We don't call someone back right away or do a chore because we are exhausted, and guilt has something to say.

So, let's tell guilt where to go when it has taken on the role of tormentor. We know it does it well; there is no competitor. But that doesn't mean we have to give in, give up, lie down and let it trample us into the ground. No, we can stand up, face it square on, hear its message and then act in the opposite manner. Yes, we are deserving! We are fighting hard in this game of life. Even when we slip and fall, we get back up, dust ourselves off and stand proudly for conquering just one more moment in our sometimes daunting lives.

ANGER

"I explode when I want. It is on my terms; if I wreak havoc for others, so be it. I don't want to be managed anytime soon, so take a hike!"

Figure 3.19. Anger.

Anger is a storm in the mind. It seizes every rational cell and disputes any of its messages. It dominates, colonizes, and sweeps, wildly bringing blame, accusation, and a righteous response. It is out to get even, and to do it now; not tomorrow, but right away. It comes with no timeout for reflection, no pause. It seeks justice and is determined to mete it out. Anger inflates us in the moment, puffs us up with vitriol, and states unequivocally that we are right and they are wrong and they deserve fully our vindictive backlash.

When we see the person with whom we are angry, we can feel the anger bubbling in our veins, building up in our blood, bursting in our mouth before we have even opened it. Then the spew begins. It is justified, so surely we don't have to sift through our words carefully. No, we can let the hate-filled message stream bitterly past our tongue and attack, demean, undermine, chasten and excoriate. This is no time to discuss my role and your role in the situation. No, this is all about you, what you did, your fault, your time to grovel big time.

Sometimes, a burning fire can spark another burning fire, and then the explosions start and all is possible: hitting, punching, slapping, spitting, attacking with implements and even guns and knives. This is when anger takes on a life of its own, when every moment of injustice in a lifetime gathers into one moment and is all focused on the other, as if they were the culprit for every wrongdoing ever suffered.

Anger, then, should come with a warning label: "Do not use in moments of intensity." There should be sell-by dates on anger. If this anger is for a wrong of five years ago, let it go. Dispense with it; quit carrying it around and projecting it onto others who may in fact be innocent.

Some cultures insist on a walkabout where one separates from the tribe if one is angry or having unsettling feelings. The wisdom in this simple practice is profound. It deals with blame instantly. If you feel it, it is yours to deal with; no one else needs to be involved. In the walkabout model, there is cultural pressure to own your feelings, and then work through them. Instead of carrying unresolved stuff, resolve it now. In many societies, this would mean a lot of walkers on long journeys. The consequence, however, may be a world closer to peace than could be brought about by any other human gesture.

So how does anger get so out of control in the first place? The root most often starts in childhood. Many of us have had less than ideal parents. On a societal level, it is only in recent times that it has become possible to air, without personal shame, the emotional problems rooted in poor parenting, and that techniques have become available to heal them. We may have suffered from emotional neglect, abuse, favoritism, absent parenting or overprotective parenting, and so the list goes on. Sometimes, a partner, friend, or colleague, having hurt us in some way, finds themselves bearing the brunt of all our childhood hurts. How fair is that? No wonder they look completely bewildered about the intensity of our reaction: for a minor misdemeanor, hell's fury is now spewing recklessly out of our mouth.

Anger needs entitlement as a kitten needs its mother's milk. Entitlement says, "I am justified in my response. I am owed. My reaction is legitimate. This is overdue, and it is my turn to collect my dues." Dues are entitlements to a rage, a full-scale breakdown. Smashing things, throwing things, hitting people, even having an affair can be symptoms of unresolved anger meted out, with entitlement paving the way.

Entitlement is often born of a time when we felt victimized. In our mind, it is a leveling of injustice that still causes us great pain; the greater the perception of entitlement, often the greater the pain from the past. So entitlement says, "Go for it! Don't hesitate. Be impulsive. Get your needs met now." Sadly, entitlement doesn't have a crystal ball and has no ability to foresee the damage inflicted by uncontrolled anger. The hurt from one violent episode can scar the deepest connection, and then one tear after another eventually shreds the fabric. Relationships fall asunder, and so meaning collapses around us. After all, if those we love aren't with us in the trenches of life, what do we have?

Anger, when controlled and reflected on, can have an enormously positive impact. First, it needs to divorce entitlement, and also develop strategies to air itself in a healthy manner. Anger then can become a friend. Its early warning of irritability can help us look within and explore what our reaction is about. Anger can let us know when we are hurt or have been taken advantage of. By airing it in a calm and cool manner, we have an opportunity to get closer to those we care about.

Voicing anger in a mutually sensitive way, owning our reactions, can also help us to heal the past. We deal with the present-day triggers and resolve the issues with those that re-trigger our past. Only from the trigger does the opportunity to heal present itself; and it is always a mystery how we unconsciously attract those who will ignite the hurts of our earlier life. Ironically, they offer us an elixir, some healing balm to soothe and mend the scars of our history. Then anger can play an important part in our liberation, freeing us from past resentment, and transporting us to a calmer place. Reactivity now becomes a ghost only furtively haunting, instead of the enraged bull on a stampede.

HOPE

"It is as if our heart is attached to a butterfly's wings, lifting and alighting us, taking us into the ether where hope builds on more hope."

Hope is like immersing the heart and soul in bubbly spring water–each bursting bubble is another spurt of energy. Optimism and possibility abound. All seems reachable. It's as if the climb up the mountain has suddenly changed to a hill, and the peak is now in view. The steps ahead are on firm terrain with a manageable ascent. Hope buoys your step, and each step boosts your confidence, and then imagination takes hold and declares that your wildest dreams

Figure 3.20. Hope.

are within your grasp. Contemplating failure is not on the radar–hope takes over the whole brain and fills every crevice, leaving no opening for doubt.

Hope says, "Think big! Imagine wider than wide! Let your eyes crave limitless horizons." Hope says, "You are not alone." It whispers, "We go forward together. May the human capacity for goodness pierce the heart of the deepest cynic and drain the toxic ooze." Hope builds on hope when we join hands.

Ambassadors of hope can only be firelighters of the flame of hope if they understand the gravity of their path and are willing to stay the course. Nelson Mandela, I imagine, surmised that he would only fit the shoes designed for an inspiring leader if he had drained all bitterness from his heart. With a cleansed heart, free of the hatred sanctioned by apartheid, each phrase of his inauguration speech hung in the air like a butterfly being suspended by wind thermals. The sun glowing behind its wings, its flutter light and unhindered, effortlessly it rose upwards and outwards on its journey.

Ambassadors of hope like King and Mandela offer their hope to us by their very presence. Their hope is hope because of its sincerity. It resonates like the string of an instrument only because it has made a resolute choice to play a single pitch. Hope knows darkness and fear well. It has made its expansive choice in full knowledge of the tricks, chicanery and manipulations of the con artists who would shrivel the human spirit. Hope has linked up with transcendence, and their relationship has endured. "Stay the course," hope encourages, "and your potential as a human being is limitless." When you surround yourself with other hope-inducers, the most intractable human concerns can be seen from a fresh angle. You no longer need to fix the potholes in the old path; with transcendence in tow, a whole new path is illuminated for all who dare to hope.

Hope is not a gift placed in your lap–you must struggle intensely for hope. Hope and discipline need each other as plants need water to survive. Each day, the hope barometer rises and falls according to your ability to make the disciplined choice that expands the spirit, challenges the mind, and soothes and nurtures yourself and others. Hope never gives up on those who have been contracted by their obeisance to fear. Hope says, "It's never too late to join us!" Hope's numbers are expanding each minute, and soon the mightiest walls of oppression will crumble in its presence. Hope says, "Yes, we can!" and "We will!"

SELF-DOUBT

"It is like living life on an earthquake with constant tremors; it is nigh impossible to know what to do or what to think from this place of turbulence."

Self-doubt is powerful, even though it often dupes us otherwise. Its power lies in its persistence and its percolator drip of attacks on self- confidence, encouraging us to question our ability to do just about anything. It encourages the imposter syndrome, where we fear we are a fraud; it is also reminding us continually that we are not measuring up in some way despite our efforts. It is a brand-new day and the hope was to enjoy yourself, or perhaps

Figure 3.21. Self-doubt.

to get something important done or to connect with those you care about, for example. Self-doubt squeezes into the moment harassing you with an array of internal questions or challenges, pricking your potential to enjoy the day with each intervention. The questions might be: Do you really have time to enjoy yourself when you have loads of things you need to do? What are you avoiding? Are those people really your friends? Are you sure you can trust them? You haven't been achieving very much lately, don't you think you should spend time doing x for instance? and Are you really deficient, or worse a loser? These are some of the brutal internal attacks you may ask yourself.

Self-doubt has two main strategies to get its way. First, it gets you to internally question everything, and I mean everything. You are so exhausted by the questions and by the time you have addressed some of them, any momentum you had has evaporated into the ether. It is not only your momentum that has gone, but also your self-esteem that helps you drive into the future, helps you to take risks, and bolsters you for challenging moments in life, are now shaky. Occasionally, self-doubt links up for a dance with shame., The two of them invite you into a vortex of self-loathing, drawing you deeper and deeper into low self-worth. Shame and self-doubt are intent on reminding you of all your past failures; it retrieves them with such ease, one after another until you are immobilized. It also has a knack of remembering any past labels you have had for yourself in dark moments and bellows them out repeatedly, so in time you wither like a vine in desert winds. The labels might be: you are an imposter, you are a fraud or an outsider, you are not good enough, you are inadequate, or you are a failure. The other strategy self-doubt uses is distraction. For instance, it encourages you to endlessly scroll on your cell phone. Self-doubt knows full well that if you get distracted it is much easier to manipulate you. At these times, self-doubt connects with procrastination and takes you on the road to nowhere. You may be stuck in a kind of glue unable to follow through, thinking about thinking, boiling, and bubbling in "I should," "I could," and "I wish."

So how did self-doubt get to root itself in our body and how can we get the upper hand? The seeds of self-doubt are often sewn in childhood or in other tough moments of trauma in our lives. For instance, they may be seeded from parents who judged you and reminded you that you should have done better. You brought home the B+ report and there is an unmistakable sneer or disappointing glint in the eye, or maybe a comment of, you should have an A. The result is feeling *less than* and inadequate, both fertile ground for self-doubt seeds to grow. There is also the parent who molly coddles a son or daughter, propelled by their need to be needed. The parent is teaching their child repeatedly that they cannot make it on their own—that they need them for guidance and figuring out life. The dependency on another lays the foundation for vulnerability or self- doubt. Another way to fertilize the seeds of self-doubt is constantly comparing oneself to others. Self-doubt loves this; it knows you will never measure up and it can worm on in doing what it does best, undermining your peace and capacity for self-acceptance.

Given self-doubt's power and its corrosive impact, how can we wrestle away its influence and take charge. Our first step in challenging self-doubt is to notice it. Over time, you will build self-awareness and make note of the signs and symptoms when it sneaks in, for instance, the self-questioning and labelling. There may be different signs for different people; we all have our vulnerable places. Knowing them and recognizing its sneaky presence can help detect its influence early on, before it can build its persuasive powers. The second step is to remind ourselves of our accomplishments despite self-doubt and its wily ways. Make an ongoing list to keep re-referring to in times when a little doubt sneaks in.

Another protective mechanism is to honor our uniqueness, writing down our list of strengths and all of our characteristics that we value, that sometimes get buried when we compare ourselves to others. Also, take a bird's eye view analysis and assess whether systems that encourage us to compare ourselves to and to be in competition with others truly reflect our values. Another way to release self-doubt is to reflect on what works for our body to release embodied emotion. For some, it is using a visualization that counters self-doubt—what visual helps you to feel at your strongest, imagining it when self-doubt slips in. Others may find movement, tapping, acupuncture, or body work helpful to release the emotion that is stored in the body and continues to play havoc with our mind. Another key piece is employing our strategies early and taking action. Also, resisting the temptation to distract for hours pretending self-doubt is not building its resources to harass, undermine, convince, and manipulate us, and move us away from the core of our hard-earned wisdom and fortitude.

ANXIETY

"It is a thief of sorts, robbing one of self-trust, shaking our core self, and undermining our ability to manage the moment and to move forward in life."

Figure 3.22. Anxiety.

It can start as a butterfly under the skin, floating around the heart or the stomach are some of its favorite places to hang out. In no time, it is a veritable flock of butterflies, flitting here and flitting there, making us feel more and more unsettled, and moving us closer and closer to the destination of panic. Anxiety, in addition to the fluttery feeling, has a loud voice. Often its messages are, "you can't cope," "something bad is about to happen," or "keep hyper-vigilant and don't relax." Anxiety also has the habit of taking over our psyche, dominating everywhere we go, undermining conversations with others and our ability to be present. Our concentration goes for a loop, and it is challenging to get anything done when its influence is so pervasive. The stronger anxiety is, the more it impacts our body, for instance, our hands can have a tremor, our voice can quaver, or our feet cannot be still tapping up and down continually—if there is enough anxiety in the body it can lead to a full-blown panic attack. A panic attack, like an erupting volcano, produces many reactions. For example, we can have a rapid pounding heart rate, difficulty breathing, a sense of impending doom, light headedness, sweating, trembling, and/or shaking.

Anxiety, if untended, can have a dramatic effect on our lives. It can stop us from working due to its impact and unpredictability; and can make it nearly or completely impossible to cope with our day. It can encourage us to isolate because of the shame we feel in trying to conceal its presence from others. It can consume our days, obsessively worrying when we are next going to feel out of control and incapacitated. All in all, it can take over our identity, substantially impact our life choices and freedoms, and it can deprive us of even a small shard of peace and enjoyment.

A key piece in dealing with anxiety is to notice the tricks it has up its sleeve. One trick is it refuses to be ignored. It is always needy for attention, wanting to take center stage in everything we do. "Focus on me," it says in a loud voice when you are desperate to move away from its impact. Another of anxiety's tricks is that it pretends it is showing up alone, and that it is only its influence that is impacting the moment. The concealment of other feelings helps anxiety stay dominant and makes it very challenging to clear its impact. Anxiety can also trick us into believing that alcohol, other stimulants, or distraction will take it away. In essence, the root cause for anxiety has not been addressed, so although there may be temporary relief, its presence is likely to build and it may, in time, ramp up for a full-blown panic attack.

So, how do we take charge and drain anxiety's influence and feel as if we have some effective way to manage and to work with our feelings? Our most powerful intervention can be deep breathing into the area of our body that we feel a build-up of anxiety. For instance, it may be in our chest or stomach, in our shoulders, or in our throat. Once we have detected the area in our body with the build-up, we can use our breath like a fishing line, retrieving feelings that may lie underneath anxiety's flutter. By breathing deeply into that area, we may detect sadness, hurt, fear, helplessness, powerlessness, inadequacy, for instance, or emotion that has been embodied due to past traumatic experiences. Now we are onto something; the more we connect with the deeper layer of emotions underneath anxiety, the more we are disabling anxiety and sending it into the ether. Detecting the other feelings is an important first step. The second step is to focus on clearing the embodied emotion. If, for example, we detected sadness in regard to a loss that has not been resolved, we may want to explore ways to move through the sadness. Releasing feelings can involve crying it out, writing it out, releasing it through body work, or vagus toning exercises, tapping, movement, or open communication are some strategies that work for some people some of the time. Clearing embodied emotion is a lifelong endeavor for all of us—and figuring out what works to clear past emotional issues from our body is an ongoing commitment to our mental health, peace of mind, and the ability to be present.

Once we have strategies to detect and to clear embodied emotion, anxiety no longer has a powerful role. Although, historically, anxiety can be seen as an undermining influence robbing us of peace and stability and challenging our capacity to manage our everyday. We could also see it as a friend and ally. Its message says loudly, stop, breathe, connect to your body. Anxiety lets us know there is something that wants to be cleared. Its butterflies alert us to the place in the body where emotion related to past trauma is now rising to the surface of our consciousness. So, anxiety can help a lot, revealing where we need to pay attention and to remember to attune to our body to do the identifying and clearing work. Therefore, the next time that anxiety pops up, see if you can treat its presence with curiosity. Where in our body do we need to pay attention? What are we needing to clear from the past, so we can move forward into the future with more optimism and a lighter way of being in the world?

ABANDONMENT

"Someone pushed us away, knowing we were vulnerable, and left us ill equipped to handle the pain of the loss."

Figure 3.23. Abandonment.

Abandonment takes us to a raw, vulnerable place. It is like we are curled up in the corner hugging our knees, trying to feel safe when the wounds are gaping, and when the pain is oozing like a river in full flood. Abandonment attacks our self-esteem and it makes us question our value, such as, who we are in the world? It also creates uncertainty on how to put our next foot forward, given the rejection we feel. Abandonment implies someone just left emotionally or physically, packed their bags, and disappeared with little to no explanation or an explanation that often does not make sense. Abandonment feelings are often big and hard to handle, as they can trigger the very same issue in childhood when our vulnerability was overwhelming and our capacity to make sense of what is happening in our world was extremely limited. For example, a mother who needed a break from the marriage just took her packed suitcase one day and came back three months later to make things work, with minimal explanation to the children. Or, it could be a father needing to go to a war zone for work and he does not return for more than six months. Either way, the child can experience the event as being abandoned. The abandonment feeling can come with other intense feelings too. Rejection, fear of loss, vulnerable, lonely, betrayal, misunderstood, confusion, loss, grief, distrust, unsafe, destabilized, adrift, shame, and a feeling of being lost can all be in the mix.

Abandonment, like other embodied emotion, can live on in our psyche, unconsciously attracting the very situation we are trying so hard to avoid. The internalized experience of abandonment can influence, for instance, the unconscious choice of future partners. An individual with embodied abandonment may be attracted to partners who are less stable, more impulsive, or who struggle with commitment or fidelity, so inevitably the embodied feeling is triggered again by a partner's actions of perceived abandonment. It is a harsh reality of the human condition; the very experience we find overwhelmingly painful is often the very experience we re-create. One asks, why would one be so masochistic? The truth is that the body wants to heal, and the body's way to heal from a history of *locked in* pain is for a new experience to re-traumatize and to re-trigger, by bringing the pain to the surface so it can now heal. Unless of course we do proactive trauma healing, and go digging or mining for embodied emotion, and then clearing what we discover deep in the cells of our body. This will help release the issues in our tissues continually.

When we are abandoned, or perceive ourselves to be abandoned, it can be a deep pit to try and climb out of. First of all, our trust in others is shattered. "How could they be so cruel?" we ask ourselves. Our fundamental truth about ourselves and our worthiness is now in question. If someone could abandon us, just like that, with the swish of a horse's tail, what is our value? We assume all sort of givens in relationships with others and one act of abandonment throws it all up like confetti getting swept up in a gust of wind, going anywhere and everywhere, leaving our sense of self in pieces. If our identity is shattered, so then are the roles we have in life. Our role as an employee, daughter, caregiver, friend, confidant, sports team partner, member of a book club, and so on, are all are affected because the ground beneath us has shifted, and life will never feel as certain again. Finding meaning in a sea of uncertainty will also be challenging moving forward.

Given the impact of abandonment, how do we get up, take the next step, and move onto ground that we now know has cracks, crevices, and potential pitfalls? First, we need to dig deep and retrieve the courage patiently sitting in our heart. If it is hard to access, review past accomplishments in your life that took both courage and a spade full of determination. When we review tough moments in our life, we can take note that our courage showed up despite fear, apathy, despair, inadequacy, not enough and destabilized for example. Therefore, exercising even a little courage can be medicine; we are already pole-vaulting over a formidable wall of barriers to progress. To take even one step at this stage is facing a great deal and committing to expansion, despite the desire to curl up and to contract for an illusory idea of safety.

Second, to face and to heal from abandonment, we need to regain a sense of control, particularly in relationships. That seems impossible given we can feel so out of control after the abandonment. The control is two-fold, it is not the illusion of control guaranteeing us that we will never be abandoned again. It is the ongoing development of confidence in our capacity to discern characteristics of those likely to abandon. It is also bolstering our capacity to heal from past trauma, as a way of developing resilience with whatever happens in life. Dealing with past trauma can be a lifelong endeavor as layer and layer of the past is revealed and then released by strategies that work for our body.

What are some of the characteristics we want to be aware of going forward that could assess someone's capacity to be in a healthy relationship? It could be a whole range of characteristics to look out for, but overall, assessing an individual's past capacity to commit to others, their ability to move through their past trauma, their ability to stay connected to their feelings, and their ability to be present with others. Discerning an individual's capacity to care for others and assessing if their capacity to care is matched by actions. Having a clear idea of the kind of people we would like to attract to our lives, all of this can help with the rolling of the dice. We acknowledge being in a relationship with another is still a gamble, but at least we can take time to discern whether the person is worthy of the risk and leap of faith we are choosing.

The other aspect of control is learning strategies and lifestyle choices that can help us heal from past trauma. Slowing down is key, so we can recognize our own triggers, and also what helps to soothe us when we are triggered. Exploring a healing integrative modality that resonates with us, will help us shift embodied emotion and integrate it into our body. Talk therapy can be limited here unless there are mind/body techniques incorporated into the sessions. Talking about trauma, particularly all the details, often activates it and we can retraumatize ourselves. Exploring then somatically based therapies that focus on the body, can facilitate ways to release trauma from the body.

So, picking yourself up again and focusing on the path ahead with discernment and also your capacity to heal in your backpack of abilities can help a great deal. It may make life's journey a whole bunch easier, knowing that you will have more wisdom at hand and some more confidence in your heart with regard to healing, no matter what happens on the unpredictable, pot-holed road of life.

SELF PITY

"Self-pity says, 'It's not fair, it shouldn't have happened, and I need to take time to lick my gaping wounds.'"

Figure 3.24. Self-pity.

Self-pity shows up when we are at our most vulnerable, and when we may be feeling victimized by life's circumstances. It convinces us from the start that it is our friend, an ally, a comfort. It pretends it is a soft blanket to snuggle into, to wrap around and shelter us from the storm of life. The blanket, however, over time smothers us, stifles our growth, and keeps us stuck. How does self-pity go about doing that?

First, self-pity agrees with us that what happened was not fair and that we are right to be angry and hurt. Self-pity is convinced that it is not your fault and that the circumstance or another person is to blame. Self-pity's consistent tune that is singing in your ears is "woe is me,'" over and over again. The combination of an injustice, others are to blame, and woe is me are guaranteed invitations down the path of victimization. Aligning with victimization is impactful, as many of us have histories where we felt victimized in the past, particularly in childhood. So, what started out as a thirty-pound problem, with self-pity in the mix, is now fifty pounds, and add past victimization, and now we are weighed down with a ninety-pound weight dragging our shoulders down and no easy way out of intense suffering.

What is it about self-pity that it can take a hold so quickly; why are we so vulnerable to its beckoning? Why is it so comforting when we know that it is taking us into a contracted place, which will intensify our aloneness and increase our tendency to feel sorry for ourselves? We know intuitively we will struggle to get out of the dark, dank room that self-pity takes us to, but we are pulled in often at a deeply unconscious level. Likely, its most seductive strategy is the place it guides us to is familiar. We know self-pity well, if we reflect on our childhood and early adulthood, and review all the times that we were hurt, vulnerable, and felt victimized by life's circumstances, we can be assured self-pity was there. So, in the past, it has offered us some bitter comfort time and time again, and so we fell into its seductive cloak effortlessly. Self-pity knows that once it has wrapped around us it will be a long, intense struggle to release its hold. It has won out once again. When self-pity has us in its grip, it is often alienating for others to be close. Often, they can see we are in its shackles, and so others can feel helpless to help or to support us, given the power of its influence.

Besides familiarity, what else makes it easy to fall under self-pity and its wily ways? We are vulnerable to self-pity because feelings such as hurt, shame, rejection, betrayal, grief, loss, helplessness, powerlessness, victimization, being bullied, loneliness, fear, and/or confusion, as some examples, are still locked into our body and have not been released. This embodied emotion, often stored at a time of trauma, contributes significantly to us being sucked down a low road in life with such ease. We are easily triggered if we have not healed from past issues, and we are consciously or unconsciously pulled into dark traps, like the one self-pity sets for us, that can lock us into deep suffering for months, and even years.

Given the influence of self-pity, how can we protect ourselves as best we can and resist being pulled into its sticky web? Self-awareness is key, noticing when we are giving into it. Being watchful with regard to the words we use when describing our challenging situation. If we are interpreting it from a victim's lens, we need to take the time to notice and be aware, and also reflect on the feelings that may be triggered and explore ways of releasing the feelings. One way to release feelings, for example hurt, because of prior rejection or betrayal by an ex-partner or ex-friend, is by writing a letter to them, not sending it unless we feel they are ready to hear our hurt and let them know how their actions impacted us and about the scars that were left behind. Reflect also on your earlier years. Does this feeling go back to childhood or early adulthood, and what other memories does it bring up? We could write a letter to those other people too who have hurt us in the distant past. Taking time to resolve the feelings helps you to heal and to move forward with more power in the future. It is also a protective shield against self-pity and its desire to offer you mock comfort and take you to a lonely place, where you will feel increasingly misunderstood and alienated from those you care about.

So next time you see self-pity beckoning to you to, tell self-pity that you are onto its tricks, that you will not be seduced by its "woe is me" song, and that you intend to exercise your power so that you are protected from its manipulations and influence.

HUMILITY

"Humility is a way of being in the world—it understands that the ego is superfluous and that showing vulnerability with others is a greater good."

Figure 3.25. Humility.

Humility comes from a deep place within us. It is not here one day and gone the next; it is an undercurrent that becomes part of our foundation. We dip into it to approach life's challenges from a place of vulnerability and grace. Guided by humility, we acknowledge that many situations encountered in life are bigger than our ability to change the circumstances. A friend, relative, or someone else is in physical pain or in deep distress, and we acknowledge that we cannot fix it or take it away. We ourselves at times face intense struggles. The helplessness and powerlessness we feel in these circumstances can take us deeper down the road of humility if we are willing to admit our limitations. That is the choice point: are we willing to acknowledge our incapacity to fix, control, or make a positive impact on the situation? Or, do we ignore it, deny it, resist it, run away, distract from it, or reject it, and pretend to ourselves that the only choice is to keep on trying. Much like an animal butting up against a wall thinking yet another butt will somehow clear the way. Looking over our lives it is helpful to notice how many times we have been in that position, adamantly and zealously refusing to admit defeat, seeing submission as weakness. Our ego is involved after all. We must prove to ourselves and others as we perceive our identity is at stake, our self-esteem, our feeling of competency, our mantra "we can manage no matter what," it is a battle, and we must and we will win. We get into a state of blind positivity, defiance propelling us, with tunnel vision so narrow we are almost cross eyed with the fury of it all. In this state, we associate humility as giving up, being weak, inadequate, small, and deficient. Humility, however, is the opposite. It is often immersed in wisdom, and in essence takes a great deal of strength and courage. Humility reaches for the bird's eye view of a situation; from the higher plane it sees realistic choices very clearly and is also acutely aware of limitations. Humility's life companion is surrender; surrender is not giving up even though many view it that way. Surrender is the capacity to let go and to acknowledge that human beings are limited in their influence. Surrender is an art form, a profound life skill. For instance, imagine a frog in a whirlpool with chaotic currents using every limb to fight to get out of a whirlpool, Its frenetic activity just makes it spin faster and faster, the struggle is so intense that it looks like it may pass out with complete and utter exhaustion. Then suddenly there is a change, it surrenders, its limbs go flaccid, its body a state of torpor and miraculously given resistance is gone it effortlessly lifts onto the sunny rock where the battle is over.

The advantages of living a life with humility are dramatic. Energy is no longer spent on senseless grasping leading to possible burn-out. Humility moves us onto the road to peace, its companion surrender helps us to face the healing grief work of actively letting go. Humility endears us to others; reflect on the Dalai Lama, Nelson Mandela, and Desmond Tutu as role models of humility. Their humility and vulnerability make them relatable; they exude a depth of calm and joy few of us likely will achieve in our lifetime. Their spirits are chiseled by adversity and the capacity to let go over and over again of forces outside of their control. Humility helps lower others' defenses. It is heart and compassion centered, and it resists ego-jostling with others. Humility contributes to resilience. Using active discernment, we decide when to put effort into effecting change or when to let go, it helps to build our strength, and thereby, we are protected from going down the rabbit hole of helplessness and powerlessness where we can struggle for ages to get out.

Humility says in a clear calm voice, "it is ok to be vulnerable, to not know what to do or how to respond, to be overwhelmed by life and all of its complexity." Humility gives permission to take risks and to experiment in life. It encourages us to lift the burden of perfectionism, of being right, of the illusions of invincibility, and moves us forward to follow our gut response instead and to see where it takes us. Humility then can take us down the unknown road, the never imagined destination, the unforeseen circumstances that contribute to our lives mimicking an adventure, where the only thing we must figure out is the next step. From this place, we can notice a bit more joy in our step, a little more lightness and humor, increased creativity, and the ability to meet others in a heart-to-heart centered place where we have the capacity for a deep connection, and together be immersed in a whirlpool of humility, grace, and surrender.

DEPRESSION

"Depression soaks our soul in a feeling that meaninglessness is everywhere and there is no point in even trying to change it."

Figure 3.26. Depression.

Depression can often sit in your heart, like a heavy piece of steel, weighing you down every moment of every day. Its heaviness impacts our face, it feels tight, our smile feels restricted, like our mouth might crack wide open if we venture to smile. It impacts our shoulders, as if a huge brick is hanging from each one. Our feet seem to drag along, barely lifting off the ground, and our spirit is shrouded by its presence. Our will struggles immensely to do basic tasks, such as getting out of bed, brushing one's teeth, and getting dressed. All seems overwhelming, and nigh impossible when depression is having its way. Depression is far-reaching; it takes over your perception, like you bought a different pair of glasses that are glued over your eyes now. Everyone and everything in your life looks less attractive, you notice faults in others more easily, crevices and cracks in your life become more apparent, and all those tasks that gave you meaning in the past now seem unimportant, superficial, and potentially meaningless.

Depression is deep, and when people say get over it, or do this or do that to fix it, or you must try harder, pull yourself up by your bootstraps, or get busy or some other superficial understanding of depression, there is a feeling they do not get it. Also, there is a feeling that they do not understand the heaviness of the load nor how pervasive it is, or that you cannot just shake it off, that it is not a choice, that you are not being slothful, that you cannot help it right now, and that it is not your fault. You seem to be trying all you can but the river you are swimming up against has an intense undercurrent, and it takes one side swipe, and you are pushed right back despite your efforts. Feeling misunderstood by others can intensify depression. In addition to feeling misunderstood, you could also feel loneliness, alienation, and feel unseen, potentially, as well as an increased desire to isolate.

There can be many contributing factors to depression. One significant factor that we have no control over is our biological make-up. We could have genetic loading for depression from our parents or could have inherited a biological sensitivity to a change in seasons, and for some, may need medication to offset the inherited imbalances. A history of trauma is another factor that impacts depression. When a range of traumatic events have occurred in our lives and we were not able to release the feelings associated with the event, the feelings are stored and impact our mood daily. For example, if we experienced bullying at school and experienced hopelessness, helplessness, hurt, and despair, each one of these embodied feelings will contribute to our thoughts, our feeling state, and will influence what we attract to our lives in the future. Thoughts from this set of feelings may be, "what's the point of trying," "I can't do anything to help the situation," "being depressed is inevitable," or "others are out to hurt me." Additionally, you might feel that "I'm unprotected," "I am not safe and there is a lot to worry about," as some examples. When we hear these thoughts repeatedly to our mind, it is understandable that we feel depressed. In addition, a whole range of other factors can also contribute to depression. Some examples are the complexity of our personal history and personality, how others impact us, where we live, societal factors, weather, how accepted we are for who we are, how sensitive we are, poverty, violence, food insecurity, our life circumstance, or if we are enabling others and carrying some of their load in life. These and a range of other issues can all have an impact on our mood.

Given the variety of factors that can impact depression, one must ask what might help psychologically, even a little bit, to lighten our load. Honoring how we feel may be an important first step in the process. This takes us out of the habit of pretending to others and to ourselves, which can drain a great deal of our energy. Depression is at times a conglomeration of feelings, all bound together in a sticky mass held in various places in our body. So, parsing them out can be very helpful. Are feelings of sadness, hurt, confusion, loss, or inadequacy, for example, leaching into depression? Sorting through the specific feelings and writing them out daily can help us to start to understand more deeply what is pulling us down. Once we have a fuller understanding of our feelings and issues, it is critical to explore clearing strategies to help release the embodied emotion. Asking the question: "what helps me soothe, calm, and clear feelings from my body?" The art of clearing out emotion is often neglected in the busyness of life, yet it can make a profound difference in how we live our life overall. The continuum of our life can range from stable misery at the low end to transcending limitations and reaching for the best version of ourselves at the top of the continuum. Most of us may lie in the middle, taking some time to honor and to release feelings, but still neglecting old, unresolved issues and related feelings. However, if we take time to clear old issues and feelings, we can liberate ourselves not only from challenging feelings that will likely be triggered time and time again, but also from fixed unhelpful patterns of behavior and limiting thoughts. What works for people to release and to clear feelings is specific to each person. It could include: artistic expression, for instance, drawing what they are experiencing and mapping out the complexity of the situation: music, letter writing to deal with unresolved issues; reading or writing poetry; or exercises for toning your vagus nerve, time in nature, breath work, tapping, yoga, massage, qigong, acupuncture, eye movement desensitization and reprocessing (EMDR); cranial sacral therapy; and other modalities that may help in the release of embodied emotion. It is different tools for different people, taking time to learn what makes your body feel a little lighter, a little more energized, or a little more grounded.

Reflecting on our lifestyle is also a key component of resisting depression's voice of "what's the point," "isolate from others," no one gets you," "you can't effect change," and "there's something wrong with you," as some examples. To drown out the volume of depression's voice we need to slow down. It is only through slowing down that we can identify specific feelings and know what clearing strategy works. All in all, working through depression can be one of the most freeing tasks we will ever do. It takes time, effort, and patience, but the outcome can be monumental in terms of the elevated trajectory of our lives and of our ability to be close with others, holding their hands in companionship in this challenging and mystifying journey of life.

BETRAYAL

"Someone yanked us off the rug of our lives with an earthshattering jolt and a steady stream of lies and manipulation."

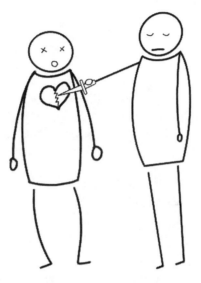

Figure 3.27. Betrayal.

Betrayal triggers deep pain, right down to the marrow of our being, and it is profoundly challenging to swallow the full impact. It can get stuck in the throat for example, perhaps for years, even decades, because it fundamentally challenges all we know about love, meaning, and relationships. Its long echo in our body takes us to a raw, vulnerable place, where for the longest time we can sit in disbelief that the betrayal actually happened. There are degrees of betrayal. For instance, there is the betrayal of a long-term partner who has an affair for months and perhaps years. We thought we were being told the truth about all those missed evenings, and now with the truth peeled back and exposed, we recall in horror all the times we were lied to, manipulated, deceived, undermined, taken advantage of, discarded, rejected, used, and devalued. How could they do that to you? You trusted and were committed to your partner, you were there for them, you were always trying to help your partner, you loved your partner, and how could they? It is bewildering, and the answers are hard to find, no matter your effort, and that increases the pain exponentially. In time, one must admit that the person you love is not the person you thought they were, that they perhaps did not love you after all, or at least not in the way you understand love. One of the challenges of betrayal is it is so easy to get caught in an obsessive betrayal vortex, thinking about thinking, fixated on the betrayal, struggling to let go and feel the full range of feelings. The tormenting question that keeps circulating is "did they really love me?" In your conflicted mind, if they did, they would not have betrayed you. The layers of loss and grief seem never ending, and who can mow through all that detritus and not get stuck in deep cynicism, bitterness, and a broken or closed heart.

Another kind of betrayal is that of a parent who could choose to stick by your side when a truth is uncovered, or when they see injustice, and yet they stand there, silent, bearing witness in some instances to you experiencing abuse in its myriad of forms. Why are they silent? They should be protecting you. Why would they not stand up for you, call out whatever injustice is happening, or state unequivocally this is wrong? The answers are often lost in the deep recesses of their being, and so again we are left with deep internal conflict in our expectations of others. Our belief in love is questioned, so too is the belief in human goodness and righteous behavior. The internal conflict puts pressure on us to revise our entire way of being in the world given the risks are so glaring.

Another form of betrayal is the betrayal of a colleague or group of people who you thought were friends, and when confronted and the heat gets turned up, they slink away, like an eel sliding into some dark crevice. They are also nowhere to be seen in a critical moment when you have to defend yourself in a situation that has been twisted, contorted, and is nigh impossible to move through. Again, the heart hurts, you nurse your disappointment, vulnerability spikes, and destabilization and uncertainty dominate. The big question looms large, like a hovering black cloud that follows you everywhere, even into your dream state. Who can I trust on the road of my life?

Given the complexity of being a human being, there is the need to take risks and to form relationships if we are going to be shielded from the ravages of loneliness. How do we steer our ship into safer waters throughout our life? What can help us develop our capacity of discernment? We can start to assess who is too risky to trust, what are some of the characteristics or behaviors that would be useful to be on high alert to, and what are some early warning signs to watch out for regarding betrayal. Additionally, it may be helpful to get clear on the characteristics and behaviors of those who are trustworthy for the most part, who understand loyalty, and who have the courage and strength to stick by your side when you find yourself in a challenging situation. These individuals are often more connected, abide by their values in life, and are steered by their moral compass and the ability to form committed long lasting relationships. Their care and concern for the *other*, and their willingness to be present to another's experience, are all assets in a relationship and make betrayal less likely.

When looking at the characteristics and behaviors for those who may betray us, there are several personality aspects worth noting. Entitlement can be a key character trait to track. Entitlement is often developed from a childhood of victimization, whereby one reaches adulthood feeling owed, feeling pay back is warranted, and often there is no amount of pay back that will fill the pit of unmet need. Entitlement can also contribute to an excessive self-focus. Therefore, in an intimate relationship, the partner may be primarily attuned to their needs at the expense of the relationship. Another characteristic worth noting is the degree of self-connectedness that the person demonstrates. If the person is using drugs, alcohol, busyness, and/or excessive work, as some examples of ways to disconnect from themselves, and they live a life with considerably more chaos and adrenalin, a betrayal is more likely, as they have lost their connection to their moral anchor in life. Other characteristics to be alert to with regard to betrayal are taking note when individuals struggle to form lasting relationships, and when they demonstrate a limited capacity to attune and be present for *another* and struggle overall with commitment. A pattern of behavior that is also worth noting is dependency. Over-functioners, those who are overly responsible for others often are attracted, consciously or unconsciously, to under-functioning individuals, who have a need to depend on others and are waiting to be fixed. When one is waiting for someone else to *fix* you, which is not possible, one has a tendency of not being accountable for one's actions, hence betrayal may be more likely.

If we have experienced betrayal, what are some ways of beginning the letting-go process. Feeling some of the feelings is challenging but necessary in the release from the body. The feelings may be anger, bitterness, rage, rejection, unworthiness, self-doubt, confusion, loss, fear, distrust, cynicism, self-loathing, distance from others, alienation, misunderstood, disoriented, unsafe, devalued, abandoned, inadequacy, depression, anxiousness, wariness, hurt, shame, and being unlovable, to name a few. Writing a letter to the person who betrayed you (you may need to write twenty or more letters to release all the pain) and not sending them unless you feel the person can hear your pain and support your process. The letter writing is about getting one's truth out, saying unequivocally what one needs to say, releasing the pain of the experience including the anger, and perhaps rage, at those whose hurtful actions have betrayed you. Developing a ritual to release the letters may also help. Perhaps, when one feels ready, burn all the letters and visualize the letting go of past pain. Body work like a deep tissue massage, cranial sacral therapy, or acupuncture can also help release the blocks in the body, and perhaps assist with opening one's heart again if one feels ready and safe to do so. What heals us? This is a question we all need to answer throughout our lives as inevitably we will experience pain. Pain is often our biggest teacher, guiding us to face what we thought we could not face, challenging us to rise to the best and strongest version of ourselves, and bringing out from the dark, dank recesses of our body, the pain and the important story that goes with it. Tackling pain can be liberating, releasing the heavy backpack of unresolved emotion, and spreading your wings and deciding who to fly with in the future with all your hard-earned wisdom and courage.

UNSAFE

"We cower in a corner, barely an eye open, too scared to acknowledge what is happening and how frightening it all is."

Figure 3.28. Unsafe.

It is like living in a permanent earthquake state, the very ground you walk on feels unsteady, filled with potholes, treacherous crevices, and steep drop-offs to nowhere. Unsafe befriends *out of control*—the two feeling states work in tandem; they are united in their efforts to remind you repeatedly of risks. For instance, their dictates are to be on high alert, that there is no escape, that they are in charge, that you are at their mercy wherever you go, that you could be thrown off balance any moment of any day, that no-one and nothing is to be trusted, and it is best to isolate, take few risks, and stay home. A life dominated by unsafe and its best friend "out of control" is a contracted existence, potentially filled with regret, stripped of meaning, barren in one's capacity to grow, and is often a friendless and joyless state where our primary focus every day is to just survive the storm of life. Our mind is consumed in this state with *what if*, analyzing every possible scenario, trying to persuade ourselves desperately that we do have some lever of control and that we should be able to guarantee our safety.

Unsafe, along with "out of control" is non-negotiable in a wide variety of complex situations. There are protracted societal conditions of war, gun violence, or tyrannical regimes, where it is expected that unsafe would have the upper hand and dictate our days. There is also the reality of living with an unsafe partner or family member where hypervigilance is protective and helps to keep one alert to threat. The unsafe feeling can also dominate when we have serious health issues, and when our mortality is threatened by disease. In these extremely challenging situations, it is expected we would feel unsafe, and our moment-to-moment pre-occupation with survival makes total sense. However, there are also individuals who have been overwhelmed with an intense feeling of unsafe, perhaps years or even decades ago, and who are no longer in a triggering traumatic situation, but who carry unsafe like a burdensome backpack wherever they go, lugging it here, there, and everywhere, so it weighs down each moment with such gravity. Past trauma related to unsafe also skews our vision with regard to what is safe or is not. If we have unsafe reverberating in our body, it is tough to act in a discerning manner and to figure out when and where we can relax and let go. This is the power of trauma, trauma that is held in the body resounds forever more until it is released. It also dictates our thoughts consciously or unconsciously, helping to create the very reality we are often most wanting to avoid. The event oh so long-ago states emphatically, "it is not safe to take risks, you can't trust others, you will be harmed if you don't protect yourself, and you are vulnerable every moment of every day."

So, what happens in our lives when unsafe has the upper hand and this panicked filled state dominates our existence? We often tend to retreat from social situations, we take few risks in life, and we try to follow a tried and tested path to get some modicum of stabilization. Given that we attract the very situations or people that would be helpful to avoid, these individuals or events can trigger unsafe in a variety of ways. All emotion locked into our body tends to draw, like a magnet, the specific conditions so they are triggered. The trigger could be a partner suddenly leaving with no explanation, or one finds oneself surrounded by others who are intent on bullying you. Unsafe could also crop up in the workplace where a boss demeans and criticizes you incessantly, creating an unsafe climate overall. When unsafe is triggered again, we are at a choice point in our lives. We can distract, numb, and disconnect as a way of pushing it down again, hoping it is buried forever. Or, we can use the trigger to explore and to honor the pain, work it through somatically so some of its layers are released from the body. Dealing with the layers of the feeling that are triggered is our path to healing, and a release from the contracted, fear-based existence. If we face the pain, tackle it head on, and release it from the body, it does not mean that it is gone forever more, there may be other layers. It does mean, however, that the sheer weight of it has been lightened, that we are now fore armed if it should show up again, and that we have experience in draining its impact. Importantly, we are not forced into a dance of attrition, taking unsafe everywhere we go, following its dictates as if we were servile toward its constant demands. We also are no longer living like a frightened bird in a cage, unaware we had the key to unlock the cage door all along and fly to newfound freedom to all those places in life that uplift us, nourish us, and bring us joy.

COMPASSION FOR SELF AND OTHERS

"Compassion comes from an ever-expanding understanding for yourself and others, and believes that you are rising to the moment with all the grace and dignity you can muster."

Figure 3.29. Compassion for self and others.

Compassion for self is like moving around life with a comforting cape around your shoulders, and for others giving them a cozy wraparound for their soothing. The cape and the wraparound remind us that we are safe in this moment with compassion by our side. They are also forms of protection in those times when life falls apart, or we made a mistake, or someone hurt, betrayed, undermined, or violated us, as some examples. Life is filled with moments of immense pain and compassion, which allow us to re-group, to move to a quiet safe place, and to take time to heal. Compassion is forgiving, it allows us to be human, and it creates space to learn from our mistakes. It is also like a mining tool searching intensely for a deeper understanding of the situation, and a more complex summation of *what happened*. Compassion is also aware that the clarity of hindsight is often challenging to grasp in the moment; it understands life can often be a storm with one hurricane after the next, and just holding our ground somewhat can be a mammoth accomplishment. If compassion is so helpful and profoundly comforting, why is it so often in short supply for both ourselves and others? The answer can be complex and take us perhaps to a history of embodied traumatic memory. If our childhood years were filled with moments from parents who implied we were not enough, that we were undeserving of, for instance, love, validation, or understanding unless we met certain expectations, then when we struggle in life old wounds are activated. Cellular memory of these wounds in the form of locked in feelings, for instance, shame, hurt, inadequacy, not enough, stupidity, being undeserving, deficiency, or incompetency will be triggered. When past embodied feelings are triggered, there is no room for anything else. We often experience the triggered feelings like a waterfall violently swamping us, taking away our capacity to cope, and moving us automatically into fight, flight, freeze, or fawning behaviors to survive this brutally painful moment. Compassion, in these times, is remote and inaccessible; we are just trying to cope as best we can with the onslaught. Alongside the torrent of feelings, embodied memory also activates a torrent of unhelpful messages to our brain. They might be "I am unworthy of compassion," "I messed up again," or "I'll never get it right," and worse still "I'm a failure or a loser," repeatedly. The activation of the triggered feelings and the cascade of unhelpful thinking squeezes compassion to the Outer Hebrides—it is no longer within reach, and without it, the unhelpful messages and core beliefs around our unworthiness for compassion are reinforced again.

Alongside unhelpful family systems, there are culturally sanctioned societal messages that reinforce self and others' judgement when we mess up or struggle. Messages like "suck it up," "you're a loser," and "you shouldn't feel the way that you do," if you are mired in challenging feelings. This unforgiving societal milieu undermines compassion for self or others. One is perceived as failing if one is not holding one's own in the competitive race for ongoing achievement, acquisition, and status. Judgement is a tolerated undercurrent on a societal level when many are perceived to not measure up.

Compassion finds competitively oriented, hyper-critical, judgmental societal and family systems hostile. Compassion wants the opposite for you; it wants you to be encouraged and reassured on life's treacherous journey. Compassion wants to commend your efforts to take another courageous step. Compassion understands deeply that we all face internal barriers and that sometimes the internal barriers are a pattern of behavior that has been dominating for decades, both within ourselves and within our family systems. Compassion totally gets how much energy, motivation, and sheer doggedness are needed to change and shift to a brighter way of being in the world. Compassion wants to hold your hand in the moments of struggle and say loudly, so you can take it in on a cellular level, "I see you, I acknowledge your struggle, your efforts are mammoth, others may not see what you are up against, but I do, your courage and strength are immense, and I am with you every step of the way."

INADEQUATE

"Inadequate is like an ever-present shadow determined to undermine our capacity to cope and it insists that we are less than we need to be."

Figure 3.30. Inadequate.

Inadequate is sneaky. It slithers and slides around, always lurking, making itself known at vulnerable moments, but not fully revealing itself, so that you delude yourself that it has gone away, and that it is perhaps tormenting someone else. It likely is, as it has spread itself far and wide, but that does not mean it has given up on undermining you. It is a long-term arrangement with inadequate; it is there consistently chipping away at one's self-esteem— a little bite here, another bite there, encouraging you to see yourself as less than, not up to the mark, imperfect and unworthy too. And no matter your effort, you never get the feeling that you are measuring up to yours and others' expectations. Even if you win the biggest award in your work, inadequate shows up when you put out your hand to reach for the award and says in a persuasive emphatic tone "you could have done better."

An important step in understanding the power and persuasiveness of inadequate is to peel back the circumstances of our life and figure out what contributed to it playing such a tormenting role. Perhaps when growing up, our familial role models had not dealt with their own inadequacy, so it was projected. They may have been well-intentioned and protective when they kept critiquing your performance. Perhaps they did not want you to suffer the ever-present reverberation of their own lived experience with inadequacy and all its consequences, or they were somewhat unaware of the impact of their criticism on you. Phrases from them that are easy to recall, and are forever haunting might be, "you must try harder," "why did you get such a low mark," "if you don't do well at school, you will never amount to anything," and "you are lazy, you should do better." These phrases can last a lifetime, as each time you heard them another deposit of inadequacy was sequestered in your body, and as it builds in the body, so the internal voice gets louder and the voice of inadequacy becomes more and more convincing.

Another circumstance triggering inadequacy may be a history of experienced racism, or another form of discrimination. You are judged by others for how you look, or perhaps your orientation or a disability, and you are subjected to others comments encouraging you to feel deficient in some way. The comments could be up front, so you can see what is happening. It could also be subterranean; you cannot quite put your finger on it, but you notice the patronizing look in their eye, their dismissive gesture when you speak up, you are passed over for promotion regularly it seems, in social settings with a particular group you rarely get eye contact, or perhaps, one person may look at your mouth when they are speaking to you, as if they are insisting on not fully acknowledging your presence. These micro aggressions can be small tears at the fabric of one's self esteem, a slow, but deliberate rejection and judgement, one may try not to pay attention to them or to minimize its impact, but it hurts just the same, and then inadequacy that has been sequestered deep in your being may be triggered once again.

A further situation that can impact inadequacy is falling short in our own eyes. We may have made some mistakes, have lived a life filled with regret and missed opportunity, and it is clear that we have struggled with life and its constant challenges. So, the inadequacy may come from an inability to let go and to forgive ourselves for messing up in some way. Each new mistake can stimulate another wave of inadequacy coursing through our system.

Given there are numerous and complex circumstances where we experience inadequacy, what can we do to face it head on, and start to drain its wily presence from dominating our mind and from finding a home in our body? The first step is to start to amass the puzzle pieces to figure out how we were impacted and what happened. Once we understand the source or sources, we can start to do some healing work around writing letters to those who reinforced inadequacy. We can let them know the full impact of their words or behavior, and how you will be taking your power back. In some instances, the letter may be to ourselves, engaging a process around forgiving ourselves for past mistakes. It is getting to all the nuanced feelings and understanding their impact that is so helpful in the process. Trauma work is often about collecting puzzle pieces; some of the pieces come from body awareness, some from recollection of feelings, and others still are shards of memory recalled, sometimes fleetingly in our dreams. Once we can create a story based on our coalesced memories, we are starting to explain why inadequacy crops up so easily, and why it is hard to shake it at times, given its long root in our body. Once we understand why inadequacy gets triggered, it is easier to put it into context, and to detach as we know it is historical, despite it being felt in the present.

Another strategy is listening carefully to inadequacy's voice. What is it saying, and in which situations is it particularly toxic and refuses to subside? Perhaps inadequacy has a story that you will always be trampled on in some way by others because you are undeserving of respect. Others then will take advantage of you, and you are helpless to stop it. Whatever the dictate from inadequacy, you now know where you can make the most change and send it on its way by taking charge. Asserting yourself, for instance, in social situations, even though your knees are buckling at the thought, and you seem to have amassed a swarm of butterflies flitting all over your body, undermining your confidence. It is at these moments, if we can pull strength from our toes, visualize our success, prepare what we want to say and blurt it out, we then take on inadequacy and stare it down and say, "get lost, quit picking on me, I am sick of you, and you are on your way out. I will drain you from my body and psyche and start to live a life where your voice gets softer and softer, and might I say, inadequate."

Chapter 4

Unlock Patterns

"A pattern has a life all its own. It sits in the unconscious, influencing our every moment of every day. If we are wise, we slow down and get to know the patterns that shape our lives, revealing themselves through our automatic reactions and repeated behaviors. Then we can choose which patterns help us and which diminish us and through this process live our lives more fully."

Patterns took hold of the steering wheel of the unconscious a long time ago, likely when humans first arrived on the planet. They are the drivers of behavior. Like most of us, you probably like to think you are making clear choices from a liberated mind, but often it is not true. Patterns passed on by your familial history and your genetic pool are the captains of your ship. If this is true, then how can you get the wheel back and start charting your own course through the darkness on this journey called "life"?

Seeing in the dark takes a great deal of illumination and self-awareness; it comes through your own tracking of what is really going on. You take note of what is repetitive, where you are feeling compelled beyond reason, where your vision is myopic. Then you choose to actively fight the pattern, to bring all of your resources to the moment.

In this chapter there are both patterns that you will want to start subverting and resisting and others that you will want to start building. For all of us, change is generally twofold: subverting and undermining what is keeping us stuck; and building exponentially those habits and patterns that keep us on the road to expansion.

CODEPENDENCY

Kahil Gibran eloquently penned his words about marriage, a warning against codependency, many decades ago. He warned;

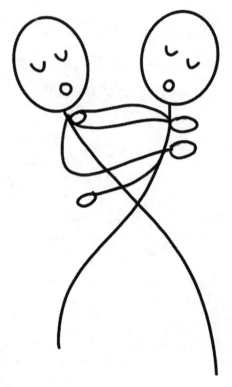

Figure 4.1. Codependency.

Love one another, but make not a bond of love:
Let it be a moving sea between the shores of your souls.
Fill each other's cup but drink not from the same cup.
Give one another of your bread but eat not from the same loaf.
Sing and dance together and be joyous, but let each of you be alone,
Even as the strings of the lute are alone though they quiver with the same music.

(Gibran, 1968:15–16)

Clearly his wise words have not impregnated the human psyche on a mass scale. Codependency thrives, a sticky web that keeps its participants locked in place, with little to no room to maneuver or grow. It is often an unconscious silent agreement: You fix me and I will depend on you. You fulfill your need to be needed and I will be sheltered from the storm of life by your shroud of protection. It's an illusion, of course, but illusions can keep you locked in place for decades. In addition to this lack of room for growth, codependency is a model with little air to breathe. In fact, it can be darn right stifling, particularly when you have to go everywhere with your codependent, as if you were joined at the hip. No freedom of movement here! Each step is a step together deeper into the quicksand of loss of self.

If this is such a trap, how do you know you are in it? Whether you are the overfunctioner or underfunctioner (or sometimes both), you are locked into fixed patterns with friends and family. If you overfunction with others, you are an ever-flowing fountain of advice. You get ever deeper into others' problems, helping them process the latest trauma, trying to prop them up, taking responsibility for their stuff, and essentially encouraging them to lean on you. You are not setting limits with them, not asserting *your* needs; this is all about convincing others that you can handle *their* stuff. Your needs go on the farthest back burner that exists; it's all about them. Their leaning gives you an identity, helps you fulfill the martyr role. Too bad if you are getting lost in the process. It is about exalted sacrifice, after all.

When you are the one that depends, or the underfunctioner, you blame others and feel victimized because your life is not where you want it to be. You are willing to receive loads of advice; in fact you seek it out under the guise of feedback. You have received plenty of feedback in your lifetime; however it doesn't mean you have to do anything about it. Your state is all about passivity, waiting for someone to fix you and watching others do what you need to do for yourself. They are running around you in dizzying circles when you have your next frustrated tantrum. Under this model, it is all about you, and you, and you. This is narcissism drowning in itself; it is hard to imagine from this place that anyone else has needs other than to please you. Self-absorption colonizes the whole being. When you talk, you are inviting others into your world. This is not about popping out of your bubble to imagine another viewpoint.

Codependency is all about boundaries, or rather lack of boundaries. This modus operandi satisfies deeply the urge to merge. What are the other advantages? Why would you find yourself in the quicksand of this type of relationship?

Well, first of all, it is stable misery, and many of us are familiar with that feeling from childhood. Few of us had parents who were striving for wholeness. If you saw the merged model in action, codependency is hardwired in your psyche; it's hard to imagine another way of being with others.

Another advantage of codependency is that it relieves you of the scary prospect of taking full responsibility for your own life. What if it doesn't work out, and then you have to face yourself fully? At least with the merged model, you can blame someone else and stay in the backseat of the car of your life. You are more sheltered there. You don't have to make any daunting choices; you can just glide along, not ever making any big decisions. It is scary to "know thyself." If the boundaries stay merged in self-sacrifice and codependency, you will not be forced to look fully in the mirror. Self-awareness can be scary stuff!

If those are the advantages of the "fix me"/"depend on me" model, then what are the drawbacks? What do you give up?

Loss of self is the biggest drawback, along with your ability to self-actualize and follow your dreams. It takes single-mindedness to strive for your deepest desires as part of a couple, single-mindedness that is only possible if you are deeply in touch with yourself. In the interdependent model, each makes his or her own decisions after consultation, asserts their needs with the other, and says "no" countless times to assert boundaries.

At first, saying no can be nerve-wracking. Soon, however, it becomes second nature. You start looking after your own needs; and so the happiness and peace thermometer starts climbing astronomically. Your life has never felt more on edge and alive. Risks are critical to the path, but there are also consequent rewards. You notice that the path has enticing views. You can see some valleys and peaks to come, but my goodness, the vista is awe-inspiring!

The path of aloneness is a daunting one, even if both members of a couple have signed on for self-actualization; respect for each other's firm boundaries is paramount. Communication is critical to this model, as negotiation and compromise are a constant, given that both members are aware of their own and the other's needs.

Another advantage of moving into the interdependent model is that you start to attract others like yourself, others who are also firmly behind the wheel in their chosen vehicle in life, figuring out the next road, highly alert to the moment, aware of the dizzying array of choices every moment of every day. The air is a swirling, vibrant mass of infused energy, blowing you here and there. Though the turbulence can be rough, you are energized by the journey. In fact, once you have climbed out of the quicksand of mass confusion and loss of self, you need never look back.

To feel self-growth is an elixir, an intoxicant available to you if you are willing to go down the bumpier road, the one with the curves that you can't see past, the road less traveled. Life starts to feel more like an adventure, each day an opportunity to carve out new territory, to expand, to exalt your being in growth beyond measure. Surely that is enough to take the first step in saying loudly in your most determined voice, "I am willing to depend only on myself. It is only me that I can count on to change, love, risk and grow in this place called Planet Earth."

DESIRE AND TURBULENCE

"Desires beg us to reach higher and further; inner turbulence states emphatically, 'This is the way!'"

Figure 4.2. Desire/Turbulence.

Desire and turbulence are married. Often we wish they were not conjoined. Desire often whispers secretly to us in a penetrating tone, "There is more." It stimulates a restless state. It encourages us extend our arm just a little to grasp something even more precious. Without desire, our lives would be static, our souls planted in dry soil. Our soul embraces desire fully, as it knows this will help with its expansion into the giant self, a state we all crave.

Desire has innumerable cravings. If you are not in an intimate relationship, your heart begs for a special connection, in which your whole self can collapse into the glory and rush of intimacy. In the pregnant pause when you are waiting for "the one," you may at times fantasize and get attached to the *idea* of someone. You can create their persona so fully that when a real, living embodiment moves into your space and sends out the "I like you" vibes, you may be oblivious to the opportunity.

If you have a partner, desire keeps you on the lookout for those patterns in the other that you feel constrain and limit you. At times, desire projects, "If (s)he/they were not so inflexible, impatient, restless, consumed, distracted, and passive (the list is endless), then I would be happier, calmer, more at ease, more confident." Overall satisfaction with your partner also stimulates or suppresses your sexual desire. When your partner is growing and expanding, they appear sexier, more alive and confident. The challenge is when they are contracting, resisting turbulence in their lives, when they settle for the hills and dales of home, instead of the icy Himalayan Peaks that require safety equipment and a truckload of courage to climb.

Desire also niggles you when you are alone. Perhaps you had planned an evening of solitude, wanting to immerse yourself fully in the moment. In a persistent voice, desire begins its escalating barrage: "How come you are on your own tonight? Do you have enough friends? What are others doing now that you are not? Are you really enjoying and making the most of your life? Have you chosen the right partner or path? Was it a mistake to have (or not have) children?" Any semblance of peace is now shattered in intrapsychic shards around you, so you decide you will go to that forum on "Building Community Networks" after all.

What it boils down to, in essence, is the ability to surf turbulence in life that affects dramatically whether you will act on your desires, or suppress them. If the small waves of change have you flailing in the surf, rendered power-less and swallowing both water and sand, you will send a message to your psyche, "Settle for what you have." However, after you have taken on the big waves of life and felt the exhilaration prior to crashing, you will be more likely to gamble with difficult decisions. You will be more willing to act on the unrelenting murmur, "You need to change your job, leave that half-baked relationship, move to that dream city or country or fulfill that passion that has always magnetized you."

Kahil Gibran wrote eloquently of the different intensity of longing and desire in all of us:

> In your longing for your giant self lies your goodness: and that longing is in all or you. But in some of you that longing is a torrent rushing with might to the sea, carrying the secrets of the hillsides and the songs of the forest. And in others it is a flat stream that loses itself in angles and bends and lingers before it reaches the shore. (Gibran, 1968:66)

Desire and turbulence also have a relationship with our willingness to love. For some people, the scars from earlier years have left an indelible mark; a lifetime is often not enough to heal the hurts, disappointment, abuse and rejection. The imprint says, "Don't trust fully. Don't give all of yourself. Hold back. Keep your expectations in check, so it will be easier when you are let down." Others, in spite of the obvious scarring, barrel forward, securing a blanket of innocence around their being, and keep taking small, risky steps.

It is a choice of sorts, and relates directly to the turbulence thermometer. When you are aggrieved, what do you say to your psyche? "I will don my hip waders and move into the pain of it and slowly, hopefully make my way to the other side"; or "That was unacceptable; I never want that experience again; life's unfair; it shouldn't have happened; I will make sure I don't find myself in that place again"? Both will occur at different times in your life, but it is worth observing the overall pattern. Is desire a persistent friend, encouraging the next risky step, or a hindrance, merged with regret, mumbling "if only," reminding you of the life you could have lived?

DROWNING IN SELF

"As the lens focuses inward, the ability to be with another diminishes. Loneliness devours the heart, and one is convinced, 'No one but no one feels the way I do.'"

Figure 4.3. Drowning in self.

It is so easy to drown in the vortex of it all, spinning dizzyingly in self-analysis. Looking outside of oneself is becoming a formidable challenge in society. The "self" conversations are everywhere–and they are not always conversations. When someone sees you, experiences you as just another set of open, flapping ears, willing to hear the latest splat churning around in them, that is not connecting. A connection needs to be two-way, and increasingly the "self" is so mired that the dual connection gets lost. Sincerely connecting comes with an unbridled curiosity to peel back the layers that hide the other's interior. How many are bringing that presence to the moment? Why are so many of us slipping inside and being seduced by our latest thought, the nuance of a feeling? Why are we finding this a fascinating destination where we not only visit as is necessary, but set up a permanent encampment?

The dates 2025 and 2050 with their predicted doom scenarios are reverberating in our collective psyches. The assault can be daily, hourly, weekly, monthly. Its messages are clear regarding climate change. Unimaginable devastation and never-experienced catastrophic chaos is on its way. One can dip into the collective unconscious and feel the turbulence building beneath the surface, threatening to burst through at any moment. This is not a hurricane that whips and plays sadistically with all in its path. It is also not a seismic shift of gargantuan proportions that tears down buildings in seconds, like a carefully crafted movie set. This force is like no other. It has the capacity to turn huge chunks of African and Australian moist, red, fertile soil into an elephant hide, parched to its core, begging for a drop that would quench the dry rasping of its last breath.

It will forever change landscapes and consequently torment the animal life remaining. Patterns that have been deeply embedded in the mammalian psyche for eons will no longer be helpful to ensure a next meal. If the ice has melted, how does the polar bear get access to the seal-abundant landscapes? Recent news footage has spoken of climate change eliminating half the world's species. That is part of the barrage that we hear: yet another species is at risk because we have sucked oil and coal from the earth's belly, and spewed it into her ever-hazier skies.

So do we face the issue head-on and admit fully that our fundamental core beliefs are destructive, and will destroy the only home we know? Do we acknowledge the void we have created, where we not only feel empty inside, but also distance ourselves from the outside world? Can we confidently ask ourselves what the point was of that last weekend, last month, year or decade of our existence? What did we do, think, and feel that was really critical, that contributed wholeheartedly to the earth's mission for us as a species? Self-nurturing time is critical, and vital to the wellspring of our soul and our ability to give, but we are out of balance. To "know thyself" is key, but that is a springboard to the bigger stuff. Somehow, most of us have found ourselves frozen on the springboard, unsure what our role may be and if we are up to the big leap.

It's easier to go into the self. It's safe—we don't need to take the big risks, or face formidable worldly fears head-on. We can focus solely on those aspects of ourselves that we can bear to know, and collectively burrow our heads deeper into that inviting sand all around us. If we have moments when we feel small, there are always invitations from sources like Facebook that can puff us up like a bullfrog inflating its frame. Facebook challenges those feelings of being lonely and disconnected from what's real. It says that you have more friends than you ever imagined. It provides a forum for mock intimacy and the self-delusion of stepping out, of being real with the world. In "Tomorrow's God" by Neale Donald Walsch, we are challenged:

> Even today, with all your powers of instant communication and total connection and advanced comprehension and increased awareness and sophisticated technology, you can't produce the simple, humble experience for which humanity has yearned from the beginning of time. You can't produce peace; you can't produce lasting joy. . . . The more you know about how to destroy yourself, the more you need to know about how to save yourself. It is time now to expand your base of knowledge. . . . .to increase your awareness, and to enlarge your consciousness. (Walsch, 2004:4, 21)

Step one for me would be putting my feet firmly on the "taking responsibility" plate and stating that my contributions matter. I am willing to suspend my need to know, swim in deep pools of powerlessness and acknowledge beliefs that inhibit my connection to the greater whole. I am willing to recreate myself anew and be part of a civil rights movement for the soul. "Take the gifts you have—they are plenteous–and share them with the world. Apply them to the challenge at hand. Use them and give them in your life as if there's no tomorrow" (Walsch, 2004:150).

If we as a species sincerely admit that the time for mammoth change has arrived, that eleventh-hour bells can be heard ringing loudly in all parts of the globe, appealing to the soul to wake up, then now is the time to examine the Western economic model. The present economic paradigm is built on the overriding tenet that the more one owns, the more power one has, and therefore the wealthier one is as a person. Consequently, the economy has to be in a state of ever-expanding growth to cater to the ever-expanding needs of billions, regardless of the earth's finite supply. "The answer would be to redefine wealth as access and availability. Shift from a 'possessions and power' economy to a 'use and cooperation' economy" (Walsh, 2004:286). Perhaps my washer and dryer could be used by my neighbors in return for the use of their electric lawn mower.

Some indigenous societies have modeled this collaboration and cooperation for millennia, but the self-righteous model of superiority and domination, brought by the advanced to the apparently "primitive," have seduced us all. The seeds for this disharmonious way of being were sown initially by philosophers like Newton and Descartes. They believed, contrary to Rousseau, that the intellect and powers of reasoning were superior to intuitive sensory perception. Thus human beings in the West began to view themselves as superior to other beings in the natural world. This led to reconstructing the environment instead of co-existing within it.

It is going to take tremendous courage to come out of the bubble we have constructed to protect ourselves from the overwhelming helplessness and loss of control we all are experiencing. The situation seems so much bigger than us, a tsunami of tsunamis in which our surfboard in life is likely to get crushed into smithereens in seconds. With all of this, it would be easy to persuade ourselves collectively that it is too late, and opt to stay "safe" in our small world, knowing instinctively that the longer we stay there the more our fate is predetermined by nature. Alternatively, we can resist the idea that the die has been cast, that we are helpless to effect meaningful change. Deep in our interior we know this idea is not true. We know too that marshaling our resources in an unprecedented way and creating a cooperative consciousness can bring about the exponential change that is needed. We can act on a new set of beliefs that honors all life–not just humankind. It is time for all of us to be stewards of the earth and of all its inhabitants. Together, holding hands as world citizens, we have the power to change the way we live and allow peace and joy to reign at last. We will be liberating our world and liberating ourselves simultaneously; we are all one, after all. When we feel and experience the harmony, peace, and joy that we seek so voraciously, it will settle like a pink sky caressing our new world.

VULNERABILITY AND NOT KNOWING

"To stew in vulnerability is to admit our humanity fully. It says we don't know what life brings, we will suffer at times, but through our vulnerability we will hold hands with all beings, united by our tenderness."

You feel exposed and raw, as if someone had peeled away the casing over your heart and laid it bare for all to see. It is scary when others witness your insecurity, your neediness, your inadequacy, your imperfection, your fragility. When you present yourself to the world, you want to have your act together. You want to strike the balance, be open, warm and engaging but be "in control." You want all your open wounds to be sealed over, and you want to be able to choose what to say at all times and what to reveal to others. In essence, the core issue is control.

Control and vulnerability find themselves on either side of the same coin: Flip to the control side of the coin and you get a proud figure with face firm, sharp eyes looking straight ahead, and lips taut. The figure also has an erect neck and back–this is someone on a mission, in charge, at the helm of their ship. They have an unswerving, formidable presence and tight boundaries. They know where they end and you begin, and there is a clearly demarcated

Figure 4.4. Vulnerability and not knowing.

line in the middle. Codependency and boundary confusion are not going to be part of this person's make-up, given the sealed-off portals. They are built on the independent model: you look after you, I will look after myself, and when it suits us both, we can get together.

Flip the coin to the other side and staring back is vulnerability. The eyes are soft and confused, the lips quivering occasionally into a perplexed frown. The figure seems uncertain where to place their hands; and the posture reveals a person who sometimes buckles under the intensity of intimacy and feelings. They invite others to merge. The boundaries keep shifting; maybe this is who I am, or maybe that. Vulnerability also triggers protectiveness from others. Many are touched by the rawness, like a mother protecting cubs, securing her paw over their newly formed bodies.

So which is more attractive? How do you present yourself to the world overall? Naturally, the situation makes a difference in how much you reveal. The question to ponder is this: When you are in the comfort of friends, family, or a lover, who do you let have a long stare at your underbelly, your vulnerable side?

For me, it is an ever-present internal struggle. Fierce independence has historically bolstered my control side and has at times created thick walls so others feel the block. They have likely sensed that the drawbridge had been hauled up in haste at some point in the past, and would not be lowered any-time soon. However, life has sent me numerous situations that have triggered my vulnerability. The easiest way through for me now has become putting all of my cards on the table for those I feel close to. I have reached out to hold their hand, knowing I needed extra support to steady my feet. I have sought their counsel and let them know that the dots are not all joined and that the direction of my life is uncertain. I have swum in the humility of it all. I have announced that my boat is determined not only to visit the "sea of the unknown" but to anchor there for some time. On the whole, it has been freeing not to seal off and suppress what needs airing, and freeing also to be able to love more fully and have a deeper connection with others. The deeper the connection with others, the larger the cushion of meaning I can lean into, nestle and embrace in tough times.

Loving others is where vulnerability and control flip back and forth the most. This is not an easy arena for you to sustain your mask for any duration. An ongoing service we can provide for each other is to create a safe place for vulnerability to dance unbridled and weave in and out of our lives. We are in this together–we need each other to love, to grow, to enrich our lives. We need to embrace vulnerability in order to reach our potential, our best self that we can then give to others who seek liberation. The Zulu word "Ubuntu" says it all—a human being is a human being because of other human beings.

MARTYRDOM

"Martyrdom is not a virtue when it serves as a substitute for true courage; true courage stands up not only for the freedom of others, but for one's own."

Martyrdom can be a trap–a formidable trap with an intense hold on you. What lures you closer and closer to its vice grip is the whirlpool of mean-ing. You think, "My life will have purpose if I submerge myself for the good of humankind." Once in the whirlpool, you get dragged down by currents of despair and confusion. The deeper you go into the vortex, the harder it becomes to swim up for air, and the more you are paralyzed by suffocation.

It can all start so innocently: You are in a relationship that from the outset appeared mutually giving. Each partner seemed to contribute to the health of the other. You were each uplifted in the other's company for the most part, and as time clicked by, the bricks of meaning solidified to form a solid foun-dation. Then something happened, not dramatically, but inexorably: new pat-terns started to emerge. Your partner was starting to lose their steady ground and some addictive patterns or distractions started to gain momentum.

Figure 4.5. Martyrdom.

At first the patterns were a wispy, ethereal shadow that appeared and disappeared in the relationship dance. The couple paid it little attention–its presence was fleeting. Soon, however, your resentment thermometer started to rise as you witnessed the pattern taking hold of your partner. Your resentment now coincides with invitations to a slow dance with martyrdom. Your needs are being increasingly ignored or "put on hold" as your partner's attachment to the addiction and distraction deepens. Martyrdom's voice, initially soft and soothing, is now getting stronger. Emphatically it says, "Stay focused on the other; their needs are the most important right now. Being invisible is good! It's necessary to 'sacrifice' for another." That's the word that gets martyrdom salivating and gloating: "sacrifice."

Sacrifice is marketed by many religions as goodness personified, an idealized state. It justifies suicide bombing, self-immolation or imposed starvation. It states that the cause is just; whether it is done for one's country or family, it is worthwhile. Many cultures analyze martyrdom through a tinted lens. Rarely is the full cost on a societal or individual level exposed for all to see.

This is not to say martyrdom is always an unhealthy choice–Nelson Mandela martyred himself with a 27-year jail sentence. However, he did not drown in the victimization of it all, an overwhelmingly tempting choice. It appears he used the imposed solitude to renew and expand himself to such a breadth that few are able to match his capacity for forgiveness. Some degree of martyrdom is at times a necessary choice. Raising children is a case in point. However, many sustain the course of self-neglect for too long. The cost is dramatic if it is not countered with some self-nurturing attention. What is forgotten, too, are the benefits for children who witness their parents' resistance to martyrdom's constant invitations.

So what is the cost? Why should you draw on every fiber of your being to wrestle yourself away from this dance of attrition? It is like a virus that leaves in its wake a shroud over your sensory organs. Heartfelt emotion is now subdued and it becomes harder to identify feelings. In time, a numb state seems "normal," albeit confusing. Without the ability to name how you feel, your ability to assert yourself and maintain a presence is challenged. Increasingly you feel insignificant, invisible and small. Your voice becomes soft, barely audible, imbued with Pollyanna lilts.

So the battle is on and martyrdom looks set to win. The fallback cushion is to justify your shrunken persona with the mindset of a victim. You encourage others to believe that you were forced into this role, stating, "Someone has to be the rock for everyone else to lean up against." Or you say to yourself, "It's temporary. My time will come; I can be patient." This is a tantalizingly sweet melody to martyrdom's ears, a signal that it can head for its final destination, the shrouding of your soul. The soul is where martyrdom can have its greatest impact; once here, it can guarantee a "lost" state for eons. Under martyrdom's influence, the soul is spun into a repetitive motion, whirring pointlessly in endless circles. This is the great irony of martyrdom: It is a state imbued with great meaning, but once its domination is secured, it leaves you bobbing on a sea of meaninglessness. Over time this state engenders waves of existential despair, emptiness and, alarmingly, at times even suicidal feelings.

How can you escape this vortex of despair? In this desperate state the soul can send out red alerts: "Wake up! Take charge! You can't look after others effectively unless you look after yourself, too. Give from a place of plenty, a flourishing garden, not a dusty, arid patch of earth." The way through is painful, but in essence less painful than a soul-spinning vortex. Slowly, your voice returns and begins to draw attention to your needs. Tentatively at first, it challenges assumptions by others. Courageously, it starts to set limits and begins to experiment with the feel and cadence of the word "no." At a glacial pace, but moving forward in a new direction, you reconnect with yourself, your values and cherished ideas. You have an opportunity to rediscover your soul's purpose. Hallelujah! It is a momentous breakthrough, and from this self-nurturing destination, martyrdom's dance of destruction at last looks astonishingly toxic.

PROJECTION

"Projection stops our growth instantly. It says loudly, 'Another is to blame, not me.' It takes the spotlight away for a while, but it is temporary. The shadows sequestered will dance on the main stage of our lives again, demanding full attention and recognition."

Figure 4.6. Projection.

It happens at times in an unconscious way. You feel a desperate need to deny, to escape from that part of yourself that triggers revulsion, dis-ease. It could also be memories that you need to escape from, memories that have the capacity to uproot your core. These memories have been nestled deep in the recesses of your psyche or body. You believe wholeheartedly that you have not only shut the door on them, but bolted the latch and maneuvered a gargantuan boulder in front of the potential opening. The unconscious quid pro quo agreement is that you will continue to live a lifestyle of distraction in order to maintain your disconnected state, if the memories will remain sealed. What you have ignored oftentimes is that memories have the power to disconnect from the whole and leak out, like a wisp of smoke. They sneak through the cracks and crevices of the bolted door, and send an alarming message to the brain. They attack like a sledgehammer dropping from the sky. There is no intrapsychic cushioning; that which you feared intensely has permeated your mind fully.

At this moment you have a number of choices (though "choice" is an odd word to ponder at this moment, given the intensity of the entrapment that you feel): You can increase your distractions and disconnect further from yourself. You can brace yourself and face the memory head-on. Finally, you can project onto another.

Projection has been part of the human psyche for eons. Projection is what germinates the seeds of war and fans the flames of division based on religion, race, class, gender and sexual orientation. The underlying tenet is that if it weren't for those people, or that person, I would feel better about myself. There are many examples of projection:

In biblical times, the poor, prostitutes and lepers were the outcasts. All manner of religious doctrine was used to support their separation from the community.

In India, the *dalits*, or untouchables, are a recognized group; various Indian religions subordinate them and validate their low-caste status.

Slavery of Africans was justified by the projection that Africans were inferior and primitive, and somehow less than human. Between 1700 and 1720, about twenty thousand slaves were imported into North America. By 1740, a further fifty thousand had been sold and transported to other countries. Their conditions were deplorable, and many died during the horrendous journey to the region that would later call itself "the free world." The projection of inferiority justified their treatment.

Over six million Jews suffered extermination because of the projection that their status was lower than animal life. Similarly, Hutus committed genocide against eight hundred thousand Tutsis. Projection, then, is a frightening psychological phenomenon on an individual or collective group level.

Some cultures are aware of projection's power and build into their cultural norms a strategy to drain its destructive nature. One important cultural belief is if anyone in the tribe is tormented by anger, jealousy, hatred, resentment, etc. they should leave and only return to the group once they have worked through the intense emotion. In this way, a person is culturally supported in taking responsibility for their internal state–a far cry from the violent offenders that exist in most cultures in the twenty-first century. If numerous cultures adopted this one strategy to handle blame, projection and all its manifestations of murder, war, rape, torture, and abuse (physical, emotional and sexual), then poisonous processes would be undermined and exposed.

For the person experiencing the projection of another, it is a moment of intense powerlessness. Desmond Tutu, a human rights champion from South Africa, who handled the cruel manacles of apartheid with heroism and grace, recounts his personal struggle to deal with racist projections. He describes a painful moment when his child requested to play on the swings in a "whites only" playground. He recalls, "I said with a hollow and deadweight voice in the pit of the tummy, 'no, darling, you can't go.' What do you say, how do you feel when your baby says 'but Daddy there are other children playing there'? How do you tell your little darling that she could not go because she was not really a child, not that kind of child? And you died many times and you were not able to look your child in the eyes because you felt so dehumanized, so humiliated, so diminished" (Tutu, 2004:46).

Projection allows the projector to delay taking responsibility for their hurts, inadequacies and suffering, and in the interim wreaks havoc in others' lives. Projection skews and contorts ideas about victimization. Ironically, some men who are violent identify themselves as victims. How could that be? They have chosen to seal themselves off from their own trauma and so are easily triggered by perceived injustice all around them. One simple transgression in traffic by another, and their response can be horrific. When a victim happens innocently to cross such a man's path, it can be a life-or-death scenario.

Therefore, on a societal and personal level, it is imperative to bridle projection, to slow it down, to reflect on reactivity, to challenge stories of "the other," to take a time-out and pause. It is also imperative to question the origins of dark streams that flood our consciousness, to skin the glazed vision of ourselves and courageously admit our flaws. The time to change the human condition is nigh. By acknowledging projection and by staring it down and battling it, we have a chance at a different human experience.

Epigraph

"Recognition of the inherent dignity and of the equal and inalienable rights of all members of the human family is the foundation of freedom, justice and peace in the world."

— Excerpt from the Universal Declaration of Human
Rights (United Nations website, Preamble)

INJUSTICE

"To live in this world is to experience injustice. At times we are deluded into thinking we are the only ones who have experienced this grievous state and so we remove ourselves from the human family. Injustice invites us to reach for our highest selves in the forgiveness process; it encourages our big-spiritedness to take over if we are willing to heal."

Figure 4.7. Injustice.

At the mere thought of injustice, your entire body prepares for a full attack. It is galling: How could they/it/he/she think they could get away with it? How dare they? The battlelines are marked out in preparation for an explosive confrontation. You are inflamed with revulsion that courses through your body with every memory of the unjust act. Injustice gets stuck in the back of your throat. You refuse to swallow, for somehow by swallowing you feel you are admitting that what happened was acceptable. It is as if you were rubber-stamping the abuse, thus paving a path for a similar injustice to revictimize you in the future. "No," you say to yourself and others, "this is a time to fight."

Injustice then has the power to pull you into a swamp bubbling with toxic fumes, with whirlpools of acid at its core. When you were at the swamp's edge, you had perspective. You had asserted yourself and if possible told the offending party their violation's impact. You might have requested compensation and declared what would be a reasonable sum or action for recompense, something that would help the toxic lump slide down your throat. When you were at the edge of the swamp, it was also a lot easier to garner support from family and friends. Hearing an injustice brings out the self-righteous king or queen in all of us, and it is natural for most to give the victim unbridled support. At this stage of the process, you could wallow in the validation and the team feeling that had hopefully been stimulated around you.

While your battle remains at the swamp's edge, you do all in your power to bring about retribution, but keep the injustice marginalized in your mind. You resist a full colonization by maintaining balance in your life, even having some moments of contentment, in spite of the violation. Sometimes, though, the injustice, like a train with many carriages, links up with all of the injustices in your lifetime, and, intentionally or unintentionally, you move into the victim role. If these circumstances come together, the cynicism thermometer rises. Generalizations are tempting at this stage. For example, based on the perpetrator's gender, you may make generalizations that account for half the world's population. If you felt small and diminished by the injustice before, you are now falling into a trap that could bring on a whole series of future contractions.

The injustice has taken over your mind. It is there like a heavy metal plate on your chest the moment you wake up in the morning. It is a backpack full of heavy stones on your back all day. It also manifests as tension in your muscles and acid coursing through your digestive tract, corroding your organs. It burns your stomach lining, and fires your heart's core. Your voice takes on a bitter tone, as you snap, retort, obsess, prickle, and rant your way through your days. The overwhelming theme is "How dare (someone/something) take my power away!" You don't realize sometimes how every day devoted to victimization pulls the plug on your energy quotient and drains your inner resources. As Houff points out, blame at some point becomes a form of self-abuse:

> Thus, when someone wrongs or wounds you, in resenting it, you re-feel the injury. And in doing so, you re -hurt yourself. . . . It confronts us with the awesome penalty we pay by nursing a grievance. The first injury may have been done to us, but via the reliving of that grievance we injure ourselves a second and third time. . . . and sometimes even blight our lives. I've seen it happen (Houff, 1991).

It is so hard not to succumb to injustice on a personal level that it is one of the greatest tests. On a societal level, it is sometimes an even more tortured internal battle. Others' painful stories corroborate your own, and the flames of revulsion are re-lit over and over again. It seems there is no escape. You start to gasp for air in the swamp's center; you sense that this experience could last a lifetime.

The human race has a long history of killing and hurting each other in reviled ways. Genocide of another cultural group, or other abusive tools like racism, sexism, homophobia, or class discrimination have all been used for oppression. They have left a wake of victims' stories of injustice, tales of profound pain, passed on through generations.

Another compelling story that runs parallel to the river of victimization is the river of forgiveness. It is not for everyone–for some the monstrous act is too enormous and their internal resources too diminished. However, if you want to forgive and have the strength, courage, and resilience to heal, forgiveness can mimic magic. You can remember, without reliving the range and intensity of feelings. The scar has formed a protective layer over the pain, and perpetrators can't use their manipulations to get under your skin as easily. With letting go and forgiveness, the sweetest justice emerges like a phoenix rising. You reclaim your life; your heart is an expansive organ of love, not a defensive battleground any longer. Peace has the possibility of entering your life more fully, building in our bodies so it eases the difficult moments and adds to our strength. Houff paraphrases Dorothy Soelle, who has written prolifically on the Holocaust: "[W]ithout in any way discounting the suffering of the survivors, Ms. Soelle argues that, whenever we look back at a time of hardship or pain, we are still free–free to choose how we will respond" (Houff, 1991).

RESILIENCE

"Resilience says, 'I am in it for the long haul. If the going gets tough, count on me. I will stay with you right to your last breath, always striving, always ready to stay in the race, no matter the struggle.'"

It would be extraordinary if you were born with an overflowing container of resilience. Soon after your arrival from the protective womb to the earthly planet, you needed to draw on its resources. You became aware of it at an early age when the love and attention you needed to feel secure in your world was not fully there. When you were a child, these moments seemed to reverberate for eons. It could be excruciating when the external world was not able to deliver the necessary balm to soothe.

Figure 4.8. Resilience.

Resilience, however, is a self-soother. Its voice whispers through the paralyzing anxiety, "You are going to be all right." Most of the time you push the sound away–it only compounds the loneliness of it all. Then you might breathe, and a shard of hope glimmers briefly for a moment. Somehow you get through, and so a credit is added to resilience's stockpile. There is only one way to build resilience, and that is to be in the trenches of life.

When life is pink with sweet icing, you glide through, much like a cross-country skier on flat terrain. There are no marked highs in this zone and no great dips either. You could almost switch into autopilot. It is a drifting time, neither good nor bad; it just is. Then all of a sudden an alarming event occurs out of the blue, something no one foresaw hurtling around the corner at breakneck speed. You feel the impact–for a while you are in shock. You had been seduced into the illusion that life was routine and predictable, as one plus two equals three. You start to slowly digest the reality of the event, then, alarmingly, another event, followed by not one, two, or three, but maybe four more. Wow! You are breathless. It feels like a conspiracy, as if life were out to get you, as if some evil plotter were dictating, "That one needs a shakeup—send another one!"

If the intention was an awakening, an internal scrubbing and a high-intensity intrapsychic exfoliation, you got it. You are on hyperalert. You move out of the passenger seat of your life, no longer a passive observer with your feet up on the backseat, staring nonchalantly out the window. If your road in life is now a precipitously snaking highway to the valley of doom, you need to change your orientation. You move into the driver's seat, tightly strapped in, with a highly sensitized airbag ready, your whole chest hovering over the steering wheel as you scour the road for the next pothole. You sense intuitively that you are going to need to draw on reserves you didn't know existed, to draw on every ounce of resilience stored in your body.

When life sends a series of shockers one after another in Big Bang style, it is a test. Some people will buckle under the weight of it all. Their resilience reserves weren't there; they have been stripped naked and exposed, unprotected from the harsh elements that whip them around like fine hair in the wind, tousling the strands this way, that way. Sadly, the buckling can last a lifetime. A person can remain beaten down, trodden upon. It's revealed in their eyes; they battle to meet others' gaze head-on, their inadequacy having shriveled their spirit, their personality muted, their focus on survival.

For others, however, who somehow got their body clumsily over the first hurdle, an adrenaline rush flickers at the core. Perhaps the resilience reserves were there after all. Maybe, just maybe, they are going to get through this penultimate challenge. The approach to the next series of hurdles is steeped in anxiety: "Will I make it, or won't I?" Each hurdle clambered over sends a direct deposit of resilience to the internal bank account. Its level is rising, as muscles often flexed retain their increasing strength in the body. Each hurdle conquered is cause for enormous celebration.

If you need role models for resilience, there are countless human stories of extraordinary challenge met with unimaginable strength. A few in the political context are Mandela, Tutu, Gandhi, and King. In the everyday world there are reports of people who struggle against extraordinary circumstances to survive tsunamis, wrench themselves from the jaws of a ferocious animal, or remain intact after civil war.

Nature also provides role models in this regard. Pink flamingo chicks in Kenya and Tanzania are a humbling case in point: Soon after birth in the salt pans, they are corralled in chattering crèches of one hundred thousand or more. Their spindly legs struggle to keep their bodies erect. They have an enormous test ahead of them; for some it is more than twenty miles to a fresh-water lake, and it is urgent that they leave before the salt sucks the last drop of moisture from the salt pans. It is a race against the odds. Their parents bear witness to the struggle from on high and bring food to them at the end of their day. When the chicks' rubberlike legs buckle, they can pick up lumps of soda. It dries on their body, huge balls of it, making it nigh impossible for them to keep their balance. Still, each time they fall, they push up automatically unless their last drop of energy has dissipated.

It is a story of resilience; it is a story of immense determination. If you need inspiration when you are in the valley floor of life staring at the momentous climb ahead, you can hear the pink flamingo chicks saying, 'Get up! Try again! You can't give up yet. Who knows? You might succeed next time."

PEACE

"Once you have felt peace you will continually strive to get more and more of it, surfing the chaos, knowing that peace beckons on the other side."

Figure 4.9. Peace.

Peace can be as elusive as grasping rain with your hands: no sooner than it has settled in your palms it runs rivulets through your fingers; it is nigh impossible to grasp and secure fully. Some are born in parts of the world that will never know peace. How can you attain it when the world around you is filled with despair, hatred and hypervigilance? You wait for the next bomb, or the terrifying whistle of a missile hurtling to destroy, or an army of invaders whose hands are stained in the blood of the last massacre.

To achieve peace in this environment is saintly, otherworldly, almost not human; the person who can achieve it is the living personification of all deemed godly, sacred and profound. We have living memories of these people; ponder Mandela, the Dalai Lama and Gandhi as just three examples. They were able to hold onto their universal human compassion, in spite of the dry desert of parched hearts all around them thirsting for vengeance. The peace that they have achieved internally shows on their faces, their softened jaws, the creases at their eyes, the subtle joy sitting on their lips. Their words vibrate with soft sounds from their mouths and sit in the color grey, acknowledging complexity, offering insight from a bird's-eye view of the world, not the harsh black and white verbiage that alienates and creates walls.

This peace-filled talk draws the opposing sides together, like cavern walls crushing in and forming a new arrangement on the valley floor. This new grouping of people is now intent on finding peace, creating harmony, supporting community, and holding hands in the struggle of it all. They see their common cause and goals, moving forward in togetherness, creating a blanket of peace for all to snuggle under at night under the illuminated sky.

For those of us living in countries that have known peace on a mass scale, peace often seeps into our hearts on a steady percolator drip if we beckon it. One moment of peace creates the craving for another. Chaos becomes increasingly repugnant. In this peace-accruing state, we note the difference between living spontaneously and impulsively. Spontaneity is best when it is moving off firm ground, a fresh moment and an action seized without paralyzing analysis. Impulsivity, on the other hand, is action taken in chaotic circumstances: the winds are swirling, the person pushed here and there, and then more chaos and storms take away all the hard-earned peace in an instant.

So how can you actually get peace to take up residence in your heart? Are some people born with more of it than others, some as infants already on the path heading for their kind of nirvana? Peace is dependent on deep self-knowledge. If you desire to "know thyself" you will be rewarded by tidal waves of peace washing over the shore of your soul. The more you plunge into the complexity of your history, and come to peace with all of the injustices suffered in your and your loved one's lives, the more the drip of peace accumulates.

Forgiveness is to peace as water is to the desert plant; the two are bonded in a close relationship. Forgiveness of those whom you are least inclined to forgive is the hardest; but the rewards are evident with an injection of peace that is absorbed into your very cells. Soon you are steeped in peace, and it is worn like a cloak shimmering incandescently in the whirlpools of hate, cynicism and revenge.

Those that shun peace and push it to the margins in their world pay the price. Their mouth reveals the bitterness that has accumulated within; their lips are tight, often turned down for all to see that something went wrong in their life and they are still suffering. Eyes, too, tell a tale; there is murkiness in the iris. Confusion, uncertainty, and hatred cover up the vulnerability within. The heart has hardened; the eyes say it all, distrust permeating more deeply the deeper one stares. Is it too late for such a person to turn things around? Is peace a lost cause when one has frozen in time and one's heart is only capable of beating blood?

No, I say, tomorrow is a fresh new day, even if tomorrow comes from the inside of a penitentiary, in a cell so inhumane that most humans could die from the discomfort. It is possible for the first step for forgiveness to be seized at any moment in any life. Each step of forgiveness lightens the body, takes away brick by brick the internal heaviness accumulated in the very cells. Then, as the load gets lighter, so too does the heart begin to feel again. It's slow, and it's painful. Who has the courage to take on a life of regret? Some do, and even though they have failed in many eyes, they have redeemed themselves in some way by humanizing themselves and feeling again, perhaps feeling some of the immense pain of their victims and their families and releasing the regret and sorrow for such a misguided path. Peace then begins to grow. The seed is in rocky ground, the soil depleted, but as we all know, hardy plants can grow even in the desert with one drop of rain. So too can a human being, once lost to hatred, take a sharp turn in the road and move one glacial step after another toward long-lasting peace.

SELF-LOATHING

"To view oneself through such a laser of darkness brings tremendous sadness. To see self-loathing in another is to suffer intensely, knowing the attack leads to the attrition of all goodness and mercy."

To hate yourself, despise yourself, and lose respect and love for yourself is a sad state, as it feels permanent in that moment. Nothing will change unless you decide to turn it around; in the meantime it's a living hell, a torment so deep that it scars the inside with oozing lacerations. These inner wounds

Figure 4.10. Self loathing.

secrete shame, and the shame you bring onto yourself is more deriding, more corrosive than the words of any other. The words of the other may hurt, but the words you take deeply from your inner world triggers a jury fierce in its critique, marshaling all of its resources to diminish you. It is your inner critic; these critics have been trained with tongues of acid, corroding any vulnerability within, burning into your psyche all that is unworthy about yourself.

It is painful to look at someone plagued by self-loathing. Their skin appears to be crawling with the discomfort, their mouth grimacing. They look desperate to escape their body, fly off to another realm and flee from the steady drip of savage inner summations. They may be hearing in a loud, derisive voice, "You are such a loser," or a growling voice of disdain, "You will never amount to anything! Surely you can see that." Other voices with echoes from childhood may say, "You are stupid. You are fat, ugly, and lazy. Nobody loves you. You really are a blight on the planet. Surely you can see that you can't do anything right. Children are better seen and not heard, and you are not the child I wanted."

To the emotionally healthy observer, these phrases seem ludicrous, abusive, cruel, and obviously untrue. However, if you suffer from self-loathing, each one comes with an arrowhead so sharp that it pierces the toughest skin effortlessly. It heads straight for an inner wound still throbbing from all those years ago. Once it pierces, it takes up residence, intensifying the wound and magnifying it in any way possible. If the voices before were loud and cutting, now they take on a whole new gusto. They are relentless; reminders are everywhere: you tried to put your bus ticket in the machine and you had it the wrong way up and people saw your mistake. "Well," the voices say. "you can't even get that right. You should go home and crawl in your bed and stay there." Or you have the courage to phone a friend to try to make a social plan, and they say they can't meet because they are busy for a while. It's genuine on their part, but you hear something entirely different. You hear rejection in their tone; you are convinced they are making an excuse, trying to fob you off. After a while you hear, "No one likes you," an echo from childhood. Now you are fearful of reaching out to anyone ever again. That one event has had such a reverberation in your psyche that it takes days to shrug off. Still it lingers, dying to be triggered by the tiniest of mistakes. Self-loathing has a microscope that picks up the slightest flaw; its appetite for error is voracious.

Well, if this is living hell, there must be something you can do. Even reducing the intensity of the choir of critics would at least be a start. First of all, it can be helpful to identify the originator of the message: who was struggling so much with themselves that they projected their hell onto you at a time when you were ill-formed and vulnerable, finding your way and identity on the rocky road of life? Once you have discovered the source of the message, you can start the path of resistance by writing a letter letting them know the emotional impact of their tormenting phrases, and telling them you are not accepting their abusive summations a day longer. This reroutes the saved-up vitriol from an attack on yourself to its rightful place on the owner.

Many people fantasize about sending their letters and having those who emotionally abused them cower and beg forgiveness. Often this can lead to more abuse; the abuser did what they did from a place of soul contraction, and it is unlikely their contraction has disappeared to give them the strength to hear the pain they inflicted. You may need to write twenty or thirty letters to the same person, getting deeper into the pain that has lain resident for some time.

As you engage in this process fully, you will start to notice that the next time you make a mistake you shrug it off more quickly. You may hear the faint echo of "You're a loser," but then you realize that everyone makes mistakes and that it is human, after all, to do so. The echo seems fainter and fainter, and then at last it disappears into the ether. There are no more piercing arrows because there are no open wounds. Sure, the memories of the wounds are still there, but they are no longer gaping; they have healed. Although their healing is still superficial, in time it will grow deeper, the skin firmer. Finally, the other's vicious tones get caught in a strong wind, swept away, and with the help of the boomerang of justice, eventually end up swirling around the one who demeaned you in the first place.

PERSEVERANCE

"Perseverance stays steady. It says it is in it for the long haul. It has held determination's hand from birth, and between them they aim for greatness in all that they do."

Figure 4.11. Perseverance.

You want what you want. There is no negotiation here; you want it so badly that you can bite into it and have it for lunch, the craving is so bad. It's not as if this is impulsive; you have thought long and hard about this thing that you want. It all makes sense in the trajectory of your life. It is the next obvious meaningful step and you can't imagine your future without it. You have tried for years now (not just weeks, months and days; we are talking years!), and you are still hoping, still burning for the opportunity. How long can you hold on? Where do you get the resources to take the next step? You look down and your feet are in sticky, clammy mud, the type that sucks at your boots and pulls you in, down, away from everything you want. Can you do it? Can you get your feet out of this mess? You hear a voice whisper so softly that you can barely hear it, "Give it a try."

That is the voice of perseverance. Perseverance is proud of you, talking you into hanging in there. It is the epitome of faith in action. My goodness, there should be some sort of award that you could apply for. Perseverance is convinced you would win the prize unashamedly.

Yet another test of your perseverance comes your way. You sign on for a marathon. You are battling and wanting to quit early on. However, in spite of your internal struggles, you decide to stay in the race. You have lost your hat, the tread has worn off your shoes, and your water is nearly finished. You know there is a water station a couple of kilometers ahead, but kilometers right now feel like light-years. Can people not see that you are struggling? Your face feels puffy; in fact your whole body is either puffed with fatigue or creaking. You are trying not to think about the cost of perseverance. They said this race was not for the faint of heart, and of course you like a challenge. Could you have bitten off too much this time, extended beyond your capability? In fact, could you crash anytime soon? Perhaps fall on your face so hard that you leave an imprint in the tarmac?

You just passed a sign that says you are three-quarters of the way there, and that your water station is two kilometers away. Was the sign supposed to be reassuring? Your body doesn't think so. In fact, as soon as you read it, you feel your body sag significantly, even though you are trying not to feel your body at all. Someone just passed by you leaping like a bunny; you can't believe the lightness in their step. You are both on the same hellish journey; you question immediately, "What in the hell are they on?" Must be some kind of drug; it is the only explanation. You wish they would run right out of your view. This is really off-putting: You are positively exhausted and now some battery-pumped bunny leaps on by, almost fluffing their tail in your face.

You feel your grimace get tighter. Yes, they said this was the run for perseverance, but you wonder if some sadist cooked this up. They figured you would likely collapse about now. Then a steep hill appears as you round the corner. "Oh my God," you say to yourself, "I am not going to make it." you hear also, "There is no way, no way that you can do it, no way." The voice is unequivocal, but your body still limps along robotically, self-propelled, as if there is no choice. You knew the stakes were high. Even though your body feels like a decrepit mass of moving flesh and muscle, and your mind a battleground of negativity, something keeps propelling you. Now you are actually moving up the hill, badly, crookedly, desperately, but you are moving. Your feet still shift one in front of the other, amazingly.

Then eventually from the top of the hill you see the finish line. It's on the flat a little way from the bottom of the hill. People are all standing around it; you get a pump from that. They are all there to celebrate those who go down the road of perseverance, who stay the course, who keep their head down, their limbs moving, and their spirit indomitable.

Yes, *you* are one of the people they are cheering for. For them, maybe you are a role model, a mentor in the high stakes of life. You feel some wind engulf you and transport you for a moment. Then suddenly it dawns on you that it is your spirit that got you here and has kept you in the race. Your body might have given up a long time ago, and unequivocally your mind lost the race a while back. However, your spirit has stayed the course, injected hope and resilience right into your veins, when your whole being was on the verge of giving up.

Your feet are now buoyant, much like the wound-up bunny who bounced past you. You are almost flying down the hill. The mob around the finish line looks bigger now. You can't remember a sight so welcome. It doesn't even compare to being rescued, starving and desperate, after losing your way in the wilds of Africa, This is positively one of, in fact *the* best moment of your life! You have run the road of perseverance, lived to testify to your efforts, and succeeded by your sheer determination. You have defied the odds against you, won out your willful mind and manufactured hope that will live in your cells, hopefully for a lifetime. Pride is now rising and falling around your heart. You feel like you may burst with the joy of it all when you hear the cries as you step over the finish line. "Wow!" you hear from the crowd. "Isn't she amazing?"

INSTABILITY

"Instability says, 'You need me like the flowers need the rain. Remember, I get you moving to the land of much beauty, where all the treasures in you will emerge.'"

In essence, instability is a good sign. It is an indicator of change, shape-shifting, potential growth, and expansion, perhaps transformation; but internally you often resist it. You can resent its presence, its unsettling nature, its pervasiveness. When instability comes, it seems to go everywhere in your body. It is rarely content with just your stomach all aquiver, or your chest filled with a sensation of a thousand butterflies beating furiously beneath the skin. No, it is all over, and it feels as if it has taken up long-term residence and signed a contract to be around for the duration of your life. That is part of your panic, the panic that instability will be around forever, taking away your enjoyment of the moment and undermining your ability to focus, be confident, and feel self-assured.

Instability has a loud voice. It can't be ignored, no matter how hard you try. It bellows from every colonized cell in your body, "You can't ignore me. I am an internal earthquake rupturing routine, predictability, and normalcy.

Figure 4.12. Instability.

It is time for big-time change, and you have no choice in the matter; I am in charge." That is what is frightening you, scaring the hell out of you. In fact, you are starting to be convinced that this is your new hell. You didn't see it coming and then wham! It arrived, took over and started dictating its terms. In your rational mind you wonder what its terms are. If you comply with its program of turbulence, might you get rid of it forever?

You hear instability again, as if it has a megaphone attached to its mouthpiece: "Never say 'forever.' I am here now. I give you no guarantees, but go with me and we will dance together to a higher level."

"Dance?" You respond, thinking instability has gone completely mad. You ask again, "Did you really mean dance?"

"Yes! Let's dance, let's go wild, let's shake up every cell in your body. Move, move, move, and you will see: I will settle. It's the quickest way to pacify me, at least until I want to rise again to your surface."

You decide to take instability at its word; you are desperate, a bit deranged, so you are willing to do anything. You heard about the benefits of a trance dance, so you put on a blindfold to go deep inside of yourself. You follow your yoga teacher's "breath of fire" technique because you know it is about rebooting you. You hear her voice: "For about five minutes, two short breaths in, one breath out." You put on some wild, wild, wild music and you let your body go, go, go. Your limbs start to move on their own as if your body knows just what to do to release this sucker of peace. Your arms are flinging away from your body, your hips gyrating frenetically. In fact your head feels like it will fall off from the chaotic moves, but you keep going. You are losing yourself; your mind has taken a hike so the body can take over fully. Shake, shake, shake—you've become a human rattle, on and on, and you lose yourself in it fully. Time escapes from you. All you hear is the music and your heavy breathing. You have entered a trance, and now there is no end.

Suddenly the music stops, and your body settles in mid-sway. You are emotionally and physically wiped, incapable of speech; you only know something big just happened. You lie down and drink it all in for what seems like forever. Tentatively you check in with instability. You hear its distant cry, almost an echo: "I have been released." Then, sleep muffles everything. A deep peace reverberates in all of you; aah, home at last! A thought flashes into your mind, a realization: This is one reason, perhaps, why people from all over the world dance until they lift off into other spheres. Many eons ago, they wrestled down instability. You smile and drift off.

INFERIORITY

"To shrink into your weakest self is a choice. It is easy to feel inferior if you compare yourself to others, but why do that? There is no one like you on the planet; that is why you are here. What could possibly be inferior about that?"

Inferiority is often worn like a skin, shrouding your spirit in self-doubt, in self-criticism. It's painful for others to observe: you crawl inside, trying to make yourself smaller, less conspicuous, different. Anything but yourself would be acceptable, or so you think. It is a profound self-rejection, born from scar upon scar that didn't heal. It has left you with the overall feeling that you are deficient, inadequate, unworthy, unlovable, and unacceptable in countless ways.

The internal conversations are cruel; even you would admit you wouldn't treat an enemy as badly as you treat yourself. Daily, hourly, minute by minute, you are on the lookout to accrue evidence that the negative story you have of yourself is undoubtedly true. For instance, you may be walking innocently down the street, avoiding puddles from the rain that hasn't stopped falling for the last week. A truck goes by; it's in a hurry, of course, and it mows through

Figure 4.13. Inferiority.

one of the puddles on the street, spraying everywhere, including on you as you run from your sense of inferiority, splashing the new dress you put on to hide from those inferior feelings. You look down and you are horrified: there is mud all the way down the front of your lemon zinger summer dress, and it is still dripping further. Any mask you had been hiding behind gets whipped off, and you feel exposed, marked, stamped as inferior yet again. You tell yourself this kind of thing wouldn't happen to a normal person; you are jinxed.

That, of course, is just the beginning. You have to face your super confident colleagues who know everything about everything, always looking pristine and shining in whatever they wear. You feel like turning around, going back home, diving into your bed (the only safe place you know), and replaying the scene over and over again. You conclude quickly that no one else would have such bad luck, and confirm that no matter where you go or what you do, you will always be inferior, really inferior.

You walk in the door because of course you can't go home; what would you say to your boss? That would really expose you. The first person you see is Sally, who always looks like she has stepped out of a magazine, in flirty, fresh, clothes that hug her lean body and spray out with femininity flouncing around her. "Oh my God," she says out loud with a high-pitched, disgusted tone. Now everyone comes out of their offices to look. Someone even says,

"Look what the cat dragged in!" You can't believe they would be so heartless. You know you will remember the phrase over and over again, now and at three in the morning, when the scales are lifted and you have to face yourself again in the horror of the night where there is no escape. It's so embarrassing that you blush, and everyone can see you are embarrassed, ashamed. When you look at their faces, the pity really gets to you. It looks like it is painful for them to look at you, take you in, and acknowledge your presence. The combination of your flushing face and throat, your pained expression, and the dress of horror is reflected in their faces. Quickly you crawl into your office like a furtive animal wanting to burrow deep for escape.

Feelings of inferiority can be pervasive, but in your heart you know it doesn't have to be that way for the rest of your life. You start to get sick of its haunting, demeaning tone, and start to focus on building some layers of esteem. You want something like armor to protect you from inferiority's derisive knocks and dismiss them into the ether. So how do you start to build the armor so it sticks around? Armor for many of us is earned link by link by facing head-on the daily challenges that come our way, even seeking out challenges, especially those that send shivers down the spine when we imagine taking them on.

Public speaking is just such a challenge, if you are one of those who sweat at the thought of being on the podium, in front of all those potentially critical eyes. If the fear is great, it is also likely to have a great positive impact. So you start small by attending a Toastmasters' meeting, a forum where your skills will be tested. Someone calls on you to speak and suddenly some creature is sitting in your throat, blocking your breathing. Your voice sounds ancient, crackly and nervous all at the same time; you barely recognize it as your voice. You have to clear your throat, and when you do, you are horrified at the distasteful gravel hack that emerges. When you catch some people looking at you, you think you pick up pity in their faces. You soldier on. What are you going to do, leave the podium midstream? You rattle on about something and eventually come to the end. You practically run to your seat, flushed, overwhelmed and shaking, but my goodness, you did it. Yes, you did! It may have sounded horrible and you may get awful feedback about your voice or your poor eye contact or your slouching posture, but who cares; you did it, and you can't believe you pulled it off.

As you walk home, still high that you did it, you feel a thinly veiled cloak come over you, like a protective sheath. It feels good. You haven't felt this good in years. You can't wait to go back to Toastmasters to give it another go. You know you have earned some esteem in the way that matters, facing down fear, esteem that will be with you now wherever you go.

Next time there is some freak event and you are the recipient, there will be the initial horror, but then, after a while, instead of sticking to some negative internal Velcro long-term, you will shake it off. It might take a while initially, but sometime soon, when you have become a Toastmaster pro, you will shake it off like water, just like a duck; only quicker.

GRIEF AND LOSS

"To lose to death someone you love is like marching forward in life without a leg. No wonder we feel lost, out of sorts, hollow. It doesn't mean we will never dance again; when we do dance, it will be with the shadow of our loss, moving together in memory that has been cauterized forever in our soul."

Figure 4.14. Grief and loss.

Grief and loss often seem bigger than you, towering over you like a mountain peak, showing that the path is a staggering uphill climb all the way. No plateaus on this venture! This is one painstaking step after another. There is slippage as well; sometimes you fall and fold into a shaking ball of overwhelming sadness, temporarily incapable of getting up. Grief takes over, and you are consumed by it. You cannot go through a day without remembering the one you loved. They may be dead, but their living likenesses are everywhere. You follow their ghost, thinking another person's hair and stature look the same from behind. For a moment, you imagine your beloved is still with you. Then the other person turns around, and you are abruptly confronted with reality; it is not them at all. No, they are gone from this world, and the dread, pain and grief rise and consume you once again.

Some relationships are too deep to get over. The person was so close to you that you didn't have to say anything, or explain yourself; they just got it. You felt understood at a soul level, all of your soul, and it is frightening to think you will spend all this time on Planet Earth without them. There is a resound-ing hollowness ringing in the very air you breathe. Even if your beliefs hold that they are still alive, existing at another level, there is still the emptiness, the hollowness, the soul's yearning. The sorrow that takes over, the shadow of their existence and memory all merging and following you around wherever you are. You long to see their face, hear their voice, have an exchange that says the world is all right again. However, it doesn't happen, and the long-ing becomes a physical ache in your heart, so big you are convinced it will never go away.

Yet, over time, if the tears are shed and the stillness is maintained for it to all wash over you, the intensity lessens. You have reached the first base camp on the mountain; and although they are not there at your side cracking some joke, the vistas are helping you feel more alive. The grief initially was deadening, burying you under it, but now there is more space in your heart and mind. You are more aware of everything now; you cry easily, even at a movie. However, strangely, you are also more satisfied when the moment takes over and you get consumed by beauty. In fact, you seem more sensitized to beauty. Loss and grief seem to leave that in their wake, like a line for you to hold onto as you climb to the next base camp on the mountain. Each step is a bigger stride in letting go and moving up the path to acceptance, even though you still struggle with the loss. Kahil Gibran captured this experience in his piece on pain:

Your pain is the breaking of the shell that encloses your understanding.

Even as the stone of the fruit must break, that its heart may stand in the sun, so must you know pain.

   And could you keep your heart in wonder at the daily miracles of your life, your pain would not seem less wondrous than your joy;

   And you would accept the seasons of your heart, even as you have always accepted the seasons that pass over your fields.

   And you would watch with serenity through the winters of your grief. (Gibran, 1968:52)

Grief and loss also relate to the loss of a partner through divorce or separa-tion. Even if you have chosen the separation, planned it, packed your bags knowing it is the right choice for your emotional health, the grief can be intense. At the moment of departure, you remember all the aspects of the per-son that you treasured. Grief has a long-term memory and seems to store all the precious moments in one region of the brain. At the moment of loss, they all gush through, confusing you regarding your decision. In that way, grief and loss can be crazy-making. At intense moments, you remember only the good stuff, as if you have blotted out the past hurts completely.

Grief and loss go everywhere, for they are related to many aspects of our lives. There is grief for your loss of dreams, loss of job, loss of self. There is the grief of the empty nest when the children leave, and the grief of unrealized potential. Grief says to you, "Stay awhile and ponder what you have lost. It is your way through to a higher path, an elevated plane." Grief reminds you, "Stick with me and I will lighten your load in time, assist you in letting go of the pain and help you remember the beauty of what has been."

OBSESSIVE-COMPULSIVE PATTERN

"The goal of the obsessive-compulsive pattern is to reduce us to our smallest self, taking over, turning us into a robot, undermining our ability to make choices. It says, 'Follow me zealously and you won't have to feel.' It's lying; in time the self-loathing and bitterness will invade our entire being and have us flailing in a hellish state of despair."

Figure 4.15. Obsessive / compulsive.

Nowadays, there are special groups for those afflicted with Obsessive-Compulsive Disorder (OCD). However, it has some things in common with patterns of thoughts and behavior shared by the entire population of troubled humanity.

We all have a tendency toward obsessive thoughts and compulsive rituals under stress. Some of us go to the extreme not leaving the house until the locks have been checked at least seven times (or was that seven times seven?). It's hard to keep up with obsessive thinking and compulsive rituals. One thing is for sure: These patterns can take over our life and colonize every rational brain cell. They turn us into fear-driven repetitive robots, following internal commands as if our very survival depended on it.

What on earth leads rational people down such a tormenting path of shame and imprisonment, whereby you are no longer free to act spontaneously? Every step is measured, the results analyzed so excessively that any risks are reduced to a minimum and hence deep fear is kept in check, well in check, for that day. There is always another day when hurricane-force, out-of-control, winds take over and sweep you away. What exactly fosters the engine of obsessive thoughts and painstaking compulsions?

In essence you feel out of control. The out-of-control feeling is directly proportional to the level of obsessive thinking and degree of compulsive rituals. A traumatic event occurs that comes as a shock. You had no warning. Wham! You were on your back with the impact of it all.

Perhaps your partner announced they were leaving, just like that; after twenty years of companionship with the usual challenges and triumphs, they are leaving. In fact, their bag is packed and their get-away program is already arranged. They have been pondering this for some time, while you sat unknowingly under the mushroom in total darkness. Or maybe someone dies with no warning, or you are shot at, or you lose your job, your home and even your pet. There is an earthquake, or a flood that drowns all your belongings in a sea of muddy, raging torrents. Perhaps it was an outbreak of war, or grinding poverty so deep that it forced you to watch helplessly as your baby starved before your eyes. Suffering is a global phenomenon, and you don't know until an event occurs whether you have the capacity to handle it, emotionally and physically. The scars remain in the psyche, the nightmares, the repetitive thoughts. Soothing compulsive rituals are intended to bring normalcy and a self-equilibrium, but equilibrium is impossible with a psychic scar contained in a stiff neck, or upset stomach or aching back. Yes, your body lets you know all is not well, that the impact is still there; it just got hidden in some weak spot in your body.

In time, the symptoms take over your life. You are reduced to a mere servant role as they command, "Think this ten thousand times, do that repeatedly, keep thinking this, do that, think, do," until you are a mere puppet dancing to their commands.

When symptoms produced by your fear of losing control have themselves seized control of every moment of every day, how can you regain control? Step one in regaining control is to acknowledge your feelings. They may be buried under a morass of thought, so writing out your thoughts and mining for feelings is a huge step in the right direction.

Step two is to admit to yourself that the trauma of that event hasn't gone away; it just got buried. Perhaps you receive trauma counseling and do some mind-body work to release it both physically and intrapsychically. Maybe you write a letter to the one that hurt you, letting them know the impact on you to this day. Perhaps the wound is so deep you need to write twenty or more letters, choosing not to send them so you don't engage with the person anymore. All in all, you start the release, and the more you choose to release, the more the repetitive thoughts start to fade. Then, amazingly, you even feel fine when you forget to check the locked door for the seventh or even sixth time. Soon you realize you don't need to keep checking; your mind is clearing. You feel the feelings of the past and you become confident enough to release them along the way. This is a new way, instead of burying, suppressing, sequestering and letting obsessive thoughts and compulsive rituals reduce you to a shame- and fear-filled automaton taking commands.

IN THE MOMENT AND OUT OF CONTROL

"To live in the now is to liberate the soul, put it fully at the helm. The soul says emphatically, 'Don't think about yesterday or tomorrow. Be in the now, right here. This moment is where the magic abounds in a waterfall of delight.'"

It is a struggle to move from forecasting and predicting your life to living in the moment, freeing yourself from a need to know. Why is it so hard? Well, the other way of living comes with an alluring feeling of having more control. You want to be in charge of the gearshift of life–none of this driving to some unknown destination. You also want to be duped into believing you are not vulnerable, in spite of daily stories all around you of unseen human disaster. What of that poor man who was just driving his car when a tree sliced him and his vehicle in half? What of the photographs from the southern hemisphere where the scenes after a hurricane or tsunami look like the apocalypse? You empathize, and then perhaps console yourself secretly that somehow people here in the North are much more protected from nature's whimsical spirit.

There is also cultural support for living "out of the moment." We arrange vacations a year in advance. We take out hefty mortgages assuming our life

Figure 4.16. In the moment / out of control.

will remain on its present track to meet our financial commitments. In romantic encounters, we meet someone, and with scant information about them start to assume relationship stability. In our conversations with each other, we talk about life as a known quantity, not realizing or even imagining it would take only one earthquake to rip it all apart. Living out of the moment also affects the way we deal with and talk about death. In the North American context death is at times smoothed over and subliminally declared an unsafe topic. If culturally we can't handle this aspect of life, then what else of import gets squeezed out to the margins in daily discourse?

An arresting moment for me while living in Africa was meeting an African who was walking from village to village in a game park in Botswana. On that trip I had many encounters with seemingly hungry wild animals from the safety of a car, but still had feared for my own life frequently. I asked him what he would do if he met a lion while moving across the land. His response was one of acceptance that his time was up. I was perplexed by the way he spoke about his death with such ease and a calm countenance. He was a living embodiment of a strategy: embrace death and uncertainty, and your life's peace thermometer will hit the peak zone.

My shift from living "out of the moment" to living increasingly "in the moment" was the breakup of a long-term relationship that I had assumed would last forever. It's surprising that experiencing a war in Zimbabwe or immigrating to three countries in a decade didn't get me there sooner. I was a hard case; analysis had been my thing, and I enjoyed my apparently astute predictive powers. The relationship breakup shattered my way of viewing the world, defied my bedrock of certainty and challenged me to the core. I worked in psychiatry and even did couples counseling. I couldn't explain to my psyche why I didn't see this coming. It was a moment Neale Donald Walsh discusses in his book *Tomorrow's God:*

> Life places you at the point of rotten choices when you are about to make an enormous breakthrough in your experience of who you are. The creation and facing of tough choices is always an announcement from your soul to your mind through your body that it is jump time for the totality of your being. . . . You bring yourself to critical choice points perhaps six or seven times a life; you can count them on both hands. Welcome these critical choice points; do not shrink from them. They offer you rare and breathtaking opportunities to leap forward in your evolution. They are always among life's greatest blessings. (Walsch, 2004:351)

During my period of immobilization in one of my critical choice points, I noticed my heart felt like it was shrinking, drying at the edges, much like a crustacean out of water. I was frightened by the sensation and realized it was critical that I start to take risks. I feared I would shrink further into a mock protective shell, living half a life perhaps for the rest of my life, being tormented daily, hourly by "if only" and regret. So I made tentative steps at first, and then bolder ones. The world felt much less certain, but I was moving, however glacially, and that in itself was cause for celebration. Instinctively I started to move out of my head (which had let me down terribly) to feeling things more in my stomach. I started to rely more on intuition.

I played mind games with my head and made predictions of how each week would unfold. Week after week, I noticed surprise encounters I could never have predicted, and so I started to stare plainly at my limitations and vulnerability. I was admitting to myself more and more that I swam in a sea of uncertainty, so paying more attention to what was happening right now made a lot more sense. Ironically, the more I was present in the moment the more I noticed subtle psychic cues and felt more in control overall. Peace was also starting to build. Waves of it washed over me, reassuring me the path was right even though the direction was uncertain.

So I have come to relish the state of "turbulent peace." Any peaceful life needs to be resting on a mat with vibrating spring coils underneath. As life shifts, so the psyche needs to shift with it. Throw out the mat with Velcro attachments that keeps you from moving! Oh, sure, you sit more comfortably on the stationary mat for a while, but when life delivers a blow, as it surely will, your static state will have you floundering. When you have more confidence in your ability to care for yourself, your feeling of self-control rises astronomically.

Asserting yourself, nurturing yourself, educating others about the internal chaos that is going on inside, can then free you to finally surrender. At last you let go of the illusions of external control that have blocked your progress and seen you quavering like a newborn on a cold day, and you can experience the moment fully. From that day on, you have seized your life back, no longer haunted by the Buddhist phrase, "As you walk and eat and travel be where you are. Otherwise you will miss most of your life"(Kornfield, 1994:80).

PROCRASTINATION

"To procrastinate endlessly is to drain all the goodness out of the moment. By the time the decision is made, the cup is dry, the motivation gone, and the desire crusty. Who knows what is the right choice sometimes, but life has a way of pointing the way when we take risk after risk on the untrammeled road."

Procrastination from the outset has refused to wear a muzzle. It was born with a garrulous tongue, and it prides itself on its monologues, especially laced with the word "should," mostly "you should." Procrastination acts as if you don't know what you should do, like some brain box always remembering what you "should do" with an oppressiveness that borders on pathological. You are not a machine, but procrastination thinks you are, as if you are a robot programmed for peak performance all the time.

Procrastination's lists are endless and don't take your fatigue into account one little bit. "You should do the dishes straight away after eating. You need to clean the house; it's appalling. You need to call some friends and get some kind of a life together. You need to lose weight now. You need to write that letter, and fix the bathroom. While you are at it, paint the outside, mow the lawn more often so you keep up with the Joneses next door, and for goodness sake do a spring clean of your closets right away." Procrastination never

Figure 4.17. Procrastination.

learned patience; procrastination was born of an age of instant gratification. That is what procrastination wants, and it wants it now. Does anyone think procrastination would ever be satisfied? If you did all the things it tells you to do, my bet is that it would come up with a whole new list in an instant. Given its wily ways, how can you tackle procrastination so you are pulling the reins on it, bridling it, so you are running your course and not following its "flavor of the month" trajectory?

First of all, you need to decide what your priorities are: Is it really important to do x when you only have a limited time to do anything at all? You need to take into account that for thousands of years, Homo sapiens have, for the most part, lived slower and much simpler lives: One slept, one ate, one grew or caught food, and one learned how to cobble a thatched or adobe hut or some such covering quickly to live in. One's "to do" list back then was pretty simple: it was all about eating, staying safe, adapting to nature and spending time with the community. There were no shops, distractions, or a thousand and something demands on one's time. One had time back then, truckloads of it, as each day went slowly, sometimes glacially.

Fast-forward to the twenty-first century and these same Homo sapiens are racing everywhere trying to do everything. Work takes up the biggest chunk; the norm for North America is about 40 hours a week. Then there is commuting, shopping, cleaning, and bonding with family and friends, as well as your favorite TV shows, then your hobbies, which of course have to be squeezed in, and the latest festival or movie. By then, you are flipping exhausted, and so the last thing you want to do is look at your "to do" list with great enthusiasm and gleefully take on another task. This is when procrastination pops up like a mole sensing time for action, rears its head, grabs onto your weak brain and refuses to let go. The "shoulds" are endless, as if you have another whole life running alongside this one. You can barely put one foot in front of another. You are wiped out. Your mood is also suffering. In fact you feel overwhelmingly "blah," with hardly the time for tackling the ever-growing list.

When you are in this nearly catatonic state, procrastination goes on the attack, absolutely oblivious to your condition, pretending you are a teenager bursting with free-floating hormonally induced energy spikes. The more procrastination has a go, the more deflated you become. Television and other distractions become magnetic in this state; you need something to take the voice away and hang out in Nowheresville for some time. Your soul is catching up with your body, just like the legend of the Africans that were helping the Dutch Voortrekkers move across the land: Day after day the Africans helped load the wagons, then one day the Africans just sat immovable. The Dutch were puzzled by the Africans' intransigence, assuming a rebellion was fermenting. Eventually, the real reason came out: "We have been moving day after day, and today we need to rest so our souls can catch up with our body."

Procrastination is horrified by the idea of slowing down for your soul; values like that undermine it immediately. It loses its power, its voice muffles, and it starts to quiver as it realizes its influence is ebbing away. The last thing procrastination wants is for you to contemplate your "self needs." If you believe you are in need of rest and you refuse a robotic, ever-achieving existence, then you can develop more realistic expectations of what you can achieve. Given that you have the same human abilities as the men and women that lived off the land for thousands and thousands of years, maybe that "to do" list can just keep growing, for now anyway. Next time you hear procrastination's dictates of "should," tell it where to go, right now!

SELF-SABOTAGE

"We say we want something, but then how come we trip ourselves up just before the finish line time and time again? To answer that question is to give self-sabotage its exit papers right here, right now."

Figure 4.18. Self sabotage.

We hate ourselves when self-sabotage happens. It is as if we have been exposed, and the deeper truth about who we are laid bare, like a sea star turned upside down, its vulnerable side revealed.

If you are like most of us, many a time you have been rooting for a certain goal, taking it very seriously, telling everyone on a loudspeaker that this is what you want. Perhaps it is an intimate relationship, someone to care about, love, hold close, share your life with and make memories together. You let everyone know you are actively pursuing online dating in order to meet the special one. When they arrive, you tell all your friends and family they are "the one"; it is unmistakable. You are getting to know them, and it is all going well, until you flirt with someone else when you are out together, or you pick a fight out of the blue and don't acknowledge it is your fault, and in fact start blaming them for hurting you before you are even hurt. The self-sabotage card just got played, laid down on the deck of life, dominating the circumstances. Your buddies are puzzled: How did this happen? How can you explain it, when you told them unequivocally all was going well? Why did you do it? The confusion of self-sabotage takes over, spiked with self-loathing and shame.

The hardest thing about self-sabotage is that often the answer lies so deep inside that you have no answers to give; you can't even answer yourself. Now, that is really tough, so tough we should get onto this self-sabotage thing rationally. It is just unacceptable to go for your dreams, and then have the rug pulled out from under you in an instant and, most painfully, by your own hands. You can't even blame another person. You may try sometimes, but self-sabotage rears its head, as it likes to be noticed. Often, too, others see that you did it to yourself, and then they give up on you a little. You have lost credibility in their eyes, and in your own eyes, too.

Self-sabotage is often rooted in childhood, a time when you were vulnerable to others' feedback about yourself. "You are lazy. You are fat. No one cares about you, and you will never amount to anything." So just when you are about to get the award, or finish the race, or get the promotion, you flop, publicly flop. You run away or go off sick, or fall down in some way. Deep down, you feel you didn't deserve it anyway, and so there is an ill-shaped equilibrium that settles again.

Self-sabotage is always on high alert. It has held onto these internalized cruel messages, and it releases their full magnitude just when you have an opportunity to transcend these historical harsh summations. It has a myriad of ways of tripping you up, so many you can't even count them. For example, you just need to pass one more exam in order to get your degree. Just before the exam, you hear a childhood message so loud it almost knocks you over: "You will never amount to anything." You set your alarm to go to the exam; you hear it, ignore it, turn over and miss the exam. You know what you are doing, and it seems insane: You studied for the exam, but somehow there is a deep comfort inside that you are not shaking up core perceptions of yourself.

How about the promotion you have been seeking forever? You know the job will be a sublime fit and that you will be happier in it for a variety of reasons. You let your boss know you are interested, and he asks you to make an appointment with him to discuss the new job. However, you can't bring yourself to make the appointment. You are aware you are having a fight with your shadow regarding a core belief of being inferior to others, and somehow not deserving the job. It's embarrassing. Your boss is looking at you strangely; he is perplexed. So are you. You can't even make small talk with him right now, you feel so exposed. It becomes harder to go to work. Your shadow just got bigger, and it seems to dominate now. All the office conversations are stilted. You know it is you; you are sabotaging yourself again. The helplessness, powerlessness and shame that go with the sabotage are turning you into a recluse.

In my own experience, the label that followed me around for some time was "You are lazy." Perhaps I was, always looking for a short cut, particularly when it came to school. However, being *called* lazy took on a life of its own, undermining my efforts when I *was* willing to dedicate the time. I

an opportunity for activation. There may also have been kids at school who inflicted their wounds with bullying, rejection, and ridicule; it led you to feel unworthy, ashamed, and full of self-doubt. Life was challenging enough, so your survival strategy was to pretend the pain of it all had gone away. With the pain in residence, however, it has been hard to take any kind of a risk, run with a new idea, strive to do something that boosts you. Anytime you reach higher or further, perfectionism is on its elevated perch, ready to unleash its acerbic voice in a tone of derision and contempt. When it attacks, beware! In seconds, it can crush what little self-esteem you mustered in good times. The words are so toxic, you're unlikely to ever imagine painting again, even though your spirit craves the release and creativity.

So, if perfectionism is so powerful, how on earth do you wrestle it down, muzzle it, pour water over its mean-spirited sounds so they are drowned into oblivion? The first way is to acknowledge its presence. If you pretend it isn't there, you'll only be caught off-guard at a critical moment. Another way is to journal, telling it to take a hike, anchoring its voice in your past; tell those that inflicted your wounds what it has been like for you to have such negativity attached to you.

You also need to get onto perfectionism's tricks. Perfectionism hates it when you take risks in spite of its warnings. Immense courage is needed but facing down the voice of doom and limitation is liberating. With consistent risk, perfectionism's voice gets softer, the tone less cutting. Eventually, the rejected painting gets dragged out and you take an honest look without the worms in your brain. Honestly, besides the background needing to be a bit lighter, it's really rather good. Perhaps there is an exhibition that will take it after all!

HARASSMENT

"Blaming, attacking, and undermining: the harasser's tricks are endless, the result the same. As they diminish the other, their own equilibrium balances. The other, wounded in battle, rises only for another onslaught. It is darkness, feeding on a frenzy of victims, never looking in the mirror to face its increasingly grotesque reflection."

Harassers have a dizzying array of strategies, but their overall intent with each one is to impact the person in much the same way. Their goal is to undermine, destabilize and trigger self-doubt so self-esteem is drained quickly and effectively. One of the perpetrators' harassing tricks is to keep you off balance. It could look like an ordinary day, and perhaps there is even a smile coming your way from your harasser, or a warm greeting. Your mind catches it instantly, and the hopeful side of yourself says, "Well, maybe things have

Figure 4.20. Harassment.

changed for the better. Maybe they have let go of their need to make me feel small. Perhaps this is a sign of a new relationship emerging, so I can relax more." The harasser often knows you are being duped by their newfound warmth, and also knows that the next sting will be more powerful if it is unexpected.

In time, the next undermining strategy comes, as you are a critical piece for their maintaining equilibrium. People project onto others in order to run away from those parts of themselves they find loathsome. If they blame others, they can put off looking in the mirror—until life circumstances dictate differently. Perhaps you made a simple mistake, something so small that it is barely worth mentioning. To the harasser, though, nothing is too small for ammunition. Perhaps you forgot to date a note that you wrote; to those on the lookout, this is an opportunity. Not only will the harasser point out your error, but they will also send the message that it was serious. So the corrosive acid starts to drip into your psyche. When enough of it collects, your perception of yourself can shift.

When you receive little to no validation for your strengths, and an intrapsychic lashing for every minor mistake, your self-esteem is in battle. Protecting yourself is critical, but some strategies at your disposal may exacerbate the problem. For instance, when you are bone tired of the steady stream of vitriol, you may challenge the harasser. The harasser is used to being dominant, so being challenged could stir them up for some sort of escalation. A strategy they may use is denial, or minimization of your experience, so you second-guess yourself. They are throwing seeds of self-doubt your way. Your challenge is to make sure you don't nourish them with self-criticism, while the onslaught of your invalidation continues.

After the challenge they may up their tricks. In meetings they may make little or no eye contact with you, as a way of encouraging feelings of invisibility. They may also not greet you in the morning so the stale atmosphere in the office starts to feel stifling and tense. Your insecurity and anxiety thermometer may start to rise, and your body senses that it is in an unsafe place, as there is a lot more tension. It is set up as a win/lose game; but in essence it is a dynamic that highlights your ability to manage stress.

Harassment can also come in the form of sexual harassment. Generally, women experience this the most. They are objectified by devouring sexual glances in spite of presenting themselves as capable, talented workers. Managers can take advantage of their power. Sexual jokes and pornography in the office can also produce an atmosphere where a woman feels intimidated and demeaned. Sexual harassment can also include rape, and asking for sexual favors as a way of securing employment or promotion. Again the strategies have the same intent to demean, undermine and belittle the worker so the harasser remains dominant.

So what do you do to fight back, to hold onto your self-esteem in spite of the intensity of the harasser's tricks? Firstly, in the wise words of Deepak Chopra, "Accept what comes to you totally and completely so that you can appreciate it, learn from it, and then let it go." (Chopra, 1997). This in no way justifies the abuse from the harasser; it means that when life is difficult, we are forced to learn more strategies. If the harasser can get you to hate them, they have been successful, so the key is to protect yourself but also to humanize the perpetrator. This was a strategy employed by Nelson Mandela with his jailers. He believed that they must have some redeeming characteristics, and so he humanized them when they were doing the opposite to him. The harasser realizes at some level that they are losing power over you if you remain respectful towards them, not lowering yourself to their level.

You also need a strategy to deal with the buildup of resentment you feel. Releasing the resentment with writing can save you from the buildup of bile and poisonous feelings. If the poison is being drained, the harasser's power is also weakened. Harassers also gain more power if their intentions are kept secret. Public discussion can help in alerting them and others that you have the courage to speak your truth. In serious situations, legal actions need to be considered.

A guiding principle to keep in mind with any harasser is that whoever angers you, controls you. "Hatred never ceases by hatred; by love alone it is healed. This is the ancient and eternal law" (Kornfield, 1994:19). Protecting yourself and forgiving and letting go is your way through. "Forgiveness is primarily for our own sake, so that we no longer carry the burden of resentment. But to forgive does not mean we will allow injustice again" (Kornfield, 1994:96). Your spirit is also enlarged by the process, and the larger your spirit, the more you are naturally protected from those who invite you into a ring of contraction.

CONFIDENCE

"Confidence bolsters the spirit in nourishing balm, saying quietly but resolutely, 'Yes you can, and you will.'"

Figure 4.21. Confidence.

Confidence is not something anyone can hand to us to help us over life's hurdles. The question is, can we jump over the obstacle, or do we trip over it?

Confidence is hard-earned; brick by brick it is painstakingly laid, each brick requiring humongous effort. It requires the effort of a body builder at the gym, pushing those pounds high above our head, our body heaving, breath held to push way past our limit to success.

Some of us, of course, have circumstances in life that have laid a foundation of cement, so that the bricks can be secured in the first place. Others of us have to dismantle what we were given because it was broken, ill-formed, and unstable, and restart the building right from the beginning. It is parents or caregivers that shape the original platform. When children are abused and mistreated, then the foundation is full of cracks. Each crack is a painful memory or a label, perhaps unworthiness, inferiority, or unlovability; the list goes on.

This is not to say that repair work is beyond you; though it takes enormous perseverance, it can be done. This is where you transcend any limitation placed on you, and build a foundation so secure, so solid, that it could withstand great tests in the future.

Confidence increases naturally when you say what you feel. You let go of the need to be liked by everyone; rather, you choose first to be liked by yourself. Expecting always to win others' approval is a bit like expecting the wind to blow in the right direction all the time; it is whimsical. Others tend to approve of us when they feel good about themselves, and are more critical when they are battling with their own self-esteem. People-pleasing is a road full of losses: loss of who you are, loss of confidence and loss of direction. You will never please enough, and after a while you don't know what you think and feel anymore. The wind has taken you somewhere else, anywhere, while you were pleasing here and pleasing there.

Confidence says, "I state my truth. People will like me or hate me, but it is my truth, and I am steadfast behind it." Confidence loves it when you are faithful to your uniqueness. There is no one else exactly like you in the whole world; you are an original snowflake. When you revel in your originality, self-esteem will build effortlessly. Confidence celebrates when your desire for growth surpasses your fear of risk. Of course you feel fear, and of course you are anxious. Maybe you feel inadequate, but confidence says with a trumpeting voice, "Yes you can!" and "Go for it!" Confidence always carries around a set of binoculars, setting your sights on the longer vision, the bigger goal and the more formidable action. From confidence's point of view, you have never arrived, never reached the end. There is always another step to a higher terrain with more stupendous views.

I have noticed too that confidence never goes to sleep. It is active in your dreams, helping you process your latest obstacle, helping you stare at the blocks in your path. Its hope is that by confronting your fears and limitations in a dream state, you will muster the strength to tackle them in the big world of reality.

The more bricks you have secured in place as you build your confidence, the more you will live as who you really are. You will follow your own values. You don't need a creed from somewhere else to guide you; you are guiding yourself, allowing your intuition to be your seer and visionary. Giving you hunches along the way do this, do that, intuition will take you to a higher plane where you become more and more yourself. Confidence is a trusted ally, a best friend. It leads you to a place of total peace, peace that you are who you are, peace and acceptance of what is. Confidence also offers you long-term protection from the ever-swirling whirlpool of projections from others of who they want you to be.

ANTICIPATION

"Anticipation hangs over the moment like a candelabra twinkling in the moonlight, each glint from a shard of light alighting our path in the mystery of the unknown, a path to the unknown destination."

Figure 4.22. Anticipation.

Anticipation forms like bubbles under the skin, often collecting in the stomach to form a mass of building bubbles about to burst with enthusiasm, unbridled joy, relief, and an eddy of elation. Whatever one has been anticipating, desiring in the soul, it has been in the body for some time. It has been getting larger. As the anticipation builds so does the intensity of the feeling held in the body. At times, it can feel as if your being is about to burst with it, as if you will be carried away on a surging river of anticipation, taking you away here and there, this tributary, that tributary, away from here, right now. To resist it, you come back to sit, almost Buddha like, blowing up exponentially but still sitting, right up to the moment before you hear that your dream has been realized. Then, in seconds, all the anticipation bursts and sprays with delight; it is finally released, until, of course, the next anticipation.

Anticipation encourages you to believe you are ready, and ready now. No more patience required, no more of this dead time in the wings. You want to be on the main stage of life, fully realizing all of your dreams this second. You forget, although your soul often has not forgotten, that whatever you desire has not arrived and is still in the anticipation stage for a reason. You think you are ready to birth the desire, bring it into full form on the earthly plane, so it is no longer a pregnant possibility but reality. However, you easily forget that life is a process, and that a birthing suggests full maturation of the state of readiness.

An elephant has an eighteen-month gestation process to birthing the calf. In the necessary time in the womb, the fetus is forming strong muscles so when it arrives it is fully prepared. So it is with desires: if you reached each one instantly you would not be prepared at times for the full outcome. The soul hears the desire, hears the impatience, hears the need to have the desire realized, but it is cautious. The soul urges that all the groundwork to be done before the dream comes through fully. The soul is intent on the dream's coming through with the best conditions possible.

For instance, perhaps you desire a different job or an intimate relationship. The craving is overwhelming. So, you do all the preparatory work. For the job, you get your resume in order, go through the necessary training for the desired profession, make contacts, send out resumes and then wait with anticipation and hope. For an intimate relationship, the preparation is unique to each person: Some get into good physical shape. Others may work through past losses so the slate is clean. Others may feel preparation is unnecessary, and just go barreling forth, hoping life sends the right person in the right form.

Although conscious preparation is helpful, there is another process that coincides. It is often not evident, for it may be underneath the surface of consciousness. It is a shadowy state; it is ill-formed but needs healing for dreams to come to birth. The all-knowing, wise unconscious mind, the inner sage in all of us, is the guide regarding desires and their realization, and it takes pains to communicate. The unconscious is aware of the internal barriers to your dreams. You say you want an intimate relationship, but then why do you keep choosing unavailable potential partners? You say out loud, sometimes on a loudspeaker, "My next partner will be an equal." How confusing, then, that you are attracted to inequality every single time, to a dependent, to someone who needs you. The unconscious knows; it could give an answer in a second: "Martyrdom. Your need to be needed is bigger than your desire for equality. There is work to do, if you really want to sit side by side with your equal."

"How about the job, then?" you ask. Suppose you want a management position. You have done the MBA, so you have the training. Perhaps you have trained and managed some students. "Surely I am ready," you say tentatively to the unconscious. "Ah, you have done your homework," the unconscious answers, "but how about the childhood memory that is sitting in your soul, untouched, telling you that you are not deserving of success? Isn't that why you fail the interviews, self-sabotage your chances? How about some healing on that front before you go for the big goal? The path will be smoother when you are ready. It will be effortless. Mark my words!"

"Yeah, yeah," you retort to the unconscious. "That's just boring." However, after five failed interviews, you are bottomed out, and its words start resounding in your brain. In fact, now you can't stop thinking about them. You dive into the work. It's hard, and it's painful, but at least you will finally get out of this state of anticipation to realizing your dreams. You have decided that in this life, now you will do all you can to play the game with trump cards. You will look for clues that your unconscious gives you, so that there are no more jokers upsetting your stride, undermining your progress.

In that way anticipation is your friend: it is saying hope is in order. Each bubble of anticipation is yet another source of reassurance that all is on track, that the preparation is occurring on a slow but sustained level, that the dawning of your dreams is over the horizon. It reminds you, though, that life is now. It reminds you to be in the present, or you will miss living your life. It states also that by being in the present you will make the necessary change and remove all obstacles for the birthing, so that the final birthing is one of joy gone mad, and exhilaration soaring to heights unimagined.

CYNICISM

"The heart that has given itself over to despair pretends that it hasn't. It puts out its cynical generalizations as fact. However, the truth is that the voice comes from a shrunken heart that has sequestered the pain and hurt of it all and drowned in bitterness."

Figure 4.23. Cynicism.

The goal of cynicism is to colonize your entire face: It takes over your mouth and turns the corners resolutely down. It glazes the eyes, so they only see through a myopic lens tinted with doom. It deeply etches the forehead with creases. The creases are everywhere, and each is a story of hurt, betrayal, disappointment, anger, despair—any charged emotion that has resulted in loss, or grief or a slipping away of your dreams. It murmurs phrases like "If only . . . ," "Why me?" "What's the point in trying?" "There's no use in hoping." "Hope is a fool's road." "Optimism is laughable; have they not woken up yet?" Each phrase is born from a moment that came with a great deal of overwhelming emotion that wasn't released. It sits deep in your body, perhaps the stiff neck, the frozen shoulder, the creaky back, the heavy heart. The longer it sits, the more cynicism becomes a way of life, a way of thinking, a way of being.

With cynicism in charge, hope and optimism are sequestered, kept in the wings, away from the everyday, so its belief that life will only produce more suffering is realized fully. There are other beliefs, too, that lie still in the unconscious but gather strength day by day, year by year and even decade by decade: "I am unlovable, I am a loser, I am never going to amount to anything, I am . . . " The impact, like the list, is endless.

An innocent encounter could challenge cynicism anytime. When it does, the choice is there: give in to cynicism, or fight back and build hope. For instance, a genuinely friendly woman sits right next to you on the bus. She is exactly the kind of woman you are looking for in a relationship. She is bright, carefree, attractive, and self-contained She radiates goodness, but cynicism kicks in the moment she sits down. She smiles; cynicism says, "She does that with anyone she sits next to." She asks your name, asks about your life, and seems really interested for a moment. You get caught up with her delightful manner. Then, out of the blue, cynicism sideswipes you, laughs at you, and says, "Come on! Who would be interested in you?" You feel yourself shrivel right there. You start to distance yourself. You feel a sneer take over your mouth that makes you look mean. She looks at your mouth, and you realize it is all over. She has seen your shadow, and it is huge. She knows it, you know it, game over. When she leaves she looks hesitant, as if she wants things to carry on in some way, but you are long gone. Cynicism has won the day and you have become yet again your shriveled self, only a bit more shriveled, now certain there is no joy for you in this life, or probably future lives, either.

If cynicism is so powerful, how can you tackle it so it doesn't take over and reveal itself every day on your face and in your body language, arms crossed, defenses high, heart closed? Just like other deep emotion, it traces its roots back to childhood. Take an honest inventory and ask yourself, have those hurts been released? If you were mistreated then, at a time when you were trusting and open, it is remembered deeply. It is a drop of poison sitting in your heart; and in time that drop seems to attract experiences that trigger the very same pain. Life unfolds that way; each trigger brings a moment of choice between healing or building more toxicity. For many of us, the toxic wasteland needs to be consuming before we are compelled to do something about it.

So, all the poisonous drops start to accumulate, and when they do, they demand expression. You start to view others as if they had grown up in some saccharine, cotton candy-filled world, with baby pink and mint green everywhere. All you can remember is the grey sky, the dark night, the barren wasteland of meaning, the desert of close connections, the grimy, rocky, potholed black road ahead. So why should you even try? Trying says hope is still sticking around in the shadows, playing a part. That disgusts you; you can't even imagine you are still holding on to something as naive as hope.

You are desperate, though. You feel so heavy and leaden some days that you don't know how you manage to even get out of bed. So, this time you do hope. Perhaps it is a hobby you have always wanted to pursue but never had the temerity to go for, like playing the ukulele. Maybe it is moving to a different part of the world, a place that calls you deeply, though until now you have been too scared to take the big leap. Whatever it is, this time you start to explore the idea and give it a try. The stakes are high now; your heart feels as if the last segment is about to give itself over to Siberian tundra.

You put yourself out there, anxiously at first. You join a ukulele group, and you can't believe what nice people hang out with ukuleles. It has changed your life, just that one gig once a week. You look forward to it as soon as it has ended. Your heart hasn't felt this alive forever; you can't even remember when it felt this way, it was so long ago. Then you pick up a travel brochure on Spain. It has called you since you were a teenager, so the least you can do is go and visit the place. You book the ticket for a vacation. Wow, it is like a hurricane of good fortune suddenly blows in. You are almost frightened by the good fortune, alarmed by it; you feel compelled to alert people around you that something very strange is happening. You say to yourself, "This feeling of elation is not going to last; doom and gloom is right around the corner." After a while, though, you forget about forecasting. You are too busy learning the latest ukulele tune and planning your trip to even notice.

Then one day you are walking home from work, and you feel a kind of silly little spring in your step. It must have something to do with your shoes, but you start to pay close attention. You notice, too, that it is mimicking the same feeling in your heart. It is lighter, you are lighter, the sky is blue, the road ahead is still potholed, but you can see a way past the potholes and the incline looks manageable. All in all, it is a somewhat magic-filled stunner of a day. Tears start to roll, a few at first and then a veritable waterfall. Each drop is a release of a bitter moment, when the hurt, or betrayal, or rejection or whatever the event that was unimaginably painful got sequestered, and hardened your heart. Now it is different, you are different, and you make a commitment to yourself: "Never again will I give myself over to a heart stewing in bitterness and cynicism. The sky may be grey again in the future, but I can always wear my new rose-tinted glasses."

FRUSTRATION

"Frustration loves high expectations; then it can have a field day, build in the body, course through every vein, take over fully."

It's no joke; life gave you a pretty rough opening set of cards, and you have played them the best you can. It's time now for some justice. You are sick and tired of holding out. The frustration is getting unbearable. You just want some justice, some just rewards for just efforts, your time at last. Is that so unreasonable?

Figure 4.24. Frustration.

Well, you don't think so–you see other people around you going for gold and getting it, so why not you? You have put in the training, hours, weeks, months, years of training, and you finally get to the Olympics in your sport. You are here, in the ceremony. You feel weighed down with expectations: your own, your family's and friends,' and also those of a whole country aware of your abilities and aspirations. Up against your competitors you stand a good chance. Your timing has been great, up until the games. You could even set a world record and bring home the gold. It's all within reach, so close now! You have done everything: You have devoted six hours a day to running and training. Your diet has been flawless, not one junk food binge, not one drink in years. You have been taking this seriously, really seriously. It means everything to you, to your family, to people who know you, to everyone you can think of. You have to do it, have to get the gold. There is no room for failure here. It is all within reach.

You line up at the starting line along with your competitors. Your heart is racing, but you are focused. You can feel the presence of the others, but you are not looking at them. Your eyes are straight ahead, imagining the gold medallion around your neck. You're off! You bolt away. You are leaping over the hurdles, clearing them with ease; it's all going great. You think you are in the lead; in fact, you are convinced of it. You can't afford to look to the side. There is no one ahead, so the gold is yours. There is one more hurdle to go and then a sprint, which you are great at; everyone knows that. You leap for the last hurdle.

Then something happens. Your foot gets caught for a moment, and then your body comes crashing down on the other side of the hurdle. It is so overwhelming; you think you are in a nightmare. You crash to your knees on the hard ground, the pain intense. You feel the wind of other bodies passing by you. You hear the crowd cheer, and it is all over.

Your dreams spread before you like fragments of glass, nothing fitting together. Someone picks you up, helps you along to the side, and the crowd cheers for you. Can you imagine? You, a broken form getting cheered, like some charity case. The tears come, burning your cheeks, releasing unbearable frustration. Four years of training for naught, your life a disaster, your financial support in jeopardy perhaps, your esteem shattered. The frustration just grows when your loved ones flock around you, making soothing sounds: "You tried your best; you got to the Olympics, after all." Nothing, just nothing, fills the black hole of frustration. It has colonized every cell of your body and has invited you to spiral downward into the abyss.

As you go down, and further down, you are becoming barely contactable by others. You remember a quote by one of your tennis heroines Chris Evert Lloyd something about the importance of reacting the same way to winning and losing. Somehow, just somehow, it stops the slide. You become alert to what is happening. You see the faces around you. This goal now becomes as important as the race. You grasp at it as you would a rope when your body is spread-eagled against a cliff's edge. It is your way forward, your incredibly hard, painful, overwhelmingly frustrating way forward, but a way forward nonetheless. Maybe, just maybe, you will pick up the shards of your life after all.

CONNECTION CRISIS

"To give over to distraction is to part with your soul and your heart (your true self) and let the head colonize every moment. The cost is high when a society promotes it, markets it as the norm, and encourages a lost species to free-float through life without an anchor."

Figure 4.25. Connection crisis.

So, the capitalist market has gotten its way after all. It has bored into the collective human psyche, and now that many of the races of "human being" have opted for a "human doing" state, its influence is everywhere: People work long hours, with little time for a friendly chat. It's hard enough to answer that next email sitting there patiently in the inbox. Friends are put on the back burner, and then the back burner gets forgotten. "Well, I will contact my friends next week, next month when there is more time." Then time gets eaten up like cheese nibbled by a voracious mouse.

Common phrases speak to a full-blown "human doing" state: Monday mornings are beset with "I don't know where the weekend went," or sadder still, "That vacation just sped by and it was time to come home." The question is posed poignantly, "I can't believe it's already July; where did the year go?" When such questions arise, the impulse for many is to speed up and distract. Then the temptations of which Aldous Huxley spoke so eloquently grab our attention. His vision was that an Orwellian big brother wasn't needed to take our power away; we can surrender it simply by giving in to our infinite need for distraction. The market relishes the soma, as then its tantalizing jewels sparkle effortlessly in a sea of abundant need for the never-to-be-satiated soul.

It has to be said that the capitalist market has worked hard, and has been impressively creative, in its infinite number of Band-Aids to paste over the gaping hole in the soul. Watch reality shows and perhaps you, too, can get a temporary feeling that those people talking at you, out of the box, are actually an extension of your friendships. After all, they often come up for discussion in the workplace, temporarily reinforcing your sense that you are not as lonely as you fear. The market is also sensitive and tries hard to give a quick fix of psychological relief by telling you that you are living your chosen life. Perhaps a bit of aromatherapy could fill the void right now. Turn on the new plug-in air freshener, turn the dial to "pine forests" and imagine you are deeply immersed in nature, as your soul yearns for you to be. Spend a day at the spa and have someone, anyone, give you the attention you so crave because you have put on hold all those ravenous feelings. So, when a spa attendant kneads your back with mothers' earth clay, or ever so tenderly paints your toenails, a little relief is felt. Aah! That nurtured feeling at last was there for a moment; you'll need to come back soon.

So why have you so often chosen to run from yourself, to distract, to drink, to numb, to shut out the world and turn to the Ipod or the next craze on the market's smorgasbord? Perhaps you are tempted by the idea that if you purchase that recently advertised household gimmick or video game, you might feel a little more satisfied. When you are looking for a quick fix, nonstop movement also becomes the desired state, instead of sitting still and feeling. Intuitively, you know that if you slow down you will need to confront your fears, and who has the resources for that internal battle? So, you carry on, pretending that the fears are not there. However, you know they have taken up residence, and at vulnerable moments they produce a crisis, just to let you know their status is permanent. Perhaps one fear is being alone. Another may be getting a peek at your full potential after feeling doomed from childhood to a life of mediocrity. Your other fears may include looking at those parts of yourself that you find unattractive, inadequate, insecure, needy and unlovable. Instinctively you know that the only way through is to embrace them, to wrap your arms around those ever-lurking, shadowy characteristics that sometimes repulse you–but who wants to step up and own that?

Fear of connecting to yourself can also arise because you may have to dive into that deep well of unresolved grief that you have carried for years, sometimes decades. There is no wetsuit on the market that can protect you for that moment of profound courage. Have you run from that time when you were hurt, or perhaps rejected or abandoned? How could someone do that to you when you were as vulnerable as a newborn chick, beak wide open, chirping out its need to be nurtured? It seems unthinkable, even impossible to open up the wound and release the pain that has been trapped for all this time. Talking about the morass of conflicting emotion is difficult too when you are met with the market's panaceas like "get busy," "go on a vacation" or "buy that new car you have always wanted!"

The confusion also sets in as to what to do to foster healing. To heal, you know you need to be still, to move back into a "human being" state in which trapped emotion has the opportunity to rise. Then you know you will need to feel the sadness, anger, despair, self-loathing, bitterness and all the festering emotions that have been there for ages. It's a mucky process, and when you are splashing around in the middle of the eddy, no one offers any guarantee that you are swimming out. But if you do go through the muck, the soul sends a wave of relief. An odd moment of self-empowerment rises like a bubble, and bursts onto the surface of your being. There are more bubbles to come if you can stay the course.

Magically then, almost as if you were spun into some new realm of earthly experience, you instinctively slow down. Your voice gets stronger and educates the world to your needs, wishes and desires. Next time that unsatisfied restless feeling surfaces, you are more likely to go inward to soothe it, than to look to the market for a quick fix. Desires, too, seem possible to reach from this new planetary plane. You then find the focus to follow through on your hunches. Your head appears to have cleared, and you no longer find distraction so enticing. In this new world, the capitalist market has been wounded in battle and has lost its arms; it has lost its power over you. You can partake of its fruits that enhance the moment, but you are no longer enchanted by the dizzying dance of "buy this, go here, and all will be well."

ADDICTION

"When drugs, alcohol or addictive behavior move into the driver's seat, you start to shrink, much like a crustacean on the water's edge no longer receiving the nourishing wave. In time the shrinkage takes you to dangerous places with little to no meaning, and to a community of lost souls."

Addiction feels as if something has devoured all of your reasoning; you know it is bad. You suffer immeasurably for the habit, feeling guilt, self-loathing, self-disgust, and incrimination. You are constantly berated by the jury in your head: "We find you guilty of being stupid, weak, a loser . . . " and the list goes on. So why do you do it? What is so frightening that it is worth this level of self-destruction?

The self-destruction is slow. It is a thief, robbing you of this, then that, not resting until you are in the ditch of life with the water rising. Even then,

Figure 4.26. Addiction.

the thief doesn't stop; no, this thief is intent on drowning its victim in sorrow, misery, and despair. Perhaps you have been diversifying your numbing program lately: excess alcohol, coffee, drugs, TV, computer games, shopping until you drop, busyness and the odd bit of gambling. The list goes on. Of course, you know you are engaging in these activities with a fervor so intense that no one can persuade you to stop. The activity gets a hold on you and only releases you when you are a limp, easily manipulated, jumbled and confused mess.

So what does the thief take away? Maybe if you could get clear about that you could muster the immense courage that it would take to face the pain you have been numbing with your array of techniques. To watch this thief is to watch a master of destruction at work. Its trick is to go unnoticed, so subtlety is the key. After the bout of numbing activity, self-loathing tapes play in the head. These voices mingle with all of your unresolved fears; and so it ratchets up the poor self-esteem index so that you are weakened, and therefore more likely to perform the addictive behavior again.

The next trick is to persuade you to isolate yourself, gradually at first, and then this is stepped up. The more the trickster can get you on your own the greater its power over you. To encourage the isolation, the thief robs you of comfort from others. The way it does this is to tell you that others don't understand, that they don't relate to you, that somehow they are different from you. The thief says they are likely "better people," so you start to form a camp on your own, as if you have moved to an island amid shark-infested water, so others won't venture over to connect with you.

"Aha!" the thief says. "I am getting my way at last." The only escape from the boredom, the isolation, the self-loathing is to do what you do best: drink, take drugs, run run run as fast as you can and forget that you ever had feelings in your interior. At first you are deluded into believing that you can pull it off; the thief encourages that delusion. Then you start to falter. You are alone, so you soon fall into the various potholes around you. You get up, of course. You have to; after all, you have a job and a mortgage to pay. You need to eat. Soon, however, even necessity is no longer a motivator. The hopelessness, cynicism, despair and occasional suicidal feelings are taking over. You ask, "What's the point?" and "Why bother?"

This is when the thief starts jumping up and down with the sheer exhilaration of winning. It knows now that only by a miracle could you move out of this place of desperation. The only thing that would pose a threat at this stage is if you got a surge of unbridled courage and reached out for help. However the thief has assessed this as highly unlikely, and feels confident it is winning this one so far. With suicidal feelings in the mix, it looks like its victim might end it all soon anyway, intentionally or unintentionally. The thief starts to muscle in a bit more with messages of hopelessness. Too many sick days inevitably lead to being fired from your job; the final stage of destruction is here.

Just when the thief is about to start the preparations for its celebration of your final destruction, something weird happens. Normally you don't talk to anyone; you keep to yourself, ignore the world around you, never answer the phone, but one day some stranger sits next to you on the bus and starts to ask questions. Well, blow me down! But you tell the stranger everything. How you feel, what you have been thinking, how you have given yourself over to a life of addiction. Then you start to cry. The crying sickens the thief, as the more sadness you release, the weaker its hold on you. You swap phone numbers with the stranger, who keeps calling, and then, if you can believe it, you reach out for help. You attend a counseling program. You start to heal, face the pain, stop the habit, and reconnect with people around you. Far off in the distance, the form of the thief can be seen skulking in its black cloak toward the horizon, binoculars poised, scanning feverishly, desperately searching for another victim.

CURIOSITY

"Curiosity fires the moment with absolute splendor. Babies know this, as does the dog chasing the ball for the umpteenth time. It means there are countless roads of exploration, never enough time to discover all the jewels on the road called life."

Figure 4.27. Curiosity.

To say that curiosity is the fire that sparks all life is an understatement. Without curiosity, relationships lose the glue that binds, and all roads of discovery have a dead-end sign. The heart crumples and sags, and desire dries on desert sand. In the land of not knowing lie unfathomable riches that make the mind ignite in explosive delight and the heart pulsate with ever-renewing aliveness. No matter what your age, curiosity can burn as brightly for a ninety-year-old as for a teenager. This is what keeps the spirit stewing in fresh juices, fully present for the next surprise, alert to all that is and all that has not yet appeared.

Curiosity is a natural state for a newborn and young child. One only has to observe and see the myriad expressions forming as they drown in the mystery of discovery of their worlds. Everything is alluring. The simplest thing becomes the deepest pleasure. They are in the "now," and their senses are like pleasure-seeking antennae, scanning for the next conundrum. Once they find their goal, they drown in it fully; nothing else can take their attention away. The shape, the smell, the touch of the item, is a peak experience multiplied day after day. Curiosity is their path to bliss; they drown in beauty and mystery, each moment overflowing with the wondrous possibilities fueled by insatiable, fierce curiosity.

Then, at some point in the child's (or an adult's) life, curiosity can take a nosedive. It plummets to a world of black and white, where all undiscovered colors are marginalized, sequestered, kept out of the imagination. The mind and the heart become trapped in the world of knowing, and knowledge is reassuring in a life that demands constant change. Life experience and knowledge are quickly reduced to facts; opinions become truths not to be questioned. The person then starts to form an identity around their "truths": this is how it is, no further debate, no further discovery needed, it just is. Anyone who questions and confronts them is confronting the person's very core. Debates then can become attacks on identity, and all manner of reactivity explodes to shut things down. The person's life is known from this point on. Any changes are seen as a threat and are sidestepped immediately. If the person chooses this state, nothing can shake up this rigid and ossified foundation of beliefs and values. Life is now viewed through a myopic lens, and the unknown world is pushed away with unbridled zeal.

This is where curiosity gets so stifled it takes a walk, leaves the scene. It scours desperately for a host that can embrace it, ride with the roller coaster of it all, and go down a road less traveled to a world of wonder and undiscovered mystery. Curiosity looks for someone who lives in the present and is open to constant change, someone whose mind doesn't cling to this or that idea, but who is grounded in intuition and their feelings. They are adventurous souls, souls willing to go down a path where the end is unseen, managing fear and uncertainty along the way. These souls know that life is uncertain when the rose-colored spectacles are removed, that nothing, not even life itself, is guaranteed. Curiosity sits proudly on the shoulders of those who allow themselves to be humbled by the acknowledgment that life is sometimes bigger than they can handle. However, they feel that with curiosity on their side, and well-honed instinct, the best course of action for the unimaginable struggle will be found.

Curiosity beckons to all souls, never giving up on anyone, even though it has been rejected for eons. "Come with me," curiosity says. "Let me open up your world to a kaleidoscope of wonder. Life is hard, but together we will stand in awe of the boundlessness of all our existences." With curiosity at your side, you realize more and more that discovery is lifelong, that you can move toward your death with all the wonder of a newborn, never having enough life for all the discovery that lies before you.

LOVE

"Love is the very thing that makes all of our lives worthwhile, and the supply is endless if we give over to it, knowing that the heart has limitless expansion for the love of all things. It is at its peak when we feel in our heart that we are all one: one with each other, one with the planet and all of her inhabitants, one with spirit."

Figure 4.28. Love.

To feel the ache of love is to join the human family fully. Love, however, is not for the tentative, for those that struggle to risk. Love is a bold act. Love is courage worn brightly, like a canary yellow shirt declaring to the world, "I am love!" Love brings softness wherever it spreads. Warm creases around the eyes and the mouth soften, and the gaze is warm, filled with compassion for all. A full state of love does not make distinctions between those who are deserving of love, and those who are not. Love transcends barriers; all are worthy of love. Love flows like warm treacle sweetening the air, leaving a trail of blessings to all who witness love in action.

Love lives in the heart of the wearer. It does not need the other in order to prove itself; it is a state of being. The heart has become like a lotus flower exposing its inner sanctum. It is transforming and softening continually in its ever-deepening understanding of love. Kahlil Gibran in The Prophet exposes the journey to a full loving state:

For even as love crowns you so shall he crucify you. Even as he is for your growth so is he for your pruning.

Even as he ascends to your height and caresses your tenderest branches that quiver in the sun,

So shall he descend to your roots and shake them in their clinging to the earth.

Like sheaves of corn he gathers you unto himself.

He threshes you to make you naked.

He sifts you to free you from your husks.

He grinds you to whiteness.

He kneads you until you are pliant;

And then he assigns you to his sacred fire, that you may become sacred bread for God's sacred feast.

All of these things shall love do unto you that you may know the secrets of your heart, and in that knowledge become a fragment of Life's heart.

But if in your fear you would seek only love's peace and love's pleasure,

Then it is better for you that you cover your nakedness and pass out of love's threshing-floor,

Into the seasonless world where you shall laugh, but not all of your laughter, and weep, but not all of your tears.

(Gibran; 1968:11–12).

Many imagine love to be the state of "falling in love," a state in which one finds an ideal friend, lover and companion and then quickly starts to lose oneself in the beloved. When you fall in love, all your unfilled desires and dreams are activated overnight as the beloved fills the void. The beloved becomes the medicine so you can avoid the struggle of self-fulfillment and self-reliance. No longer do you need to stare into the mirror of self-inadequacy, the broken shards chipped on the road of your life. Days and months are consumed with the beloved and with the miracle of the co-joining in facing life's everyday hurdles.

Then, at some point, you begin to feel the consequences of filling the void. Slowly, glacially, but in time the illumination occurs, and all is revealed in a stark bright light. Dis-ease sets in. As Shakti describes,

We bleed because we are afraid to lose our lovers and be alone. We bleed because we are addicted to whatever our lovers supply to us. After "falling in love" comes the phase of "being in love." "Being in love" suggests that there is "being out-of-love" and that the two states are co-existing. This is why even in the peak of our love we cannot experience inner peace; we know that potentially we can always find ourselves "out of love" (Shakti, 2011: March12th).

This is not to say that the lover, friend, companion is not a rich addition to your life. However, the time comes when it is evident that the gaping holes can no longer be filled by their presence. Then a deep disappointment can set in, which is often confused with some failing in the lover. "If they were different in some way," you think, "I would still feel full and complete, as I did at their arrival." Illusions build on illusions, and then perhaps a time is reached when you say, "If they go, then my life will feel more complete; somehow, my present state is their fault." Sometimes this can be the moment of when you fully recognize the desert that has formed in your heart, your need for "the other" to complete yourself.

The path to love is the path to self-discovery and healing. The greater the healing, the more love is contained in the very cells of the heart. In this state, you can feel a love that is not dependent on another but is a state of existence, as Deepak Chopra states: "Real love gains complete satisfaction simply by flowing out to what is loved; if love comes back that is an added joy, but isn't required or demanded" (Chopra, 1998:July 19). In this state, you are moving toward wholeness, and this spiritual love builds exponentially, effortlessly, and spreads its tendrils to all who step on the road of life, softening the way for all.

In a "state of love" loving feelings ooze out of the heart to an animal in need or to an elderly man gingerly crossing the road. Heartfelt compassion flows to the mother that lost her child and the father that lost his job. Your capacity for love grows: It starts out as a candle's flame, flickering and illuminating a darkened room. In time, with self-love propelling its growth, it becomes a bonfire of beauty, lighting others' path with ease, showing the way. Love builds on love. Its bounty is endless, vast and boundless.

So let us all join hands in moving to self-love, to a state in which we acknowledge the pain gathered in the storm of life and release it so that beauty can take its place in our hearts. We will then be able to squeeze another's hand from a state of abundance. We will have the knowledge that life is hard on us all, but with love-filled hearts, together we can do our part to create a world of peace at last.

STABLE MISERY

"We find ourselves in sticky mud, incapable of the smallest movement, trapped and stuck for ad infinitum in an escapable pattern."

Stable misery is so powerful that it can keep us in its steel-like vice grip for decades, at times going undetected, and locking us into patterns that are

Figure 4.29. Stable misery.

ever tightening, ever deepening, and that make it harder and harder to free ourselves. The looming question then is "what makes it misery and why is it so stable?"

Stable misery can come in a variety of forms. For instance, it could be that one is tethered to a partner who is trapped in a slow dance of attrition, slowly succumbing to addiction and giving up the fight, and one is bearing witness. It can show up often in dynamics with couples or with family relationships when the way of relating is repeatedly undermining, draining, controlling, or worse, abusive. The dyad is entrenched in a pattern, and neither can see any options to escape the suffering, as separation is not considered an option. Stable misery can also relate to being stuck in, for example, a dead-end job, loathing it and constantly reliving the stress related to it. However, blinkers are glued to one's forehead and therefore any remote possibility of finding alternative employment is sequestered from view.

There are also situations in life when sustained misery shows up and it is outside our capacity to change the circumstance. Poverty, war, racism, impact of climate change, and structural discrimination can dominate a society, and one's existence, and there is no path out. A terminal medical diagnosis can also lock one into a feeling of stable misery when one envisions one's capacity to live life in a comfortable way is now inexorably fading. Countless situations of suffering in life challenge our ability to exercise any meaningful control.

A critical piece when dealing with stable misery is using discernment to parse out those situations where we can exercise some influence, even if we can only have a modicum of impact, and to acknowledge those outside of our locus of control. When we have established the situation and some levers of influence, the next step is to identify the feelings that are triggered by the situation. This can be a powerful awareness to help us track the history of the feelings and to understand the intensity of our reactions. In a situation, for example, where we are watching a partner giving in to an addiction, the feelings that could be triggered are helplessness, powerlessness, being out of control, inadequacy, and fear. Our next step of self-enquiry could be asking, "were there times in my childhood or earlier on in my life when I felt the very same feelings?" This is a critical question, as we often tolerate the torment of the situation longer than we would like to because of childhood experiences.

These experiences had us reliving some of the very same feelings again and again. Hence, they are familiar, and at that time in our lives there was no way out; divorcing our parents, for instance, was not an option. It is these experiences that give stable misery its stability. Therefore, consciously, or unconsciously, we can associate the feeling with immobilization, feeling trapped, stuck, and powerless to change the circumstance. For example, with the situation of our partner succumbing to addiction, perhaps we had a parent who also gave up in some way. The giving up could be related to food addiction, drugs/alcohol, over-involvement in others' lives to avoid facing one's own issues, excessive social media and cell phone use, gambling, busyness, having affairs, workaholic issues, and obsessive-compulsive rituals, as some examples. The point is that the person (our parent in this example) gave up; despair and hopelessness were palpable even if they never voiced it. These experiences communicate a great deal to our bodies and our bodies tend to retain the message until the emotions related to the situation are released. Our bodies also automatically go into behavior patterns related to the feelings. For instance, if inadequacy was a feeling that got stuck in our body at the time, it may later show up as procrastination and perfectionism, due to us doubting our ability to manage our life in general. If the feeling was "out of control," we may be mired in obsessive-compulsive patterns as a way of dealing with the uncomfortable feelings.

So, what should we tell stable misery next time it shrouds us with a grey gauze, and traps the air that we breathe, and the life that we want to live? "Get lost!" for starters, voiced at the highest decibel possible. Then, as a next step, we can marshal our full outrage at its domineering presence, and at its messages of doom and entrapment, and then get onto to its wily tricks and seductive messages. Once we have our outrage mobilized, we have our fire power to fight back. Now, it is time to make a list of all those actions and behaviors that reveal how we gave up and gave in to its misery laden voice. Also, spend time making another list that exposes its constant bombardment of messages to our brains. The messages to our brain may include, "what's the point in trying, you will never amount to anything; you are a loser; you are powerless and helpless to change your life; and just suck it up." Knowing how it tricks us by these incessant messages is another step toward empowerment. Another key area in taking back power and control, and putting one's life on an elevated path of expansion, is to take risks that undermine the messages and the overwhelming state of immobilization. Action, even a small step, says loudly and confidently to stable misery, "go and torment yourself; clear out of my life, you are not welcome here; I do have power and I can take control." Also, it reinforces that your actions will make a difference to creating a path where your life grows, and expands, and has a destination long term of hope and fulfillment.

GRATITUDE

"The heart is splashed in thanks, thanks for all one has received and whole-hearted thanks for being so fortunate in life."

Figure 4.30. Gratitude.

Gratitude has perspective, it has been around for some time, a veritable old soul if there ever was one, and it has gathered a great deal of wisdom along the way. It has the bird's eye view in life, the big angle, the all-encompassing understanding of where you have been and where you are going. Gratitude also gets that our lives have intense struggles, that there are times that we must put on our crampons, grip our ice pick tightly, peer upwards, feel immobilized by the terror of the steep climb, and take one step forward, regardless of the intimidating mountain peaks in life. Gratitude has so much to offer; if we embrace it regularly, it can take us on the road to peace and contentment as long as we keep it with us as a trusted companion, best friend, and trusted ally.

If gratitude is so helpful and has so much to offer, why is it so hard to grip it and hold on, and to remember its valuable offerings, particularly when we are being challenged in our lives and feel stuck in a deep hole with no way out in sight? To find the answers, we often need to peel back some deeper layers of our unconscious and expose our expectations and what may have shaped them. In our family of origin, if we experienced neglect, victimization, or abuse, for example, or on a societal level experienced trauma, these past encounters can shape us and we can enter adulthood with a strong feeling of *being owed*, with our expectations sky high for reparations or some acknowledgment of the injustice that had occurred. Also, if we were spoilt, perhaps as an only child, molly coddled, or overly protected from adversity, we will have a strong sense of entitlement with the world needing to be excessively concerned with our needs. High expectations and entitlement are a recipe for frustration, anger, relationship disharmony, mood lability, conflict, self-absorption, confusion, and overall dissatisfaction with our lives, and all a far cry from gratitude. High expectations with regard to our needs being met regularly, by the world around us, encourages gratitude to slide away and to disappear, to hide in the crevices of our mind, or to sequester in our heart, perhaps not be aired for months, maybe for years and even decades. What can be left in its absence is bitterness, cynicism, sustained disappointment, and perhaps, an overall feeling of confusion and self-pity that life has not turned out the way we wanted.

If this is a pattern we have fallen into, how can we turn it around and bring gratitude back into our lives? Welcome it like a long-lost friend and much appreciated life companion with outstretched arms, allowing it to remind us gently and consistently that we can take time to appreciate what we do have. Also, being open to gratitude's reminders that there is a velvet cushion beneath us at times that we can muscle into when life gets tough, and our adaptability is stretched over and over again. The velvet cushion is all that we have with us in this moment of time. It could be a loving friend or a faithful animal companion. It could be the stability of our health, our capacity to rise and meet challenging circumstances, or that we have access to the food we need and are able to meet our basic financial commitments.

It could be giving support to someone you really care about; gratitude sees giving love and support as just as important as receiving it. Gratitude does not get stuck on our lofty dreams nor hold them as a benchmark. Gratitude is not focused on wealth accumulation, status, ego aggrandizement, competing with others, or getting a badge of honor. Gratitude aligns itself with the heart and is focused on what is being experienced in the present moment. For example, gratitude is paying attention to what is creating some meaning in a challenging time in one's life. Gratitude will also note who is genuinely supportive of you and in your corner as you struggle around the next lap of your journey. Gratitude softens the heart. It springs forth from a well of vulnerability and humility, where we understand and take note of what is helping us to take the next step on our often-torturous road, fraught with potholes and formidable terrain. Gratitude helps us resource ourselves, by taking stock of all that is helping us marshal our strength, and it reminds us of all the good that is flowing so we can move forward, even with intense trepidation in our hearts.

When gratitude is held close and paid attention to, the results are remarkable. Resilience soars, the mouth and heart soften, peace splashes onto the face. We can also trust more because on a deep level we experience being held, even if it just a feeling we feel. Gratitude reminds us, even in the darkest times, to look for all we are grateful for; gratitude wants you to rise, to not look back and to not give into fear. Gratitude has provided and it will continue to provide as long as we have our eyes peeled back to see the small things that make a difference. We need to take time to acknowledge all that we do have and the gifts that encircle us every day of our lives.

SOMATIZATION

"The torment is real and the panacea far off and elusive, leaving a trail of pain in its wake."

Somatization is like working with a wily snake—it slithers there, you come close to outing it, it slithers somewhere else, it is always on guard to be caught. It is most comfortable sitting in the dark, in the subterranean layers in our cells, wanting to stay hidden but formidable in its power to convince its carrier that *fear of feeling* should be avoided at all costs. So instead of feeling, somatization or hypochondriasis conjures up a headache instead, or back pain, sore knees, generalized aching in the muscles, paralyzing fatigue, a sore stomach, dizziness, and the list goes on. Anything, absolutely anything, to take one away from feeling what is going on emotionally at that time. The

Figure 4.31. Somatization.

problem is never sadness, confusion, lost, self-loathing, regret, grief, despair, helplessness, misunderstood, hurt, for example, or other embodied emotion from past trauma. The emotion is suppressed and replaced with a physical sensation. Somatization is a highly developed avoidance technique; it assists the person in numbing, staying frozen, and helps to put thick walls around any feelings held in the body, so as much as possible, they are not able to leach. The impact on the body is dramatic, sequestered emotions build tension and so, in time, the act of compartmentalizing feelings repeatedly can contribute markedly to the range of maladies the sufferer experiences. So, *what* causes *what* becomes lost in the ever-present woeful dance of suffering, sequestration, and despair.

Why else is somatization used? Somatization is also a distancing technique. If one talks about physical complaints and not feelings, one is able to also avoid the vulnerability that comes with intimacy (into-me-see). Somatization successfully blocks intimacy; therefore, one does not need to be truly open with one's inner world. It short circuits the path of openness. Somatization is also intent on the sufferer getting attention, attention for yet another physical ailment, which the sufferer is often willing to talk about ad infinitum. The conversation can have a circular feel, like one has heard this all before; the possibility that that is true is strong, and it is likely the same record that is put on the turntable over and over again, and the central message on the record has common themes. The overriding message may be "woe is me," "I am a victim in life," "life's not fair," or "no-one gets how hard it is for me," as some examples. The point, consciously or unconsciously, is to bring someone into your bubble of pain and turmoil. The hope is that another person can understand how tough your day-to-day life is and to observe the challenges you have regularly. Inviting someone into your bubble also helps to meet some social needs and helps to keep one primarily focused on self, also hyper-alert to the latest physical sensation, tension, or pain.

Given the dance can go on for months, years, or even decades, what is the cost on "the other?" Why would someone be attracted to try and help a person consumed with somatization? Martyrdom or the "need to be needed" can play a role. Martyrdom is often about losing oneself in another's pain so one does not need to look at one's own issues. This can be another effective avoidance technique. If I stay focused on another's pain, and with somatization locked in another person's constant pain is almost guaranteed, then I can avoid looking at myself, my issues, and my unresolved feelings. Martyrdom looks for opportunities to be fully immersed in another's world at the expense of self. Over time it is challenging to acknowledge one's own needs, or the cost of the pattern of martyrdom, as the self can get buried so deeply that the efforts needed to retrieve one's inner world is mammoth.

Given that somatization and martyrdom lock into ever deepening rigid patterns of codependent behavior, contributing to pain and suffering and leading to a dead-end road of increasing instability and disconnection from self, how can one find an off ramp to this dance of attrition? The journey to self-connection starts for many with a bird's eye view of one's predicament. With regard to somatization, an acknowledgement that one is sick and tired of being *sick and tired* is an important start. The whirlpool of desperation and despair one has been submerged in can provide an impetus for change. Many human beings only contemplate change when the option of maintaining the status quo is increasingly untenable. Another important step in the liberation process is an increased awareness with regard to the concept of choice. Choice will inevitably mean wrestling with one's intolerance to feeling feelings, because at the end of the day, our body accumulates what is forced into sequestration. It does not go away, and in time, will produce panic attacks, depression, anxiety symptoms, consuming obsessive-compulsive rituals, or other unhelpful rigid patterns, and these will all contribute to hurtling down a very dark and lonely road of contraction.

A further step on the path to undoing the shackles of somatization is being curious about the feelings that one finds abhorrent, and investigating whether those feelings may be part of a childhood trauma history. In some instances, this can explain why the intensity of somatization is so hard to undermine. Joining the dots of our present struggle to our past can illuminate a great deal and can contribute to us understanding the root cause of somatization. Perhaps we can write a letter, or countless letters, in order to peel back the layers of what we felt back then and to start to face and integrate unresolved past pain, and the share it openly with others, bit by bit. All these steps help to beat down a path of freedom and protection.

More impetus to freedom comes from learning about the impact of somatization on those around us, particularly those hoodwinked by martyrdom. When they can tell their truth about how they have been impacted, drained, frustrated to no-end, exhausted, burnt-out, angry, and outraged at times by somatization and its wily manipulative charade of avoidance, and are willing to self-connect, they free themselves and the shackles fall from their feet too. If one's martyred dancing partner bales, this helps to illuminate the consequences of staying stuck. Moving forward maybe awkward for a while; feeling feelings that have been blocked for eons can be fear inducing. However, the terrain is clearer. There are less obstacles and the potential of momentum and growth is there if one is determined to set up long-term protection to somatizations tricks and tyranny.

ENTITLEMENT

"The desire for more and more of everything is pervasive and the overwhelming feeling is it is owed to you throughout your life."

Figure 4.32. Entitlement.

Entitlement says "I am owed," with such zeal and a bellowing voice that it almost blows you over. Entitlement is not joking, and it is not owed for this one thing here or there. No, entitlement is owed everywhere in countless situations, raising its head in the most unexpected places, demanding attention, and wanting a total focus on its needs right now. Entitlement does not like to negotiate or compromise; it wants what it wants now and it gave patience the boot long ago. Entitlement is a bit like communicating with a bully. They may hear your voice in the far-off distance, but they are distracted and so did not really get what you said and are not interested in adjusting their needs or in compromising. Entitlement may also go underground for a while, but one should not be seduced into thinking that it has disappeared or dissolved. Sometimes it is taking time to cook up its latest plot on a subterranean level around getting its needs met. It will pop up soon with the plan congealed, regardless of what others think or feel. Entitlement joined hands with determination oh so long ago, and so the dual push to get needs met has a veritable bulldozer behind it.

Another aspect of entitlement is that it influences the lens with which we view the world. Entitlement, along with determination, are commonly seen out with "if only" taking it most places as a friend or ally. Entitlement and "if only" are generally unsatisfied with what they just experienced. It could be a carefully chosen hike by one's partner, a special day planned for the couple. At the end of the hike, the partner is overflowing with joy and contentment after a deeply pleasurable experience. However, the recipient, seduced by entitlement and "if only" states, "it was nice, just a pity it wasn't higher, or a shame about those switchbacks, I would have preferred a longer hike, if only it had better views or more trees along the way," and the list goes on and on. By the time the list is exhausted, the partner feels drained and the joy that had accumulated found a leak and has leached away, and perhaps confusion and disappointment are left in its wake. The partner's challenge is to keep *people pleasing* in check regularly, as it should be crystal clear by now, the one dancing with entitlement is unlikely to be satisfied anytime soon. Many a time, they will blame some external situation, event, or circumstance for their dissatisfaction, rarely seeing that it could be them, with their unresolved pain from the past leaching into the moment and how they view the world around them. Their list of gripes is likely bottom less; one addresses one but then another pops up out of nowhere. It could be a gripe about being with the wrong partner, or that others do not seem to acknowledge ones needs fully, or that no one, just no one, gets how hard one's life is and can see the intensity of the struggle. It could be a deficient bank account and entitlements beady eyes are fixated on another's wealth and is strategizing about accruing some of it. All in all, it is a generalized malaise that the external environment is just not willing to address needs that are perceived as critical to life's contentment.

Given entitlement's insatiable nature and evasive contentment, it can be helpful to bore down and to uncover some of the circumstances in life that would have given birth to entitlement as a way of being in the world. Entitlement is often a consequence of tough circumstances in childhood; it could be related to trauma whereby needs were neglected constantly, or there were abusive circumstances, or a child experienced being invisible by parental or family figures. Years of these tough circumstances produces an adult that *feels owed* on a cellular level given all they endured. The ongoing desperate urge, with little to no satiation, is that payback is warranted to deal with the enormous pain of the past accumulated in the tissues. The challenging piece is that entitlement inevitably leads to more alienation, and more and more disappointment, as others learn soon enough that the cup has a massive hole in it and no amount of giving will ever be enough for the endless stream of needs. Therefore, others distance themselves or give less, given the ongoing feedback.

So, what can one do if one recognizes that entitlement impacts one's relationships, activities, general contentment, life's goals and achievements, and overall feelings on a day-to-day basis? The first piece in any change process is awareness. Start to become aware of where entitlement crops up and what it says. It may say frequently, "they should have done more, I wish people would take my needs seriously, don't others see how tough it is for me, and I must fight for everything," and so on. The next step is to be curious about what contributed to entitlement having such a loud voice and overwhelming presence in one's psyche. Perhaps it was a father that was too busy working to acknowledge ones needs, or a mother that was self-absorbed with her own pain that she paid scant attention to your needs. Maybe it was years of bullying when you just had to suck it up with little to no support. These experiences may have contributed to a build-up of feelings like, grave injustice, sadness, humiliation, deep hurt, neglect, feelings of unworthiness, inadequacy, unimportance, shame, despair, and low self-worth, as some examples. The constant grasping for more is a desperate attempt to pull a bandage over the wound so it is not bleeding heartache all the time. However, if one is sick and tired of entitlement ramping up demands and its trail of dissatisfaction, one can choose to deal with the wound. Over time, tackling layer upon layer of it and resisting following its interpretation of "what is happening," eventually entitlement starts to fade a bit, or is recognized and outed quickly, and its "more for me" rant is barely heard as a whisper through the winds of change.

AUTHENTICITY

"To be soaked into the deepest part of your being and to express yourself from this place of authenticity and genuineness is a gift to the world."

Figure 4.33. Authenticity.

Authenticity has a feeling of arriving at a major destination in life and saying, with total relief, "aaaah at last." Or, "At last peace is attainable, at last I am plugged in so deep that I know who I am, what I stand for, what I value," and so on. It is a tremendous milestone, and the tsunami of relaxed feelings is palpable, particularly as the journey to get there has likely been tumultuous. Most of us get to authenticity through countless challenges, unending hurdles, a roller-coaster ride of uncertainty and pain, a sticky web of confusion, and an ongoing earthquake of relationship struggles, particularly ones of conflict and all its ramifications.

We all, every day of our lives, must steer our way through complex situations at home, work, and other social situations. What makes the difference with regard to authenticity is how we handle each of these events. For authenticity to grow, build a firm foundation, and thrive, we need to treat *our truth* as sacred. Knowing our truth is one of the most powerful shields we can wear, like steely fortified armor against the forces of mass confusion, manipulation, and uncertainty. Knowing our truth and knowing when to speak our truth are two different advanced life skills. The ongoing act of choosing when it is appropriate to share or not, requires a high level of discernment constantly needed in life's whirlpool of challenges. Speaking one's truth in situations of political oppression and repression can be dangerous and put us in harm's way. The same applies to an abusive relationship where domination and control are evident, and when resistance is met with violence. However, there are many complex situations we find ourselves in where stating our truth drills down and grounds us, and then moves us into our power. It can also ground others and steer us away from the whirligig of cerebral overload, whereby talking about talking spins us continually in a vortex of mock communication. Each time we state with a steady voice, an undeniable tone of gravity and a confidence that pierces through like an arrow of sound, "this is what I think, this is what I believe, this is who I am, this is what I care about, this is my position, my conviction, my truth," our soul leaps about, a veritable jig beneath our skin, elated for a moment that another truth that aligns with core values has been affirmed. Each situation tackled by stating our truth with all the grace and dignity we can muster, gives us another brick in a solid foundation. This is what resilience is all about—brick by brick laid down on a firm ground and each brick earned with a test of courage, self-awareness, determination, strength, and empowerment. Complex, challenging situations mired in conflicting positions and ambivalence now become easier to move through. Authenticity shines strobe lighting through the convoluted maze of it all. Authenticity helps us dig deeper into the subterranean layers, and much like a miner with a lamp piercing the utter blackness, it searches for resolution and for actions that align with our true nature.

What might other advantages of authenticity be? Well, authenticity attracts and attracts again. Others are drawn to authenticity because they instinctively feel safe and know deep down, "what you see is what you get." There is not the subterfuge and power plays of an off-balance person, who may speak from both sides of their mouth, dripping in insincerity, confusion, or from a state of being lost and unmoored. Authenticity says boldly with a firm voice, "you can trust me, I will tell you what I think and feel, I am loyal, guided by an inner knowing and I state my truth, even when it is not welcomed, respected, or honored." Authenticity links steadfastly with boundaries; they are a team act and one never leaves home without the other. Those striving for authenticity also exude self-respect, and that helps stealth arrows of projection to bounce off their shield, sometimes exposing their throwers ill intent for others to see. Another advantage of authenticity is leadership, those who are authentic are naturally chosen as leaders, even if it is in an informal role. They are the same qualities that attracts others and that moves them effortlessly to leadership positions. Effective leaders lead from a place of firm convictions and stated truths, and most often their leadership style is collaborative. Another benefit of authenticity is healing, by stating one's truth continually, acknowledging feelings, setting boundaries, and clarifying the nuances of one's convictions. Authenticity climbs to the highest peaks in life and when on high says with a resounding voice, "be who you are, celebrate your uniqueness, there is no-one like you and the world needs your true nature to shine and elevate us all."

SELF RIGHTEOUSNESS AND JUDGING

"To look down one's nose and see others as less than, undeserving, and to pass razor-edged judgement, impacts others self-worth and leaves a trail of scars."

Figure 4.34. Self-righteousness / Judging.

Self-righteousness and judging elevates self as superior; they put a thick velvet cushion under their posterior and they take it wherever they go. With disdain contorting their mouth, they peer down to those perceived to be hovering below. These self-appointed demi-gods have decided a long time ago that most human beings are unworthy of their attention, and that undeniably they have come to educate from this higher position for those they deem worthy. They view others as pitifully sitting in the dark at the back of the cave, desperate for their help and illumination. Their central tenet is that they are better than others. Their assumption is, for instance, that they are more intelligent, wealthier, more attractive, are from a higher class, more skilled, more refined, and the list goes on and on. They are not looking to others to validate their status; it is generally self-proclaimed—they had their very own anointing ceremony, crowning themselves with zeal for their overall sophistication and elevation. Their principal pastime is judging, although they may not admit it, their eyes are trained to find fault, any fault, and their gaze demands perfection and so they find imperfection everywhere. When they find fault, they are quick to point it out, their tone dripping in condescension. They do not spend time worrying about how the person is impacted by their criticism, and at some level they may perceive they are doing a service by spending their precious time pointing out the glaring mistake or egregious error.

Self-righteousness and judging, if you peel away the layers, often forms the foundation for beliefs that propel an invasion into a foreign land, germinate the seeds of war, colonization, classism, racism, slavery, structural discrimination, and political policies that divide human beings into camps of the deserving, and the undeserving, to name a few. Colonialism was built on the tenet that somehow the colonizers were superior, more cultured, more educated, and more sophisticated, and on a belief that the indigenous land dwellers would benefit from their advancement. Being curious about *other ways of being* in the world, was not part of the consideration; it was all about domination, bringing foreign flags, and piercing the native land with all the zeal of saviors arriving from on high. Self-righteousness and judging also stoked religious fanatics to descend on foreign land, take the indigenous under their wing, impose their religion, with self-appointed disciples imparting their beliefs with blinding superiority. The land has also suffered a great deal under this "way of being" in the world. Nature, also under the dominion of this mind set, has suffered irreparably from the assumptions that humans are superior to nature and that they need not show reverence and work steadfastly to align with the natural world. Self-righteous and judging also plays havoc in relationships. The constant undermining feedback chips away at trust, and the lack of vulnerability makes closeness as far off as a fleeting horizon, nigh impossible.

Given the catastrophic impact this mindset has had on the world around it, what are the seeds that helped it form in the first place and what waters the seeds, so they grow exponentially? The seeds are birthed in an experience of pronounced inadequacy. Often experiencing neglect, feeling unseen, invalidated, unlovable, unworthy, and deficient are some of the emotional experiences that contribute to a self-righteous and judging mental state. The superior orientation is a mask, a carefully crafted cover up to fill the gaping holes in the self-esteem of the wearer. If one holds the mask tight enough, perhaps no one will detect the inadequacy leaching through. To be convincing and ward off any detection of deficiency, it is key to promote oneself as an expert with an ever-expanding skill set. Also, in topics of discussion, one wants others to see how clever, how knowledgeable, how competent one is, and to make sure the defense is always tight and forever persuasive. What can contribute to the growth of this mind-set is a non-questioning audience; generally they find themselves surrounded by lackeys, who are willing to nestle under their wing and to have their actions dictated. They give advice, tell others how to think and feel, and offer a critique wherever they go and hold it up as the only analysis that should hold weight and dominate in a variety of ways.

If we relate to this state of mock elevation, the question to ask is, "are we willing to face and to acknowledge the impact we have on others fully and admit our vulnerability?" Each of us wrestle with change in our own inimitable ways and have unique circumstances with regard to the depth of our courage, our accumulation of suffering, and a sense of desperation to make a significant shift. Many of us need to be sick and tired of being sick and tired before we are open to change.

If we find we tend to be self-righteous and judging are we capable of change? Also, what does it take to take one's power back? To those undermined by this mindset and wanting to shift the power dynamic, wrestling back power is challenging. It most often requires confrontation, or perhaps one can side-step and give feedback through disengaging. Also, moving away from leaning on others and seeking their advice, and instead relying on one's own, often neglected, gift of intuition and accumulated wisdom in the trials and tribulations on planet earth.

MANUFACTURING CHAOS

"It is a way of being in the world, leaping from one chaotic moment to another, leaving a long trail of destruction behind."

It is so easy to get caught up in the vortex of it all. This is a way of being in the world and it requires immense creativity, consolidated dramatizing skills, a receptive audience, and a willingness to go on yet another precipitous roller coaster of chaos. The chaos can be a quixotic mix of factors all congealing together in a sublime moment. The chaos manufacturer, who is highly attuned to the necessary ingredients for the full ramp up, has detecting radar switched on all the time. They do not want to miss an opportunity and are ready, every cell on high alert, for the big moment. When it arrives, they will go down a well-trodden path. It may start with, "you can't believe what just happened, wait until I tell you about my day, oh my goodness I nearly didn't . . . " The tone of their delivery is critical; it is a mix of incredulity, highly charged adrenaline, and conveys helplessness that comes with experiencing a tsunami of bizarre circumstances. The scenario could be any number of events

Figure 4.35. Manufacturing chaos.

all conspiring to occur at an auspicious moment. You recount the details: for instance, you were innocently taking Brutus for a walk when somehow, he managed to wriggle out of his collar and went running into traffic, a car stopped and a male driver behind the stopped car started to shout out of their window. Then the woman in the front car got out and started shouting back at him. The next minute the man got out of the car. I thought he was going to hit the woman, then you can't believe what happened next, Brutus ran up to the man and bit his shoe. He went ballistic and was shouting at me to get the dog off the street. I quickly reattached Brutus's collar and started running home. I thought the man was going to chase after me and I was about to call the police, but I got in the door and locked it. Fortunately, the collar stayed on this time and Brutus was able to run at my speed. We both got home and I heard a lot of beeping in the distance, but I don't know what happened to the man fighting with the woman, I hope he didn't hit her. Can you believe it? I was lucky to get away, it could have got ugly, and I didn't know what to do when he started shouting?

The story goes on and on, for as long as the audience can hang in there. The raconteur has endless energy to go into minute detail and is willing to analyze the scene repeatedly, exploring any new angle, any other dramatic moment that needs mining fully, the purpose is to maintain the adrenaline for as long as possible. The audience initially gets taken off guard and they are swept up in a torrential river, the currents going this way and that. That is the point; disorienting the audience is also a well-used strategy. A successful regaling is measured by the extent to which the audience is captured fully and their attention is sustained on the raconteur for as long as possible.

So why would one be caught up in this pattern? And, it is a pattern; look over a chunk of time and amazingly the same person seems to attract one chaotic event after another. Is it truly a coincidence or is it the result of cocreating, perhaps at an unconscious level, one event after another? What would be the point of it all? One reason is the adrenaline; note that every event has a super charged quality, with an undercurrent of excitement running through it. The excitement is not only in living through the event, but also in the retelling. The recounting speaks to other secondary gains, such as a receptive audience where attention is guaranteed for at least a while. Other clues with regard to attention-seeking are the minute detail needed to tell the story, the rehashing at every opportunity, or the absolute delight when an unsuspecting newcomer who has not heard it all before comes along. With the tendency to obsess on minutiae and the ramping up of any potential danger, the slippage over time to hyperbole is almost inevitable with the story gaining embellishment along the way.

Seeking out adrenaline and attention seeking are often a potent combination for disconnecting from self, staying trapped in one's head which can be a place of intense loneliness, hence the need for an audience, inviting them into your bubble for a while to reduce the struggles around aloneness. The ongoing chaos can be a way of staving off embodied pain or trauma, sequestering it internally, so we do not face it for another day, another month, another year, and potentially another decade. Given the pattern, what could be the cost on the manufacturer? One obvious cost is the sequestration of trauma and the resulting disconnection. Any unhelpful pattern of behavior over time contributes to the loss of self, an inability to name a feeling, a struggle to form relationships from a numb place, an increasing stripping of meaning overall in life and ongoing immersion into feelings like depression, despair, lost, confused, numb, self-absorbed, anxious, fearful, and helpless to name a few. The cost could also be an increasingly aware audience, who have heard it all before, and so are not willing to engage in the predictable game, hence distancing and an increased alienation from others potentially occurs.

If the manufacturer starts to tire of the process, is increasingly uninterested in searching for drama, and the consequent long-winded storytelling, it is a good sign. The patterns impact is starting to be felt and there is potentially an opportunity to start connecting more with self on an emotional level. The big challenge is when one has been sequestering trauma for some time a veritable waterfall of feeling has built up, so anxiety can now be experienced as panic attacks, other feelings like despair, helplessness, and fear, and can be overwhelmingly intense to feel. Critical then is pacing and support. Biting off chunks of trauma, starting with little "t" trauma and building from there if possible. Also vital is support, support from others who will hold ones hand in a tumultuous time and also support for one's body, perhaps massage, acupuncture, rigorous movement, yoga or Pilates routines, as some examples, so that the body can find a way to discharge the build up and move over time to equanimity, where it can take a breath, start to heal and sigh at last.

NOT GOOD ENOUGH

"It is an overall feeling of not measuring up, no matter what you do or what successes you accomplish. It is a ball and chain lugged everywhere, draining energy and sapping strength."

Figure 4.36. Not good enough.

"Not good enough" is painful, very painful, and it sprays its feelings of perhaps inadequacy, self-doubt, fear, incapability, shame, worthlessness, or deficiency at any moment that it can. It is a new day, a new experience, but with "not good enough" in tow, the moments can all feel the same. The second guessing is exhausting, also the critical piece of masking, pretending to others and sometimes self too, that you are enough, that you are coping well, and that you can manage the situation. However, when you get home and have time alone, the harsh self-criticism starts to spike all over the place. It may start with, "couldn't you have responded differently, others saw you battling, what will they think?" And "you always let yourself down, when are you going to get your act together so others can at least respect you, how can you expect others to respect you when you act in such an inept way?" And so, on and on and on. By the time the spikes of self-criticism have attacked you repeatedly, you feel like a lump of dough, lifeless, dragged down. You have lost your energy to fight back hours ago, the root of "not enough" is so long and it is so easy for it be activated. When it is activated, it feels so big, like it has the capacity to take over your whole being, grind you down so any accomplishment is smashed against the rocks, crumbles into shards of memory; therefore, it is nigh impossible to recall the feeling of self-pride.

Intuitively, you know this is a childhood struggle and it is not going away anytime soon until you get to the bottom of it. So, you start pondering, when did "I am not enough" first appear? What were the circumstances that encouraged the seed to grow and take sprout, spreading its tentacles everywhere it seems? You get a flashback to your parents faces when you bring home your first report card and a B+ seemed fine to you, no problem with it at all, but in seconds their wrath emerges. You remember them saying, "how could you let us down when we work day and night for you." They went on "this is shameful for the whole family, your mother and I always got high marks. You have let everyone down; I am too ashamed to discuss it anymore." The silence around it was as painful as the excoriating attack. You remember deflating, feeling bad about yourself, and thinking back, there must be something wrong with you that you are disappointing your parents so much. You remember it went on, there were haunting criticisms of how you did in sports, ongoing attacks on your marks for a wide variety of subjects, and painful reminders that you were not shaping up, unlike your sister who was an A student. So, what do you do about the gaping wounds that have accumulated, how can you start healing the root of "not enough"?

You do not want to have it out with your parents again because now they are okay; they are more likely these days to throw in the odd praise. They have made some changes since then, and although they will never be the affirming parents that would give ongoing validation, your relationship with them has improved a lot lately. Unfortunately, making peace with them does not seem to stop the toxic core belief from growing, flourishing, and expanding its reach, like boring tentacles. You still view life through cracked spectacles that are trained to see "not enough" and deficiency from miles away. So, you decide to start a letter writing campaign, an ongoing one. Every time "not enough" sneaks and slides into your psyche you write a letter to it, telling it how it is impacting you right now, and you write out all of your feelings and then state clearly, in unequivocal terms, how you will take back your power. Through this process you notice your awareness building, you are more detached, and from this perspective, you also become cognizant that "not enough" has been one huge motivator. You can see the countless achievements that you engaged in to prove to "not enough," once and for all, that you are enough. This is a revelation as looking back "not enough" has stimulated a far reach for success in many areas of life. You also find a trauma counselor who helps you connect with deeper feelings and uses a variety of techniques to tackle the roots of the issue, chipping away, one memory at a time, clearing embodied emotion, that you think got stuck in your hips and shoulders.

Over time, you notice you are a little lighter, although "not enough" still squirms in wherever there is a tiny crevasse, though it does not stay for as long. Its presence is detected quickly, so it does not have time to link up with self-doubt, inadequacy, shame, or worthlessness. It seems that hanging out with them for long periods of time really had given it the power of a bully, and the ability to push and steam roll its depressing opinions with brute force. For now, it feels like the momentum is on your side and the "not enough" antenna is highly attuned, and finally the fight back is marshalling more and more energy. You seem to have more spring in your step these days. You are also taking more risks, getting out there, and telling "not enough," when it slides in like a worm, to get lost, find another victim, and to leave you alone. You shout from on high, "how dare you take away my joy, my celebration of all I have achieved, and most importantly, my ease with myself. The world will be a brighter place now that the cracked spectacles are disintegrating in the garbage, exactly where they belong."

ART OF PACING AND SELF DISCIPLINE

"To pace in life, taking small, considered steps forward, is a way of aligning with the body, and living with grace and patience to see what unfolds in the mystery of life."

Pacing and self-discipline have a specific vision in mind, and it is hard for them to shake it off. Their destination is that far-off elusive prize of balance: balance in work, in leisure, in expectations, in health needs, in giving and receiving, in self-love and loving others, and in taking on a challenge and then retreating for restorative time. The art of pacing and self-discipline are forever relevant, much as we would like to go hurtling into the now, giving over to unbridled recklessness and impulsivity and seeing where we

Figure 4.37. Art of pacing and self-discipline.

land. Pacing and self-discipline says with a strong clear voice, "let's build a firm foundation first, spontaneity is great, with one caveat, let's leap from a grounded place." What they mean is that a solid foundation will give you a launch pad to build on exponentially, brick upon brick of effort, carefully paced and timed, so that it is on steady ground, veritable marble, and then any future endeavors can flourish and reach for their full vision of brilliance.

If pacing and self-discipline are so intricately tied to reaching high, to taking steady steps toward our penultimate desires, why is it so hard to flex these traits at times? Impatience plays a role; impatience says "let's get it together now, and I mean now." For instance, after a couple of months of hit and miss connections, you meet a potential romantic partner online. They seem to tick all the boxes and your eagerness to get together and fire up the romance is intense. You meet them right away; who needs to do any pondering when it looks like they are *the one*. Wow, what a find, you cannot believe your luck, the adrenaline is coursing through your veins and so too is oxytocin, what a potent combo, each day feels like fireworks are going off and any contact you have with the new person is electrifying and they seem to feel the same way. They say things like; "I have never met someone who I click with so instantly" and "I have been looking for this kind of connection for a long time." You wake up in the middle of the night one night and a surge of doubt surfaces, the doubt is all about pacing, taking it slowly, being careful what you are getting yourself into, and exercising a bit of discipline to get to know the person a bit better before you jump into the tumultuous river. You shrug it off. Why slow down when things are this exciting? You are thinking you should move in together at some point. In your mind, you start to plan months ahead, perhaps a vacation together and your new found love meeting your family sometime soon. Then, out of the blue, they seem to retreat, you do not know what is going on. It is incredibly confusing and they seem to make more and more excuses about getting together. You initially shrug it off, but then the pattern cannot be ignored and you confront them. Turns out they are in a long-term relationship; they were only interested in having a fling. Yes, of course, they still have feelings for you but naturally they are not going to end their relationship. You are devastated, absolutely heart broken. This has happened before in your life when someone betrayed you, and looking back you should have slowed things down, got more information, taken it step by step to discover who they really are. You curl up in a ball feeling depressed about it all, and it is hard to face friends and family for a while too. You are totally embarrassed because they know your impulsivity well and they would not be at all surprised you got into such a pickle.

You reflect a bit more and now remember the disastrous business deal you got yourself into. It seemed at the time exactly the kind of project that would meet a lot of your interests. The person selling you the franchise was a sort of a friend, someone who knows you and seemed to be caring. They gave you all sorts of impressive figures and explained why they needed to bale at this time. So, you took out a big chunk of your savings and sent off a check to them. Well, long story short, it was a disaster, you did not do your homework, the market in the franchise had already plummeted, and you lost a big chunk of your savings. The sort of a friend was nowhere to be found, scampered into the night with a fat wad of your cash, never to be seen again.

Seeing the pattern you realize is a big step. You have joined the dots on all of the occasions that you leapt with little information, with impulsivity driving you forward, and with recklessness hell bent for action. You reckon now is the time to make a change, that pacing is going to be your new best friend, and that you will start to flex the ill-formed skill of self-discipline. You start to realize self-discipline is a loving act, it is a way of valuing yourself, seeing your commitment of energy to anything as sacred in some way, also as an action that needs serious consideration. As after all, your life is made up of these sorts of commitments and you do not want to look back in your later years and see one deflated balloon after another. You want your projects, interests, hobbies, passions, and commitments to rise, like a bird circling ever higher and higher, attaining new perspectives and experiencing the glory of a well-nurtured, lovingly crafted, and carefully tended venture in life.

VICTIMIZATION

"Victimization sees the world through a lens that insists we are going to be undermined no matter what, that we do not have the power to stand our ground, and that we are helpless with regard to what happens in our lives."

Figure 4.38. Victimization.

Victimization is deep in the marrow of one's body; often, it had carved out its perspective oh so long ago when we were small, vulnerable, and experiencing horrendous events with little to no protection. It was hard at the time to explain these events away, or take an adult, detached, birds-eye view lens that would have offered some explanations or at least some understanding of what was happening. As a child, if we experience one tough moment after another, we can develop a lens that sees the world through a victim standpoint and at times blame ourselves, even though we were innocent bystanders. Victimization can also occur later in life due to a traumatic event, or events, that surpass our ability to manage the moment and our capacity to deal with the emotional impact of the trauma. Each event can trigger the same set of feelings, for instance: helplessness, victimization, disrespected, self-blame (even if it was not our fault), despair, anxiousness, self-loathing, inadequacy, shame, guilt, hopelessness, sadness, vulnerability, fear, self-pity, or being overwhelmed. These sets of feelings start to form a pattern that impacts our worldview and skews our vision of the world around us.

It is a new day, a new week, or a new year, and yet we still find a feeling of victimization pervasive. We got a new job and within weeks it feels as if you are being disrespected by colleagues and by your boss, just like the last job. No one seems to value your opinion. This is also how you feel with your group of friends, and you had to raise it with your girlfriend recently too. Victimization is very skilled at following its hosts, much like a sinister furtive shadow, popping up in so many unexpected places. You do not want to see yourself as a victim; it seems weak somehow, but the evidence is convincing when you think about it. Looking at the last social gathering of your friends, everyone was consulted with regard to the next get together except you. Your boss also picked on you in the staff meeting and implied that you had not been following up leads quickly enough, and it was humiliating to be singled out. Then, your girlfriend's parents ignored your request to keep the dog in the back room when you visit because of your allergies. So disrespectful, you feel the resentment rising and coursing through your veins; it feels like at some point something horrendous will happen and some deep dark liquid will burst through your skin and explode everywhere. Come to think of it, victimization also popped up at Aunt Sally's birthday party. The whole family was there and everyone seemed to be having a good time but you. You were in the corner looking at her photo albums. No one bothered to reach out to you or ask you anything about your life or even about your new job, just typical, you surmise internally, as you seethe even more.

You realize now, once the feelings related to victimization are triggered internally, thought patterns seem to take on a life of their own, like a flame being fanned continually until it becomes a raging fire within moments. The first thought may be, "here we go again, I am being ignored and no one is respecting me," followed by cascading thoughts one after another. For example, "no one is interested in what I have to say, no-one is looking at me, others are judging me, life's not fair, I am not liked by others, I always get the leftovers, I'm broken, nothing is ever going to work out for me, and no-one gets how tough life is for me and I wish someone would help me fix my situation." The list goes on. It is hard to track them as they fall on top of one another, bombarding the mind like stealth missiles determined to undermine the victim as quickly as possible. If one felt victimized prior to the trigger, now with emotions activated and thoughts cascading, it feels like you have dropped into a well, it is dark and dank inside, lonely too, and you are frightened, overwhelmed, and terrified that you will never get out. When others say, "see the bright side," and more nauseatingly, "be positive," you almost want to heave. Are they really that clueless? "Don't they realize it will take all my strength to get out of this pit of despair, and when I do, I will likely want to cower in a corner and lick my gaping wounds continually."

There is another complex piece in the victimization puzzle you ponder as you are joining more dots. Feeling victimized puts one in a vulnerable state to those who offer quick and easy solutions, and who seem to give tons of attention and advice to satisfy their own *need to be needed*. You remember relying a lot on Tom, depending on him almost, and he was always there and never minded hearing your latest rant. You sometimes wondered what is in it for him, to be so available for your latest victim story to play out repeatedly.

Over time, although it was comforting that he was there, you realized the process of venting and him giving tons of advice was not helping at all. In fact, by the time your rant was finished you felt flattened, like gum sticking to the sidewalk, and all the awful and painful feelings and thoughts were now dominating. If you felt in a hole before chatting to Tom, now the hole was at least ten meters deeper, and his advice was toss away from that vantage point.

So, if others advice, and a bended ear to hear all the venting does not work long term to release the trauma, what does work? Acknowledging one's feelings is often the first step in the process, naming despair, hurt, or shame as some examples is an important start. Perhaps a reflection then on the root of the feelings, what were some of the most challenging moments in one's life to date that solidified the feeling of victimization. Tackling the situation in some way, perhaps writing a letter to the person or persons whose actions or words most reinforced the victim feeling, letting them know how they impacted you and how you are going to take your power back. Also, chipping away at the feelings, layer by layer, releasing them through tapping, journal writing, body work, visualizations, or another clearing technique can be beneficial. At the same time, it is helpful in our healing process to practice copious amounts of self-care and have anti-victimization experiences. By taking small manageable risks, we tap into our strength and start to shock our system with how empowered we can be. We start asserting ourselves wherever we can, even a mini assertion, if possible, by taking charge of situations in some small way the opposite is reinforced. This action reminds us that we are resilient, we do have choices, we can chip away at the past, and we are not victim to the old story. It says emphatically that we can create anew, step by deliberate step, and move onto a new path that says, "yes you can, and you will go to where you want to go." The path may be circuitous, or you may regress at times, and you may not be able to see around the corner, but you do know that despite your past, the path is one where you will build yourself into a robust version of yourself where you start each day eventually with, "I am struggling somewhat, but I've got this."

Chapter 5

Release it

These visuals or images are intended to help in releasing trauma by engaging our right brain. We cannot think or talk our way through trauma we need to experience it briefly so we can feel it, to heal it. A right brain orientation assists in bypassing the conscious mind and helps us access our somatic memories, this includes sensations as a way of knowing, feelings, urges, desires, and other somatic reactions in the body. An image helps us connect with trauma induced embodied emotion and the image provides a bridge for the pre-frontal cortex and limbic system to communicate, which assists in the healing process. Putting as many feelings as possible into the drawings is key, in releasing the build-up of embodied emotion, and filling in the drawing with as much complexity as possible, so you can understand your situation from a bird's eye view perspective.

SELF DOUBT

This visual is designed to assist you when you are consumed with self-doubt and are struggling to get out of its vice-grip. The visual captures a state of immobilization where one is stuck and challenged regarding making any decision. Start the drawing by drawing a chair and put your body in the chair with a heart on your body. Draw a line down the heart, put an arrow on each side of the heart one says at the end 'should I' and the other says 'shouldn't I.' Some questions to ask yourself to fill in the image are:

1. What are some of the other feelings I am feeling while being consumed with self-doubt? They could include confusion, fear, lost, uncertain, self-rejection, self-loathing, lonely, inadequate, stuck, undermined, judged, loss of self, misunderstood, alone, desperate, and hopeless.
2. What are some of the patterns of behaviour that are contributing to the immobilization? Place the list under the chair. They could include

5.1 Self-Doubt

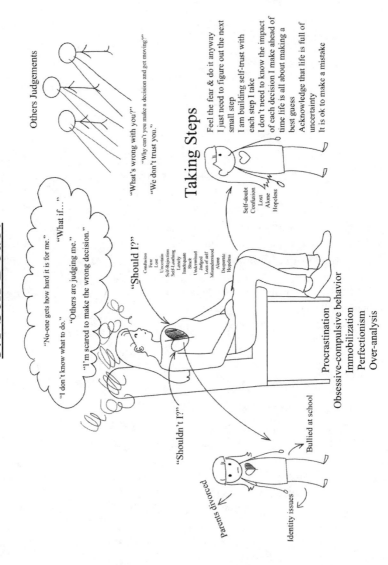

Figure 5.1. Self-doubt.

procrastination, obsessive-compulsive behavior, immobilization, perfectionism, and over-analysis.

3. Put a cloud over your head and write in the cloud some repetitive thoughts that you are having. They could be "I don't know what to do, no-one gets how hard it is for me, I'm scared to make the wrong decision, what if. . . . , and others are judging me" as some examples. Also add a lot of squiggly lines around the head indicating 'thinking about thinking.'

4. Now link your heart to a younger version of yourself—draw a younger version of yourself behind the chair. Do you remember being consumed with self-doubt at an earlier time in your life—if so, how old were you? What were some of the feelings you felt back then besides self-doubt link them to the heart of the young figure? What were some of the events that happened back then which impact your ability to make decisions now—use arrows to the head to capture the events?

5. In the far-right hand corner draw several figures and put a label above the figures of *Others judgments*. Put 2 lines coming from the eyes of each figure indicating their judgements. What do you fear they are thinking? Perhaps it may be, "what's wrong with you? Why can't you make a decision and get moving? You fear they think, he / she / they don't seem to be able to commit to anything and are untrustworthy." Any other thoughts to add?

6. Now put a figure in the distance and link the figure with an arrow to the figure stuck on the chair. Above the figure in the distance is a label namely, *Taking steps*. Now draw up a list of all the actions you are taking to make movement away from the immobilization of self-doubt. It could be, feel the fear and do it anyway, I just need to figure out the next small step, I am building self-trust with each step I take, I don't need to know the impact of each decision I make ahead of time life is all about making a best guess, acknowledge that life is full of uncertainty, and it is ok to make a mistake. What might other examples be?

SELF-PITY

Start the visual by drawing a body hunched over their knees as an indication of being consumed with self-pity. Now draw a heart on the body to acknowledge other feelings that come alongside self-pity. Draw a bubble over your head to understand self-pity's voice. Also put some arrows going towards your head to record what is contributing to self-pity. Some questions to ask yourself to fill in the image are

5.2 Self-Pity

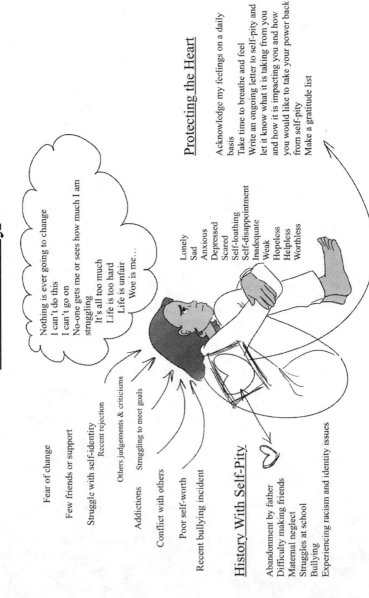

Nothing is ever going to change
I can't do this
I can't go on
No-one gets me or sees how much I am struggling
It's all too much
Life is too hard
Life is unfair
Woe is me...

Lonely
Sad
Anxious
Depressed
Scared
Self-loathing
Self-disappointment
Inadequate
Weak
Hopeless
Helpless
Worthless

Fear of change
Few friends or support
Struggle with self-identity
Recent rejection
Others judgements & criticisms
Addictions   Struggling to meet goals
Conflict with others
Poor self-worth
Recent bullying incident

History With Self-Pity

Abandonment by father
Difficulty making friends
Maternal neglect
Struggles at school
Bullying
Experiencing racism and identity issues

Protecting the Heart

Acknowledge my feelings on a daily basis
Take time to breathe and feel
Write an ongoing letter to self-pity and let it know what it is taking from you and how it is impacting you and how you would like to take your power back from self-pity
Make a gratitude list

Figure 5.2. Self-pity.

1. List all of the feelings that you feel beside self-pity and link them to the heart. They could include, lonely, sad, anxious, depressed, scared, self-loathing, self-disappointment, inadequate, weak, hopeless, helpless, and worthless as some examples.
2. Now capture what is contributing to self-pity with arrows to your head, describe each arrow, some arrows might be, recent rejection, others judgement and criticisms, struggling to meet goals, addictions, conflict with others, poor self-worth, fear of change, few friends or support, struggle with self-identity and recent bullying incident.
3. Now write all dominant thoughts in the bubble over your head. They might be, "nothing is ever going to change, I can't do this, I can't go on, no-one gets me or sees how much I am struggling, it's all too much, life is too hard, life is unfair, and woe is me."
4. Draw a small heart and put it behind the figure and link it to the heart on the body. Now brainstorm one's history with self-pity. History of self-pity could include traumatic events such as abandonment by father, maternal neglect, difficulty making friends, struggle at school, bullying, experiencing racism and identity issues as some examples.
5. Put some lines around the heart indicating protecting the heart from drowning in self-pity. Now list on the far-right hand side of the page all the actions one can take to protect your heart and create a shield from self-pity. They could include, acknowledge my feelings daily, take time to breathe and feel, write an ongoing letter to self-pity, letting it know what it is taking from you, how it is impacting you and how you would like to take your power back from self-pity. List other actions that you can take that undermine self-pity, be as specific as possible and do a regular gratitude list.

ANXIETY

This visual is helpful if you experience anxiety on a regular basis and would like to explore the root cause of anxiety and help release it. Draw an anxiety filled figure on the page and another figure in the distance that is named *new and emerging self*. Link both figures with an arrow going from the anxious one to the other, name the arrow -*releasing anxiety from the body*. Put an anxiety thermometer numbered 1 – 10 next to both bodies –put it at 9 next to the anxious figure and at a 3 to 5 range on the other figure. Draw a heart on both figures and a bubble over each of their heads. Some questions to ask yourself to fill in the image are

5.3 Anxiety

New & Emerging Self

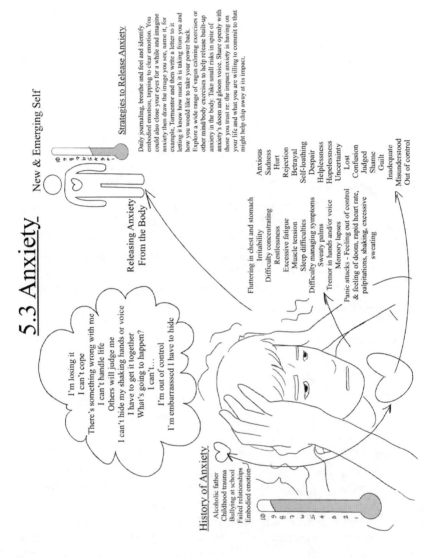

Strategies to Release Anxiety

Daily journaling, breathe and feel and identify embodied emotion, tapping to clear emotion. You could also close your eyes for a while and imagine anxiety then draw the image you see, name it, for example, Tormentor and then write a letter to it letting it know how much it is taking from you and how you would like to take your power back.

Explore a wide range of vagus calming exercises or other mind/body exercises to help release built-up anxiety in the body. Take small risks in spite of anxiety's doom and gloom voice. Share openly with those you trust re: the impact anxiety is having on your life and what you are willing to commit to that might help chip away at its impact.

Releasing Anxiety
From the Body

Anxious
Sadness
Hurt
Rejection
Betrayal
Self-loathing
Despair
Helplessness
Hopelessness
Uncertainty
Lost
Confusion
Judged
Shame
Guilt
Inadequate
Misunderstood
Out of control

Fluttering in chest and stomach
Irritability
Difficulty concentrating
Restlessness
Excessive fatigue
Muscle tension
Sleep difficulties
Difficulty managing symptoms
Sweaty palms
Tremor in hands and/or voice
Memory lapses
Panic attacks - Feeling out of control
& feeling of doom, rapid heart rate,
palpitations, shaking, excessive
sweating

I'm losing it
I can't cope
There's something wrong with me
I can't handle life
Others will judge me
I can't hide my shaking hands or voice
I have to get it together
What's going to happen?
I can't...
I'm out of control
I'm embarrasssed I have to hide

History of Anxiety

Alcoholic father
Childhood trauma
Bullying at school
Failed relationships
Embodied emotion

Figure 5.3. Anxiety.

1. Draw an arrow from the heart to the open page, take a moment to breathe as deeply as possible and connect to your body, take time to notice any sensation you are feeling, for example, fluttering in your stomach or chest. Breathe into the sensation, sense, and intuit any feelings you feel in that area of your body, or any other area. Write down the feelings, anxiety is often at the surface, see if you can breathe beneath the anxiety to discover the underlying feelings. The feelings may be, sadness, hurt, rejection, betrayal, self-loathing, despair, helplessness, hopelessness, uncertainty, lost, confusion, judged, shame, guilt, inadequate, misunderstood and out of control as some examples.

2. Put a bubble over the anxious figures head—write down your thoughts particularly when anxiety is high. For instance, "I am losing it, I can't cope, there's something wrong with me, I can't handle life, others will judge me, I can't hide my shaking hands or voice, I must get it together, what's going to happen, I can't. . . . , I'm out of control, I'm embarrassed, and I must hide."

3. Now put an arrow from your body onto the open page and name the arrow anxiety symptoms. Now list all your anxiety related symptoms they could include, fluttering in chest and stomach, irritability, difficulty concentrating, restlessness, excessive fatigue, muscle tension, sleep difficulties, difficulty managing symptoms, sweaty palms, tremor in hands and / or voice and memory lapses. The anxiety may lead to panic attacks which could also include, feeling out of control and feeling of doom, rapid heart rate, palpitations, shaking and excessive sweating as some examples.

4. Put an arrow from the heart on the left-hand side of the page and name it *history of anxiety*. Underneath *history of anxiety* put embodied emotion from past trauma. List any emotion you can recall that is linked to traumatic events for instance, helplessness may be a repeated emotion in your life linked to past trauma, are there others embodied emotions?

5. On the far-right hand side of the page put a heading, *strategies to release anxiety*. Now list the range of strategies that you could try that would help release the build-up of anxiety. It could be daily journal writing, breathe and feel and identify embodied emotion, using a clearing technique for instance tapping, visualization or movement to clear the emotion. Another strategy could be, close your eyes for a while and imagine anxiety, draw the image you see. Name the image, for example, *tormentor* and then write a letter to it letting it know how much it is taking from you and how specifically you would like to take your power back. Explore a wide range of vagus calming exercises, or other mind / body exercises that help release the build-up of anxiety in the body. Explore other healing modalities for trauma and use one's intuition to

choose which one seems to resonate the most. Take small risks despite anxiety's doom and gloom voice of foreboding and share openly with those you trust how anxiety is impacting your life, and what you are willing to commit to that might help chip away at its impact.

DEPRESSION

This visual is intended to help when you feel low, unmotivated, excessively tired, you have difficulties sleeping, you experience loss of purpose or meaning in life, and have difficulty concentrating or making decisions, experience lack of appetite or over-eating and weight gain and unexplained aches, and pains. Your depression could include a wide range of feelings including suicidal feelings, guilt, dread, hopelessness, worthlessness, sad and empty as some examples. Draw yourself in the middle of the page looking depressed. Put a wavy circle all around you representing a sea of meaninglessness. Put several vortexes at the bottom of the figure representing getting pulled into a dark hole. Put a small heart off on the left-hand side of the page indicating past trauma. Put a bubble over your head to capture your thoughts. Some questions to ask yourself to fill in the image are

1. Link an arrow from your heart to the open page and list all the feelings you feel at this moment. It could include, small, worthless, contracted, unmotivated, empty, lost, confused, weak, guilty, depressed, sad, inadequacy, unworthy, helpless, hopeless and despair as some examples.
2. In the sea of meaninglessness all around you put in some descriptors in the sea to describe your experience. Some examples might be, my relationship sucks, I have no friends, I hate my job, I have no purpose, I have lost interest in everything, its challenging to even get out of bed in the morning and I could sleep my life away. Keep adding to the list any other issues that compound your present situation.
3. In the bubble over the head capture your dominant thoughts. For instance, "what's the point of trying, there's no escape from this hell, I don't care about anything anymore, I'm going down, it's all too much effort, I can't fight it this time it's too big and I can't snap out of it, and no-one understands what I am going through."
4. Now put an arrow linking all three vortexes and in a column on the far-left hand side capture your experience in the vortex. Some examples could be, being stuck, immobilized, in a state of fear, isolated, little to no direction, giving up, feeling of being swept down further into despair and hopelessness and surrendering to the vortex.

5.4 Depression

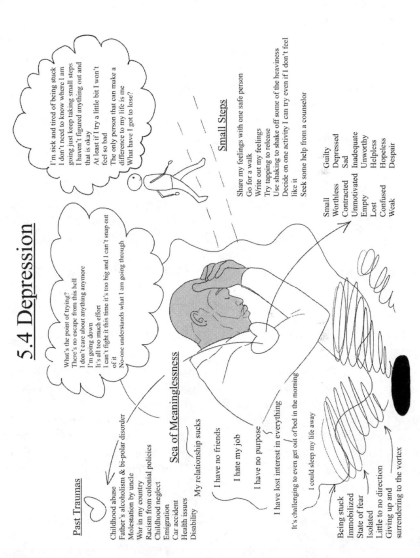

Figure 5.4. Depression.

5. Put an arrow on the left-hand side of your figure to the open page and draw a small heart. Put a title above it, *Past trauma*, depression can be a symptom of past trauma. Now list all the past traumatic incidents that have happened in your life. The list could include, childhood abuse, father's alcohol addiction and bi-polar disorder, molestation by uncle, war in my country, racism from colonial policies, childhood neglect, emigration, car accident, health issues and disability challenges as some examples.

6. Now draw a figure off on the right-hand side that is ready to take small, tentative steps out of the sea of meaninglessness. Small steps could be, share my feelings with one safe person, go for a walk, write out my feelings and try tapping to release them, write down some small healthy risks I could take to shift the stuck feeling, use shaking to shake off some of the heaviness, decide on one activity I can try even if I don't feel like it and seek some help from a trauma counselor.

7. Put a bubble over this figures head and capture some of the thoughts that might help, even a little, with motivation. They could be, "I'm sick and tired of being stuck, I don't need to know where I am going but keep taking small steps, I haven't figured anything out and that is ok, at least if I try a little bit I won't feel so bad, the only person that can make a difference to my life is me and what have I got to lose."

UNSAFE

This visual is helpful when you are being triggered from past trauma and are *feeling unsafe* and perhaps out of control. Start the visual by drawing a figure in the middle of the page that looks unsafe, and out of control, and whose feet are on steps that are collapsing. Put a heart on the figure and an arrow to the open page on the left-hand side. Now put a bubble over the head to capture present thoughts. Put a heart on the right-hand side of the open page with a heading *Past trauma*. Some questions to ask yourself to fill in the image are:

1. Write a list of all the feelings that have been triggered with the unsafe feeling? They could include, terror, unsafe, destabilized, disoriented, disassociated, unhinged, out of control, helplessness, hopelessness, despair, ashamed, ungrounded, humiliated, confusion, lost and fear as some examples.

2. Put an arrow from the heart to the right-hand side of the page and title the arrow *Past trauma*. Now write a list of events that have occurred in the past that have been traumatic. Some examples may be, child-hood neglect, absent father, history of racism, sexual abuse by uncle,

5.5 Unsafe

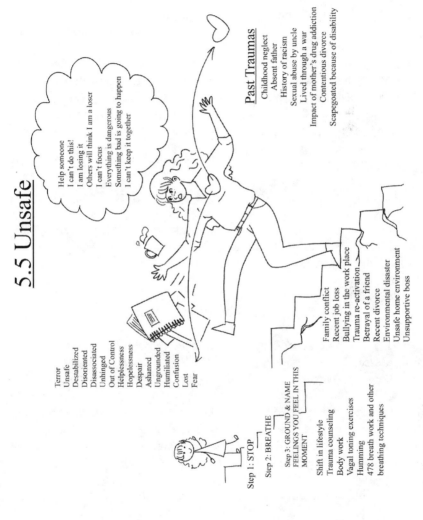

Figure 5.5. Unsafe.

lived through a war, impact of mother's drug addiction, history of bullying, contentious divorce and scapegoated because of disability as some examples.

3. In the bubble over the head capture thoughts that you are experiencing right now. They may be, "help someone, I can't do this, I am losing it, others will think I am a loser, I can't focus, everything is dangerous, something bad is going to happen and I can't keep it together."

4. Now put arrows under the steps describing what is contributing to the present unsafe feeling. It could be, family conflict, recent job loss, bullying in the workplace, trauma re-activation, betrayal by friend, recent divorce, environmental disaster, unsafe home environment and unsupportive boss as some examples.

5. Now put some steps away from the standing figure. Name the steps—step 1, step 2, step 3 and so on. Under the first step put in capital letters, stop, breathe, ground and name feelings you feel in this moment.

6. Now put a figure on the path walking down the various steps. Put under the other steps *strategies for taking future steps* and list the strategies. They could include shift in lifestyle, trauma counseling, body work, vagal toning exercises, humming, 478 breath work and other breathing techniques, visualizations, acupuncture, cranial sacral therapy massage, eye-movement desensitization and reprocessing (EMDR) and movement.

ENTITLEMENT

Start the visual by drawing a person with a look of entitlement on their face and expressed in their body. Put a bubble from their mouth onto the open page. Now draw arrows on the right-hand side towards the figure with a heading above the arrows of *Core beliefs and internalized drivers*. On the left hand-side put a title of *Past contributing experiences* and draw an arrow linking the body to the title. Also, on the left-hand side of the page put a lightbulb and link it to arrows from the head that are titled *Building awareness*. Some questions to ask yourself to fill in the image are:

1. In the bubble from the mouth list common phrases you think, or convictions that drive your behaviour that indicate entitlement. The list could include "I want it now, I'm owed, what about my needs, if only. . . . , I wish. . . . , what about me, I must fight for what I want, it's not fair, and others need to pay more attention to my needs."

2. On the right-hand side of the page under *core beliefs and internalized drivers* write a list that reflects entitlement. It could include I never get

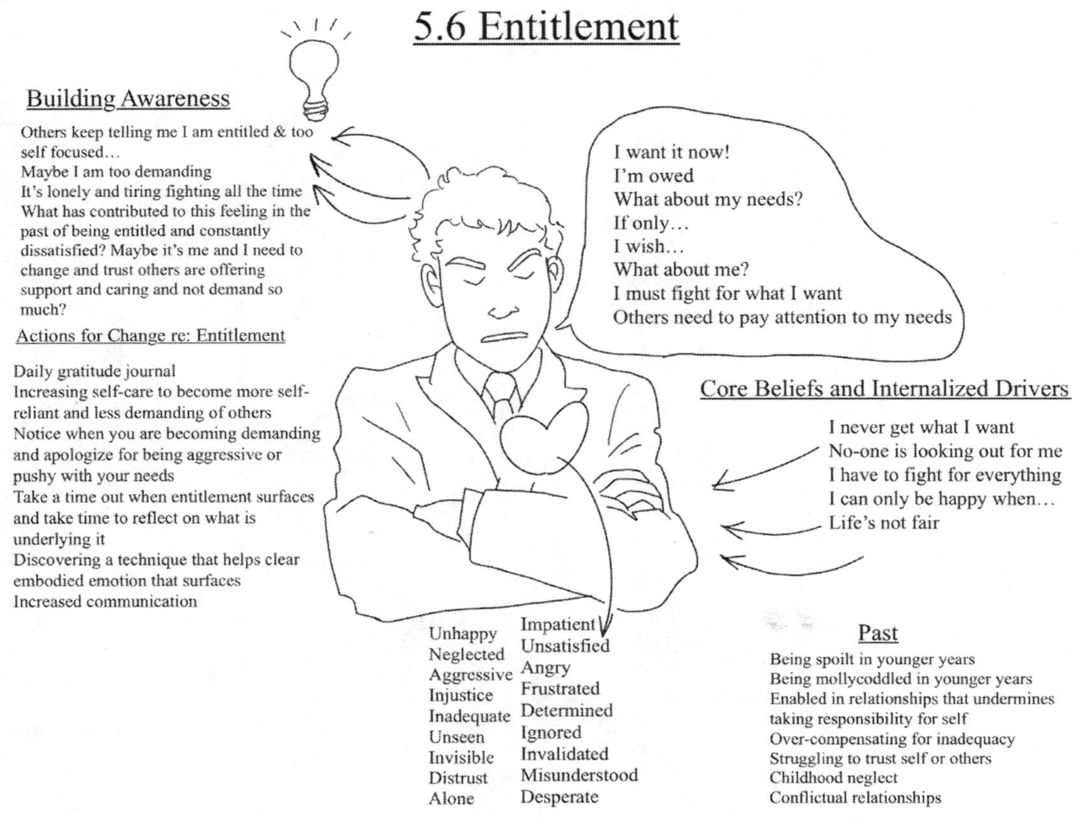

5.6 Entitlement

Building Awareness

Others keep telling me I am entitled & too self focused...
Maybe I am too demanding
It's lonely and tiring fighting all the time
What has contributed to this feeling in the past of being entitled and constantly dissatisfied? Maybe it's me and I need to change and trust others are offering support and caring and not demand so much?

Actions for Change re: Entitlement

Daily gratitude journal
Increasing self-care to become more self-reliant and less demanding of others
Notice when you are becoming demanding and apologize for being aggressive or pushy with your needs
Take a time out when entitlement surfaces and take time to reflect on what is underlying it
Discovering a technique that helps clear embodied emotion that surfaces
Increased communication

I want it now!
I'm owed
What about my needs?
If only...
I wish...
What about me?
I must fight for what I want
Others need to pay attention to my needs

Core Beliefs and Internalized Drivers

I never get what I want
No-one is looking out for me
I have to fight for everything
I can only be happy when...
Life's not fair

Unhappy   Impatient
Neglected   Unsatisfied
Aggressive   Angry
Injustice   Frustrated
Inadequate   Determined
Unseen   Ignored
Invisible   Invalidated
Distrust   Misunderstood
Alone   Desperate

Past

Being spoilt in younger years
Being mollycoddled in younger years
Enabled in relationships that undermines taking responsibility for self
Over-compensating for inadequacy
Struggling to trust self or others
Childhood neglect
Conflictual relationships

Figure 5.6. Entitlement.

what I want, no-one is looking out for me, I have to fight for everything, and I can only be happy when. . . . . and life's not fair.

3. Put a heart on your figure and brainstorm all the feelings you feel at times when life doesn't meet your expectations. Some feelings that may be pertinent are impatient, unsatisfied, angry, frustrated, determined, ignored, invalidated, misunderstood, desperate, unhappy, neglected, aggressive, injustice, inadequate, unseen, invisible, distrust and alone.

4. On the right-hand side under the heading, *Past contributing experiences*, list past experiences that may have contributed to feeling entitled or owed. The list could include experiences such as being spoilt in your younger years or being mollycoddled, enabled in relationships that undermine taking responsibility for self, over-compensating for inadequacy, struggle to trust self or others, childhood neglect, difficulty bonding and conflictual relationships.

5. Now, on the left-hand side of the page link an arrow from the head to the open page with a title *Building awareness* and a light bulb to represent it. Some indicators of building awareness that could undermine entitlement could be, others keep telling me I am entitled and too self-focused, maybe I am too demanding, its lonely and tiring fighting all the time, what has contributed to this feeling in the past re being entitled and constantly dissatisfied? Maybe it's me and I need to change and trust others who are offering support and caring and not demand so much. Now create a list under the title *Actions for change re entitlement*. These could include, a daily gratitude journal, increasing self-care to become more self-reliant and less demanding of others, notice when you are becoming demanding and apologize for being aggressive or pushy with your needs, take a time out when entitlement surfaces and take the time to reflect what is underlying it for example, name feelings you are feeling that may be driving entitlement. Experiment with different techniques that help to clear embodied emotion and make an effort to increase open communication.

SOMATIZATION

This visual is focused on illuminating the trap of somatization and exploring ways to break through the pattern so that healing can occur. Draw a figure with a body. Put a heart on the figure and add walls around the heart. Also, draw a circle in the stomach area, put the word *pain* in the circle and 20 lbs. Now draw downward arrows from the pain circle that loop around the pain circle making it bigger and bigger. Name those circles 40lbs, 60 lbs and 80

5.7 Somatization

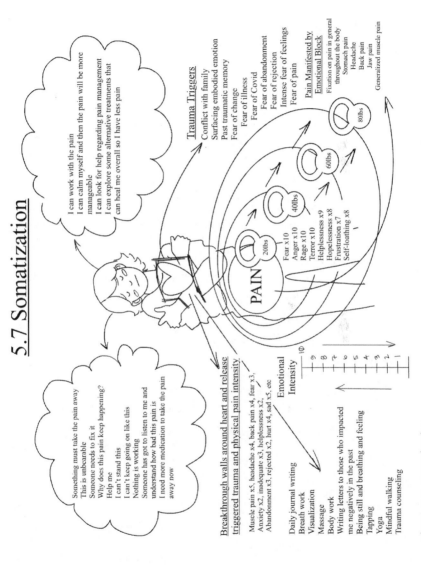

Figure 5.7. Somatization.

lbs. Also draw 2 large bubbles around the head one off to the left and one off to the right. The following questions can help to fill in the visual image

1. In the left-hand side bubble write in thoughts that are consumed with the trap of somatization. They could be, "something must take the pain away, this is unbearable, someone needs to fix it, why does this pain keep happening, help me, I can't stand this, I can't keep going on like this, nothing is working, someone has got to listen to me and understand how bad the pain is and I need more medication to take the pain away right now."

2. In the right-hand side bubble put an alternative response that resists somatization. The thoughts could be, "I can work with the pain, I can calm myself and then the pain will be more manageable, I can look for help regarding pain management and I can explore some alternative treatments that can heal me overall, so I have less pain."

3. Now put a title *Trauma trigger* and link the title with walls around the heart. List some possible trauma triggers that have initiated the somatization response. The trauma triggers could be, conflict with family, surfacing embodied emotion or past traumatic memory, overwhelming fear of feeling feelings, fear of change, fear of pain, fear of illness, fear of Covid, fear of abandonment and fear of rejection as some examples.

4. Put a barometer off to the left-hand side of the page numbering it 1–10. Alongside the barometer put emotional intensity. Another arrow going down the barometer could indicate 10 is for high intensity and 1 is for low intensity.

5. Put a title of '*Unconscious emotional response*' underneath the arrows located under the 20 lb pain circle that are then leading out to increasing circles of pain. Describe feelings and intensity that may be felt given the feelings are being suppressed by somatization. The feelings could be, fear x 10, anger x10, rage x 10, terror x 10, helplessness x 9, hopelessness x 8, frustration x 7 and self-loathing x 8 for example. The point is to record the intensity of emotions felt given the suppression.

6. Now put an arrow from the pain onto the open page on the left-hand side. Put a title, *Pain manifested by emotional block* and describe the symptoms felt. It could a fixation on pain in general throughout the body, or stomach pain, headache, back pain, jaw pain, generalized muscle pain and so on.

7. Now put some passages out from the walls around the heart indicating a heart opening. Link an arrow to the passages and take the arrow to the right-hand side of the page. Put a title of *Breakthrough walls around heart and release triggered trauma and physical pain intensity*. Brainstorm the impact of releasing in terms of feelings, pain, and

physical intensity. Some examples could be, muscle pain x 5, headache x 4, back pain x 4, fear x 3, anxiety x 2, inadequate x 3, helplessness x 2, abandonment x 3, rejected x 2, hurt x 4 and sad x 5.

8. Lastly, link an arrow from one of the passages opening the heart to a list of *strategies that help to open the heart*. These could include, daily journal writing, breath work, visualization, massage, body work, trauma counseling, writing letters to those who impacted me negatively in the past, being still and breathing and feeling, tapping, yoga and mindful walking.

VICTIMIZATION

Start the visual by drawing a person who is appearing dejected and beaten down by life. Put a heart on their body and an arrow onto the open page. Also, put a bubble over their head to capture thoughts that they are thinking related to feeling victimized in life. Now add hands in several places all around the figure each hand has a pointed finger that appears to be accusing the person of something or saying something derogatory. Draw a younger version of the person and link their heart to the heart of the figure. Ask yourself the following questions to fill in the image.

1. What feelings are you feeling, list the feelings at the end of the arrow that links to the heart. The feelings could include, self-pity, misunderstood, bullied, betrayed, scared, dejected, isolated, lonely, alone, despair, hopeless, helpless, dismayed, small, inadequate, and unsafe as some examples.
2. Now write out thoughts you are thinking they could be, "I'm a victim, I can't go on, I can't cope, no-one gets me, life's too hard, help, everyone judges me, there is so much injustice, everyone picks on me, when will somebody help, and I need someone to fix me as some examples."
3. Next write down some the judgements you think others are making of you and link each judgement to an accusing hand. Some of the judgements might be, what's wrong with you, you never get anything right, you're a failure, you act like a victim, you're a loser, you can't be trusted and when are you going to get your act together?
4. Now draw a younger version of yourself. Regarding the feeling list put an asterisk next to those feelings you felt at a younger age, what age were you? Now put that age above the younger version of yourself, draw an arrow and put the relevant feelings at the end of the arrow linked to the heart. The feelings could be, victimized, scared, unsafe, alone, helpless, hopeless, inadequate, and small.

5.8 Victimization

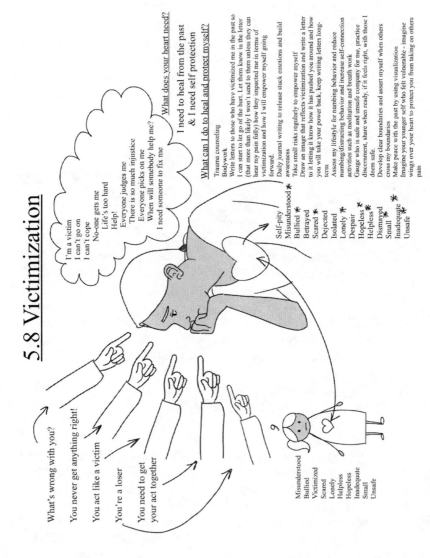

What's wrong with you?

You never get anything right!

You act like a victim

You're a loser

You need to get your act together

Misunderstood
Bullied
Victimized
Scared
Lonely
Helpless
Hopeless
Inadequate
Small
Unsafe

I'm a victim
I can't go on
I can't cope
No-one gets me
Life's too hard
Help!
Everyone judges me
There is so much injustice
Everyone picks on me
When will somebody help me?
I need someone to fix me

What does your heart need?

I need to heal from the past
& I need self protection

What can I do to heal and protect myself?

Trauma counseling
Bodywork
Write letters to those who have victimized me in the past so I can start to let go of the hurt. Let them know in the letter (that more than likely I won't send to them unless they can hear my pain fully) how they impacted me in terms of victimization and how I will empower myself going forward.
Daily journal writing to release stuck emotions and build awareness
Take small risks regularly to empower myself
Draw an image that reflects victimization and write a letter to it letting it know how it has pushed you around and how you will take your power back, keep writing letters long-term
Assess my lifestyle for numbing/distracting behavior and reduce numbing/distracting behavior and increase self-connection activities such as meditation and breath work
Gauge who is safe and unsafe company for me, practice discernment, share when ready, if it feels right, with those I deem safe.
Develop clear boundaries and assert myself when others cross my boundaries
Make peace with the past by using visualization
Imagine your younger self who felt vulnerable - imagine wings over your heart to protect you from taking on others pain

Self-pity
Misunderstood ✻
Bullied ✻
Betrayed ✻
Scared ✻
Dejected
Isolated
Lonely ✻
Despair
Hopeless ✻
Helpless ✻
Dismayed
Small ✻
Inadequate ✻
Unsafe

Figure 5.8. Victimization.

5. Next put a title *What does your heart need?* in a heading and link it to the heart. What comes to mind may be, I need to heal from the past and I need self-protection.

6. Now under a heading *What can I do to heal and protect myself* write out a list of all the actions you can take that may help you in your healing process and offer some self-protection. The list could include, trauma counseling, bodywork, write letters to those that have victimized me in the past so I can start to let go of the hurt. Let them know in the letter (that more than likely I won't send to them unless they can hear my pain fully) how they impacted me in terms of victimization, and how I will empower myself going forward. Daily journal writing to release stuck emotion and build awareness, take small risks regularly to empower myself, draw an image that reflects victimization and write a letter to victimization letting it know how it has pushed you around and how you will take your power back, keep writing the letters long-term. Assess my lifestyle for numbing behaviour—reduce numbing / distracting behaviour and increase self-connection activities for instance, meditation and breath work. Gauge who is safe and unsafe company, practice discernment, share if you would like with those you deem to be safe. Develop clear boundaries—assert myself when others cross my boundaries. Incorporate a wide range of self-soothing activities into my daily practice, make some peace with my past by using visualizations. Imagine your younger self who felt vulnerable and victimized– what can you give them now that would help them deal with the historical situation, what would help them even a little bit? For instance, imagine wings over your young heart to protect you from taking on others pain.

NOT GOOD ENOUGH

This visual can be helpful if you feel haunted by the persistent feeling that *you are not enough*, no matter what you do. Self- doubt and inadequacy are likely common feelings, and this way of being may have permeated your life for some time. Start the visual by drawing an image of yourself reflecting *I am not good enough*. Draw a small box in your head and put in the box *I am not good enough*. Now put a heart on your drawing and a bubble over your head. Also put an arrow from the box in your head to a small figure on the left-hand side of the page. Ask yourself the following questions to fill in the image:

1. At the end of the arrow from your heart to the open page list all the feelings you feel given the core belief of *I am not enough*. Some of the

5.9 Not Good Enough

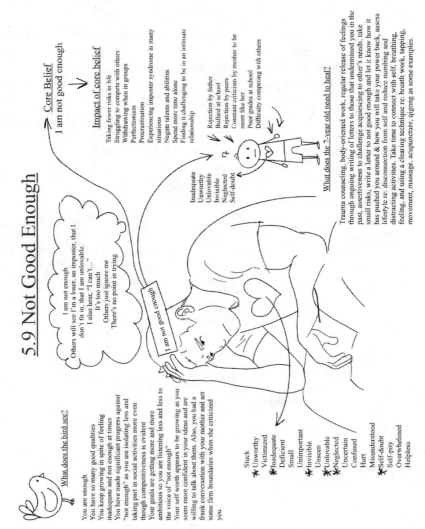

What does the bird see?

You are enough
You have so many good qualities
You keep growing in spite of feeling inadequate and not enough at times
You have made significant progress against "not enough" as you are isolating less and taking part in social activities more even though competitiveness is evident
Your goals are getting more and more ambitious so you are listening less and less to the voice of "not enough"
Your self worth appears to be growing as you seem more confident in your ideas and are willing to talk about them. Also, you had a frank conversation with your mother and set some firm boundaries when she criticized you.

Stuck
*Unworthy
Victimized
*Inadequate
Deficient
Small
Unimportant
*Invisible
Unseen
*Unlovable
*Neglected
Uncertain
Confused
Hurt
Misunderstood
*Self-doubt
Self-pity
Overwhelmed
Helpless

I am not enough
Others will see I'm a loser, an imposter, that I don't fit in, that I am unlovable.
I also hear, "I can't ..."
It's too much
Others just ignore me
There's no point in trying

I am not good enough

→ Core Belief
I am not good enough

Impact of core belief

Taking fewer risks in life
Struggling to compete with others
Withdrawing when in groups
Perfectionism
Procrastination
Experiencing imposter syndrome in many situations
Negate talents and abilities
Spend more time alone
Finding it challenging to be in an intimate relationship

Inadequate
Unworthy
Unlovable
Invisible
Neglected
Self-doubt

Rejection by father
Bullied at school
Rejection by peers
Constant criticism by mother to be more like her
Poor grades at school
Difficulty competing with others

What does the 7-year old need to heal?

Trauma counseling, body-oriented work, regular release of feelings through ongoing writing of letters to those that undermined you in the past, assertiveness to challenge acquiescing to other's needs, take small risks, write a letter to not good enough and let it know how it has pushed you around & how you will take your power back, assess lifestyle re: disconnection from self and reduce numbing and distracting activities. Take time to connect with self, breathing, feeling, and using a clearing technique re: breath work, tapping, movement, massage, acupuncture, qigong as some examples.

Figure 5.9. Not good enough.

feelings might be, stuck, unworthy, victimized, inadequate, deficient, small, unimportant, invisible, unseen, unlovable, neglected, uncertain, confused, hurt, misunderstood, self-doubt, self-pity, overwhelmed and helpless as some examples.

2. Now write out all the thoughts you hear that keep swirling around your mind. They could be, "I am not enough, others will see I'm a loser, an imposter, that I don't fit in, that I am unlovable. I can't. . . . .,it's too much, others just ignore me and there's no point in trying."

3. With another arrow from the head to the open page put a heading, *Core belief*. underneath it write, *I am not good enough*.

4. Take some time to reflect which feelings on the feelings list did you feel at an earlier age? Put a star next to the ones you remember feeling a long time ago. How old were you when you first felt these feelings? Put a heart on the younger version of yourself and put your age above the figure. Now list all the feelings you felt back then that may have been embodied due to experiencing trauma. The list could include inadequate, unworthy, unlovable, invisible, neglected, and self- doubt as some examples.

5. Draw in some arrows to help explain what events triggered the feelings *I am not enough*. Some arrows may include rejection by father, bullied at school, rejection by peers, constant criticism by mother to be more like her, poor grades at school and difficulty competing with others.

6. Next link an arrow to the core belief, *I am not enough*, and put a heading, *Impact of Core belief*. The impact could include, taking fewer risks in life, struggling to compete with others, withdrawing when in groups, perfectionism, procrastination, experiencing imposter syndrome in many situations, negate talents and abilities, spend more time alone and finding it challenging to be in an intimate relationship.

7. Put an arrow from the younger version of yourself (for example 7 years old) and put a new heading, *What does the 7-year-old need to heal*? This list could include, trauma counseling, body-oriented work, regular release of feelings through ongoing letter writing to those that undermined one in the past, assertiveness to challenge acquiescing to other's needs, take small risks, write a letter to *not good enough*, let it know how it has pushed you around and how you will take your power back. Assess lifestyle re disconnection from self and reduce numbing and distracting activities. Take time to connect with self, breathing, feeling, and using a clearing technique for instance, breath work, tapping, movement, massage, acupuncture, qigong as some examples.

8. Lastly put a bird at the top of the page in the right-hand corner and a heading above the bird, *What does the bird see*? Now list all the insights and awareness's from a higher perspective such as, you are enough as you have so many good qualities, you keep growing in spite of feeling inadequate

and not enough at times, you have made significant progress against 'not enough' as you are isolating less and taking part in more social activities despite others competitiveness, your goals are getting more ambitious so you are listening less and less to the voice of *not enough*, your self-worth appears to be growing as you seem more confident in your ideas and are willing to talk about them, and you have a frank conversation with your mother and set some firm boundaries when she criticizes you.

STABLE MISERY

This term encapsulates the intensity of feeling stuck and trapped that we experience at times. The feeling can be linked to immobilization, a symptom of autonomic nervous system dysregulation, along with other symptoms of hypo-arousal. *Stable misery* describes a state whereby we feel stuck, trapped, paralyzed, or immobilized and we experience very little wriggle room to move and change. This image helps to unpack why we can experience this state, the complexity involved in shifting it, and some ideas re our struggle to make movement.

Start by drawing a figure stuck in a box with layers of the box around the figure. Draw a heart on the figure and put a cloud over their head to indicate consuming thoughts. Now draw a small figure near the bottom of the right hand of the page and put the small figure in layers of a box as well. Draw a heart on the small figure and a cloud and link the heart of the adult figure to the figure of the younger version. Also, put arrows around the small figure indicating events and circumstances that a younger version of ourselves experienced that added to the psychological state of *stable misery*.

Some questions to use to fill in the image are:

1. Ask yourself what circumstances in your life would explain the predicament of *stable misery*? Some examples might be, relationship that feels stuck, defensiveness by partner, family conflict, mediocre job that has few prospects, unstable friendships, muted enjoyment in activities, structural discrimination that undermines hope, distancing teenage children, alienated from societal values, limited financial funds and violence in city.
2. Now ask yourself what feelings you feel in relation to *stable misery*? Put the title *feelings* out on the open page to the right and write a list of your feelings, they may be, hopelessness, despair, helpless, confused, lost, unwanted, judged, lonely, rejected, betrayed, stuck, trapped, paralyzed, distant, unseen, invisible, small, and misunderstood.

5.10 Stable Misery

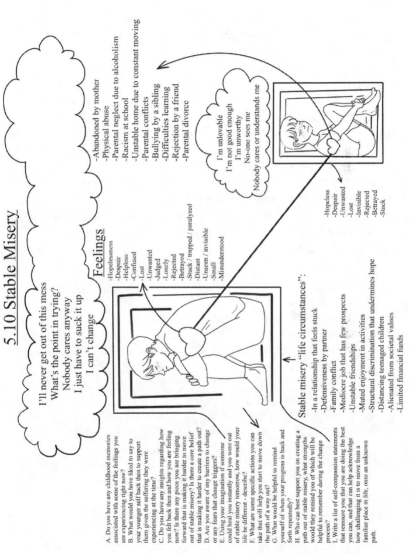

I'll never get out of this mess
What's the point in trying?
Nobody cares anyway
I just have to suck it up
I can't change

Feelings

-Hopelessness
-Despair
-Helpless
-Confused
-Lost
-Unwanted
-Judged
-Lonely
-Rejected
-Betrayed
-Stuck / trapped / paralyzed
-Distant
-Unseen / invisible
-Small
-Misunderstood

-Abandoned by mother
-Physical abuse
-Parental neglect due to alcoholism
-Racism at school
-Unstable home due to constant moving
-Parental conflicts
-Bullying by a sibling
-Difficulties learning
-Rejection by a friend
-Parental divorce

I'm unlovable
I'm not good enough
I'm unworthy
No-one sees me
Nobody cares or understands me

-Hopeless
-Despair
-Unwanted
-Lost
-Invisible
-Rejected
-Betrayed
-Stuck

Stable misery "life circumstances":

-In a relationship that feels stuck
-Defensiveness by partner
-Family conflict
-Mediocre job that has few prospects
-Unstable friendships
-Muted enjoyment in activities
-Structural discrimination that undermines hope
-Distancing teenaged children
-Alienated from societal values
-Limited financial funds

A. Do you have any childhood memories associated with some of the feelings you are experiencing right now?
B. What would you have liked to say to your younger self back then to support them given the suffering they were experiencing at the time?
C. Do you have any insights regarding how you felt back then and how you are feeling now? Is there any piece you are bringing forward that is making it harder to move out of stable misery? Is there a core belief that is making it harder to create a path out?
D. Are you aware of any barriers to change or any fears that change triggers?
E. Using your imagination if someone could heal you instantly and you were out of stable misery tomorrow, how would your life be different - describe?
F. What are some specific actions you can take that will help you start to move down the path of a way out?
G. What would be helpful to remind yourself of when your progress is back and forth repeatedly?
H. Who can best support you on creating a path out of stable misery, what strengths would they remind you of which will be helpful to remember during the change process?
I. Write a list of self-compassion statements that reassure you that you are doing the best you can, and that can help acknowledge how challenging it is to move from a familiar place in life, onto an unknown path.

Figure 5.10. Stable misery. *Alyson Quinn, Experiential Unity Theory and Model: Treating Trauma in Therapy* (Lanham, Maryland: Lexington Books), 2022.

3. Now ask yourself which of those feelings did you feel in childhood? Write out the list and link it to the heart of the younger version in a box. Some feelings might be, hopeless, despair, unwanted, lost, invisible, rejected, betrayed, and stuck. Now ask yourself what *core beliefs* about yourself emanated from these embodied emotions. They could be, I'm unlovable, I'm not good enough, I'm unworthy, no-one sees me, nobody cares or understands me.

4. Brainstorm and add thoughts in a bubble above the adult version of yourself that consume you at times. Some thoughts mentioned maybe, "what's the point in trying, nobody cares anyway, I'll never get out of this mess, I must suck it up and I can't change."

5. Write out the list of events, or circumstances, that happened to the younger version of self that contributed to the embodied emotion and core beliefs. Use arrows to indicate them. It might include parental neglect due to alcoholism, physical abuse, abandoned by mother, unstable home due to constant moving, parental conflict, racism at school, bullying by sibling, difficulties learning, rejection by friends and parental divorce.

6. Now answer the following list of questions. The questions engage a process regarding *stable misery* and may help develop insight and a detached perspective that may help to create some shifts or change.

   a. Do you have any childhood memories associated with some of the feelings you are experiencing right now?

   b. What would you have liked to say to your younger self back then to support them given the suffering they were experiencing at the time?

   c. Do you have any insights regarding how you felt back then and how you are feeling now? Is there any piece you are bringing forward that is making it harder to move out of *stable misery*? Is there a core belief that is making it harder to create a path out?

   d. Are you aware of any barriers to change or any fears of changing yourself?

   e. Using your imagination if someone could heal you instantly and you were out of stable misery tomorrow how would your life be different—describe?

   f. What are some specific actions you can take that will help you start to move down the path of a way out?

   g. What would be helpful to remind yourself of when your progress is back and forth repeatedly.

   h. Who can best support you on creating a path out of *stable misery*? What strengths would they remind you of which will be helpful to remember during the change process?

i. Write a list of self-compassion statements that reassure you that you are doing the best you can, and that help acknowledge how challenging it is to move from a familiar place in life, onto an unknown path.

Conclusion

I have many hopes for you the reader of *Heal Trauma: How to Feel It, Unlock Patterns, and Release It.* My hope is that, by facing emotions avoided and feared in the past, you will have more courage to face them head-on in the future. That every feeling will in time be seen as an ally, a best friend and companion in life, showing you the next step, the future road, the higher path; and those feelings will increasingly lose their labels as "good" or "bad." They are all there for sincere reasons; their absence would mean you had lost your way, lost the most precious gift you received when you came into the world: your connection with your unique self, with all of your complexity.

I hope too, that as you build awareness of helpful and unhelpful patterns, that you will be more protected when life gets challenging. With greater self-illumination, you can see the potholes up ahead, and instead of falling in again, walk around them with some degree of ease. Also, when you feel stuck or bogged down by feelings and patterns you can draw on the visuals in chapter five and use these examples to work through your situation. Constructing a visual that encapsulates all of your experience may help you get a bird's eye view of your predicament. You can then use the drawing to release feelings and illuminate patterns so the intensity of your situation may be eased, and discerning action illuminated.

I also hope you will find a new way of being in the world, a way that allows you to transcend being a victim drowning in life's circumstances, but a surfer on the waves of all the experiences on the open ocean, always willing to learn new techniques to ride the intense waves of life, with all the dignity and grace you can muster.

Bibliography

Badenoch, B. (2018). *The heart of trauma: Healing the embodied brain in the context of relationships. Norton series on interpersonal neurobiology.* W. W. Norton & Company.

Canadian Policy Research Networks. (2010).Weekly hours worked and indicators of well-being in Canada, at JobQuality.ca, pp1–7.

Chopra, D. (1997). *365 days of wisdom and healing.* New York: Workman Publishing.

Durning, A. (1991). How much is enough. *New Age journal* (July/August), 45–49. Adapted from the State of the World 1991, Washington, D.C.:Worldwatch Institute.

Engels, F. (1969). *The condition of the working class in England.* London:Granada.

Gibran, K (1968). *The Prophet.* New York: Alfred. A. Knopf.

Hawkins, M.(2011). How does violence in media desesensitize children? Livestrong. com, May.

Houff, B. (1991). *Forgivenss as self healing. Blame as self abuse.* Sermon for the Unitarian church of Vancouver. November 17th, 1991.

Jacques, M. (2004). The death of intimacy. *The Guardian,* September 18.

Kornfield, J. (1994). *Buddha's little instruction book.* New York: Bantam books.

Lapham, L. (1988). *Money and class in America.* New York: New Directions.

Mhi, S (2011). *Falling in love.* Shakti's blog. March 12th.

Miller, H. (1945). *The air-conditioned nightmare.* New York: New Directions.

On the virtues of slowness. (2012). *Politics of the Hap,* January 4. Blog on the virtues of slowness.

Postman, N. (1985). Introduction. In *Amusing ourselves to death: Public discourse in the age of show business.* New York: Penguin.

Some, M.P. (1993). *Ritual: Power, healing and community.* New York: Penguin Compass.

Tutu, D. (2004). *God has a dream: A vision of hope for our time.* New York: Doubleday.

UN Website, Preamble line 1 and 2.

Walsh, N.D. (2004). *Tomorrow's God. Our greatest spiritual challenge.* New York: Atria books.

Williamson, M. (1992). *A return to love: reflections on the principles of a course in miracles.* New York: Harper Collins.

Index

Page references for figures are italicized.

About the Author

Alyson Quinn has been an adjunct professor at UBC School of Social Work for seven years and has taught in the UBC Faculty of Education, in Education and Counseling Psychology, in the Fall term of 2020 and the Summer of 2022. She has been a clinical counselor for over thirty years specializing in trauma in both individual therapy and group counseling, and in conflict resolution. In addition to a wide range of experience as an individual counselor and group therapist she also has worked as a couple's counselor. She has a master's degree from the University of British Columbia and a diploma in conflict resolution from Royal Roads University. Alyson has taught students in a trauma informed counseling class, in a group work class, and also in Integrative Seminars. She has authored four published books and a chapter. Her textbook *Experiential Unity Theory and Model: Reclaiming your Soul* was first published in 2012, the second edition *Experiential Unity Theory and Model: Treating Trauma in Therapy Second Edition* was published in 2022 and aligns with the principles of Trauma Informed Practice. Alyson has taught her model at both International and Canadian conferences. Her self-help book *Reclaim your soul: Your path to healing,* published in 2014 also builds on trauma-informed principles. Additionally she published a chapter namely *Pedagogy for an Integrative Practice* in a textbook *Holistic Engagement: Transformative Social Work Education in the 21st Century* published in 2016. Alyson was born in Zimbabwe and trained as a social worker in South Africa. She launched her social work career in London, England and then emigrated to Vancouver, British Columbia, Canada. Her websites are www .alysonquinnwrites.com and www.traumainformedpracticeinstitute.com.